MY SCOTTISH YOUTH

MY SCOTTISH YOUTH

SCOTLAND

MY SCOTTISH YOUTH

SIR ROBERT BRUCE LOCKHART

EDINBURGH
B&W PUBLISHING
1993

First published 1937
This edition published 1993
by B&W Publishing
Edinburgh
Copyright © 1937 R. H. Bruce Lockhart
ISBN 1 873631 26 X

The publisher acknowledges subsidy
from the Scottish Arts Council towards
the publication of this volume.

British Library Cataloguing in Publication Data:
A catalogue record for this book is available from
the British Library

Cover design by Harry Palmer
Cover illustration: *Young Boy on the Shore, Iona*
by FCB Cadell, courtesy The Fine Art Society.
Photograph of R. H. Bruce Lockhart
by kind permission of Robin Bruce Lockhart.

Printed by Werner Söderström

CONTENTS

"LET TORRENTS pour then, let the great winds rally,
Snow-silence fall or lightning blast the pine;
That light of Home shines warmly in the valley,
And, exiled son of Scotland, it is thine.
Far have you wandered over seas of longing,
And now you drowse, and now you well may weep,
When all the recollections come a-thronging,
Of this rude country where your fathers sleep."

NEIL MUNRO

BOOK I

SON OF THE SOIL

"WHEN I was yet young,
Or ever I went abroad."

CHAPTER ONE

HAVE YOU FOUND Strbske Pleso? Or Smokovec? Or Lomnice? Or the Lake of Morskie Oko, which means "Eyes of the Sea"?

These words may be found every summer in the front-page advertisements of the more serious London Sunday newspapers. And, as far as I am concerned, the answer is "yes"—long before these exotic beauty spots were discovered by Sir Henry Lunn, Cook's, Hickie's, or the official tourist agencies of foreign governments. For it is in the nature of Scots to spread themselves over the world, and I have been no exception to the general run of my countrymen.

I have had more than my fair share of adventure: in Malaya and in Russia both before and during the war and in the first years of the revolution when I was head of the first British Mission to the Bolshevik Government. For nearly ten years, both as a Government servant and as a banker, I was an eye-witness of the post-war turmoil in Central Europe and the Balkans. I completed my education in the foreign universities of Marburg and the Sorbonne. I have set foot in every capital in Europe and I have encircled the globe. In various capacities I have served ambassadors, ministers of the Crown and captains of finance and industry, and for nine years I was a highly-paid professional journalist writing an anonymous daily commentary on people and events for a London evening newspaper. During the last quarter of a century I have met many men in exalted positions including most of the kings and rulers of Europe. And I have had the good luck and the misfortune to write what is popularly known as a best-seller.

The misfortune lies in the fact that I have had the label of adventure attached to me. My readers, especially my American readers, expect from me stories of international intrigue with great figures strutting across the stage and the adventurer

3

himself pulling the strings in the background. And to-day certain critics have accused me of having lost my sense of the adventurous and of having exchanged it for the dubious values of a gossip column in a London newspaper.

The charge may hit the outside of the target but it does not pierce the heart. Life is or should be a constant struggle to escape from the trammels of the commonplace. I have not lost my spirit of adventure. The plain truth is that I have at last begun to discover my own country.

Scotland is the land that bore me. The seventeen and a half years that I spent there are by far the longest period that I have spent in any one country, and how deep my roots lie in Scottish soil may be gauged from the fact that I had lived for a year in Continental Europe before I had ever seen London or set foot across the English border.

My nine years of journalism in London were the penalty of my youthful capacity for self-indulgence which put a load of debt on my shoulders and increased what Kipling has well called the initial payments on one's policy of independence. During those nine years my visits to Scotland have been my one great solace. I have gone back whenever the slightest opportunity has presented itself. I have travelled the country from the Borders to Caithness and the Outer Hebrides. This exile's return has brought a peace to my mind which I have never known previously. And, to-day, at the age of fifty, I realise that what sent me abroad was the restlessness of youth, a restlessness which in my case expressed itself in an incapacity to settle down and in an inability to distinguish between happiness and mere excitation of the emotions. I do not know if this is true of other Scottish exiles who too often justify their emigration by the national virtues of materialistic forethought and honest industry. I do know that too few of them go back to their native land. But by my own ability to return to Scotland I am prepared to measure my success in the battle which with varying fortunes every man wages with himself for the retention of his self-respect. By return I mean a permanent return. And this will be the greatest adventure of my life.

This book is the story of my boyhood in Scotland. It is something more than a mere chronicle of my early life. In it I attempt not merely to describe the influences which, for better or worse, have determined my character, but also to recapture a past that has gone beyond power of return and, through the eyes of an exile who has visited many countries, to compare the Scotland of that period with the Scotland of to-day.

I was born at Anstruther in the East Neuk of the Kingdom of Fife. The house in which I first raised my voice to the four winds was the Waid Academy, a small grammar school of which my father was then headmaster. Although I have always been told that I was a precocious child, I have no recollection of my entry into the world. It was a difficult birth, partly because I was the first-born and an exceptionally large baby and partly because my parents were poor and unable to afford an experienced nurse. The local doctor brought me into the world, and his assistant was Lily McLean, a young Highland housemaid lent by my maternal grandmother for the occasion. She was my first nurse and I was her first and only baby. She is alive and well to-day and, when I saw her recently, she was celebrating her seventieth birthday in her cottage beside the Spey.

The East Neuk is that portion of the county of Fife which lies east of a perpendicular line drawn from St. Andrews to Largo. Anstruther itself bears the proud title of an ancient royal burgh. The truth compels me to admit that it has never been much more than a poor fishing village. In the dim past it belonged to the Priory of Pittenweem and its church, dedicated to St. Nicholas, goes back to the eleventh century. Here I was baptised in the Presbyterian faith. Although I howled loudly at my immersion, I should like to believe to-day that St. Nicholas had some influence on my Russian destiny, for in the days of the Tsars he was a benevolent saint and a kind of Santa Claus who on his name's-day brought presents to good children. But I imagine that he must have turned his back on Anstruther long ago, for John Knox preached in the local church in 1559, and his eloquence was so persuasive that the population went out and demolished all the Catholic churches in the neighbourhood. This statement, taken from the chronicles of those times, does not seem to be strictly accurate, for the churches remain. The images of the saints, however, have disappeared.

The town, which has a picturesque harbour, is lashed by the cold North Sea and has always been conscious of its poverty. In 1617 King James, VI of Scotland and I of England, decided to visit his royal burgh, and the inhabitants were ordered to provide cattle for beef. The canny burghers replied: "Our town is ane very mean town; yea, of all the burghs of this realm the meanest. Neither is there ane flesher in our town, nor any other person that is accustomit with the feeding of beef, we being all seafaring men and fishers."

Anstruther fisher-folk made a name for themselves as far back as the days of Edward I of England, to whom they supplied large quantities of herrings for the provision of his garrisons in Scotland. The herrings were caught off the Isle of May at the entrance to the Firth of Forth. To these delectable fishing-grounds came also English, Dutch, Danish and French fishers, and hand-to-hand fights were frequent. The local hero of those days was William of Anstruther whose boat-hook had a battle-axe at the other end and who has gone down to history as "Fisher Willie".

Fishing remains the chief livelihood of the population today, and Anstruther men retain the sturdy independence of their forefathers. Indeed, although Scotland has produced fewer admirals than great generals, most of her well-known sailors come from Fife. They include Sir Andrew Wood, who in his famous "Yellow Carvel" was a highly successful harrier of the English, Sir Philip Durham, a hero of Trafalgar, and Sir Samuel Greig, whose services to the Tsars in the eighteenth century against Turkey and Sweden earned for him the name of "Father of the Russian Navy". During the Great War, Lord Wester Wemyss became First Sea Lord. Like Lord Haig, he too was a man of Fife.

But the most famous Fife sailor was Andrew Selkirk who was marooned for four years on the island of Juan Fernandez and whose misfortunes inspired Defoe to write *Robinson Crusoe*. Selkirk, who finished his career as a naval lieutenant, was the son of a shoemaker and a native of Largo, a straggling little village on the coast about ten miles from Anstruther. There is a Selkirk statue and a plaque in his memory, put up by a local netmaker, on the site of the cottage where he was born. The town continues to benefit by his fame, for it still attracts a considerable number of American tourists, and there is a modest Crusoe Hotel close to a rocky promontory where in winter the cormorants settle to seek shelter from the storms.

There is a proverb that every great and clever Scot must be a Fifer. In addition to those whom I have already mentioned, great men of Fife include Adam Smith, the author of *The Wealth of Nations*, Sir David Wilkie, the Scottish painter, and Andrew Carnegie, the Pittsburg steel king and Scottish-American philanthropist. But, taken all in all, the best of the famous men whom Fife has produced is Dr. Thomas Chalmers, the founder of the Free Church of Scotland. He was an Anstruther man and was born in 1791, within a stone's throw of the Waid Academy, in a back-street cottage which still stands. He had a curious ancestry for a Presbyterian minister. The sixth of fourteen children, he was the son of a small shopkeeper. His mother was the daughter of a local wine-merchant. Nor as a very young boy did Chalmers himself show any promise of the Calvinist seriousness to come. At his Anstruther school he gained the character of one of "the idlest, strongest, merriest and most generous-hearted of boys". But his father had the best library in

Anstruther, and Chalmers, who concentrated on mathematics, was licensed as a preacher when only nineteen. And, although he was a fine scholar, it was as a preacher that he was to impress his contemporaries. By those who heard him preach, his oratory was described as "unapproached in our day", a striking testimony to the magnetic eloquence of a man whose personal appearance was dingy and uninspiring.

To the effect of this eloquence on a family with which I have been closely connected I myself can bear witness. In the "forties" of last century a young boy called Aitken walked from his father's croft near Torphichen to Edinburgh in order to hear Dr. Chalmers preach. He saw a tall, gaunt, pockmarked man ascend the pulpit and give out the text in a rough, husky voice. The boy was bitterly disappointed and thought that he had made his long walk in vain. Then the preacher began to speak. The words seemed to come straight from God, and the soul of the young Aitken was uplifted. He made up his mind to enter the Church. In due course he became the Rev. William Aitken, and later received a call to go to Canada. Himself an eloquent preacher with the magnetic eyes and flowing beard of a prophet, he spread the word of God among the Scottish pioneers of New Brunswick. Between sermons and his long-distance parish work he found time to marry and to produce a large family of sons and daughters, to whom he gave a thorough grounding in Bible knowledge and Shakespeare. Some of the seed which he sowed fell on good ground, for one day the village schoolmaster found one of the sons, then a boy of nine, scrubbing the kitchen table and muttering as he polished: "Out, damned spot." The boy's name was Max. But for the fiery eloquence of Thomas Chalmers there might to-day be no Lord Beaverbrook.

Apart from his powers as a preacher Chalmers established a minor literary record by his writings. A volume of his sermons, published under the title of *Astronomical Discourses*, sold 6000 copies in the first month and 20,000 in the first year. As the sale was confined to Scotland, it was a remarkable tribute to the hold which he had on the mind of the Scottish people.

Although his works have not lived, Chalmers, "a solar man who drew after him a firmament of planets", was a far more vital force in Scottish history than scores of Scots who fill more pages in the history books and whose names are better known to the outside world. He founded the Free Church in 1843 and died in 1847. By that time the new Church had 700 ministers, 600 schools, a college of nine professors, two seminaries for training teachers, a whole army of missionaries in every corner of the globe, and a vast fund established by voluntary contributions. It was a triumph of organisation of which even a modern dictator might be proud.

But to my mind the finest illustration of Chalmers' character was his decision in the last years of his life to take over a church in the West Port district of Edinburgh. It was the quarter in which Burke and Hare carried out their callous murders and was so depraved that contemporary writers described the inhabitants as "the very sediment of the Edinburgh lower orders".

To the Chalmers-Aitken connection I owe a considerable debt. A year or two ago Lord Beaverbrook suggested to me that I should write a modern biography of Chalmers. The subject made no appeal to me, but it sent me back to Chalmers and to Anstruther, and, by the spur of Lord Beaverbrook's suggestion, what had long been a vague idea in my mind, to wit, this book, has become a realised ambition.

Among folk who, although not Fifers, have had some connection with Anstruther and have had a certain influence on my outlook on life, is Robert Louis Stevenson. While I was on my way into the world, he spent a few weeks in Anstruther with his father, the famous lighthouse builder, who was then engaged on constructive work on the Fife coast. Soon afterwards he left Scotland for good, and it is one of my greatest regrets that, even as a child in arms, I never saw the man who, more than any other writer, has kept Scotland alive in my heart and given me unfailing comfort in my years of exile. It was the proudest day in my life when in 1935 I delivered in Edinburgh the annual oration to his immortal memory.

A more distant and shadowy Anstruther figure is the 5th Earl of Strathmore, of whom our present Queen is a direct descendant. He is one of the heroes of my Jacobite enthusiasms and came to Anstruther in 1715. Here, at the beginning of the Stuart rising of "The Fifteen", he proclaimed James VII, known to the English as the Old Pretender, King of Scotland. The patriotic Earl avoided what the history books would call a traitor's death in the Tower of London by perishing at Sheriffmuir, a battle which was a victory for neither side, but in which the advantage lay with the Government troops—led of course by a Campbell, for the Jacobite forces retreated. The Commercial Hotel in which the Earl read his proclamation still stands and is one of the finest old buildings in Anstruther. The proprietor has a long list of records dating back to the days of Queen Anne, and, if you win his confidence, he will tell you, and give chapter and verse for his veracity, that in the excitement of the moment Lord Strathmore forgot to pay his wine-bill.

Of the morals of Anstruther I am not qualified to write, but at one time the little town had a reputation for hard drinking, caution in marriage, and aristocratic immorality. The reputation for drinking is recorded in various old rhymes, one of which pays a tribute to the strong heads of the women:

> "The lasses of Anster
> They drink strong ale;
> There's green grass in Cellardyke,
> And crabs intill Crail."

Caution in the selection of wives is expressed in the old saying: "A woman shouldna wed till she can win her guid man's bread", a practical aphorism which means that to fisher-folk a wife is of no use unless she can mend his nets, bait his hooks, and, above all, sell his fish.

The immorality is another matter, and my reference to it casts no reflection on the virtue of the good people of Anstruther. But the truth remains that during the most of the eighteenth century and the first part of the nineteenth there flourished in Anstruther an erotic club called "The Most Ancient and Puissant Order of the Beggar's Benison and Merryland". The club is said to have had its origin in one of the amorous exploits of King James V of Scotland. On one occasion, when, disguised as a piper, he was on a visit to Anstruther, he found the Dreel burn so high in "spate" that he could not ford it without wetting his hose. While he stood considering what to do, a beggar wife came up and, lifting her skirts, carried the King on her shoulders to the other side. For this act of gallantry the King rewarded her with her "fairing" and in return received the damsel's blessing. Hence came the title of "The Beggar's Benison" which was invented at a subsequent orgy in Anstruther in which the King took part and at which the club was founded.

Devoted to the phallic cult, it was attended by the cream of the Fifeshire nobility and even by some parish ministers. Among the original founders was Sir Charles Erskine, a loyal friend to Bonnie Prince Charlie and an ancestor of the present Earl of Rosslyn. The rites of the club were highly pornographic. The president was called the Sovereign and wore a wig said to be composed of the privy-hairs of Royal courtesans. New members were initiated on St. Andrew's Day and had to march in naked and to pass a test of physical virility. The club had its own record book, blasphemously called "The Bible", and on the title page were the coats of arms of the aristocratic members. They included the then Duke of Gordon and Lords Kellie, Erroll, Lothian, Balcarres, Crawford and Haddington! Many of their direct descendants occupy high places in British public life to-day. As

Regent the subsequent King George IV was enrolled as a member and is said to have taken part in a meeting of the Edinburgh branch of the society.

The club records, still kept in the National Library in Edinburgh but not available to the public, are too indecent to quote, but they show that the proceedings were far coarser than those of the notorious Hell-Fire Club founded by John Wilkes at Medmenham in England. The Club had a fine collection of gold plate with pornographic designs. Gold medals, too, were given to prominent sexual athletes. For the most part they portrayed scenes from the lives of Venus and Cupid and of Adam and Eve and bore such mottoes as "Lose No Opportunity" and "Be Fruitful and Multiply". This last motto has suggested to sociologists that the club may have had its origin in a perverted desire to raise the birth-rate, which in Fife was then very low owing to the appallingly high incidence of infant mortality. A careful examination of the records has convinced me that the theory is far-fetched. One of the avowed objects of the society was the enjoyment of pleasure without the risk of procreation, and the best that can be said is that the club's existence provides a curious sidelight on the rude morals of those days.

In trying to determine the pre-natal influences which have affected my character, I should like to give Anstruther something more than its due. It would please me to think that to Dr. Chalmers I owe the strain of Presbyterianism which, although I have long been a Catholic, my friends say lies at the bottom of my nature; to the sturdy fishermen of Anster my insatiable love of fishing and to their native canniness the streak of Fifeshire caution in my character, which, as Harold Nicolson has written of me, always pulls me up when the referee's whistle blows, and to the shade of the Earl of Strathmore in the Commercial Hotel my sentimental enthusiasm for the Jacobite cause.

The theory might be carried still further to the Benison Society and to the drinking capacities of the fisher-folk, but it will not bear even a cursory examination. My connection with Anstruther was purely accidental and has no roots. When my father left Cambridge he was appointed Sixth Form master at Merchiston Castle, one of the six Scottish public schools. Soon afterwards, during a reading tour in the Highlands, he fell in love with my mother and, in order to marry quickly, accepted his post at the Waid Academy as the first opportunity which presented itself of giving him a house to live in and a slight increase of salary. The truth is that I remember nothing about Anstruther. Even Caesar, the huge St. Bernard, who, when I was a baby, used to carry me by his mouth, is only a post mortem memory, for my first recollection of him dates from several years later when his stuffed head adorned the hall of our new home. The reasons for this ignorance are not to be ascribed to defective memory. I left Anstruther when I was ten months old. Until this year I have never revisited it.

CHAPTER TWO

THE REASON FOR my departure from Anstruther was the appointment of my father to the headmastership of Spier's School, Beith. The school was a new one and owed its foundation to the benevolence of the son of a rich local lawyer and banker called Spier who in his will left a part of his fortune for the establishment of a school in his home town. By so doing he has added his name to the long list of rich Scots who, since the days of "Jingling Geordie" Heriot, the jeweller of James I of England, have taken out immortality policies by leaving funds for the establishment of educational institutions. This practice, so much wiser than the English custom of buying peerages, has endowed Scotland with many of her famous day-schools, including George Heriot's, Daniel Stewart's, and George Watson's. In recent years Watson's has provided Britain with more Cabinet Ministers than any other British school except Eton, the more famous of them being Sir Auckland Geddes, Lord Strathcarron, Sir Robert (now Lord) Horne, and Mr. "Shakes" Morrison.

In his early manhood the original Mr. Spier who made the family fortune wrestled with the bottle. He married his housekeeper and with her aid finally conquered his addiction. His son, who left the money for the foundation of the school, was a pious and delicate young man. But he did not inherit his father's legal precision, for in his will he failed to make his instructions clear. For some time after his death it seemed doubtful if the school would come into being. Fortunately he had a taste for marble statuary and before he died had begun to order the set-pieces which were to perpetuate the memory of the founder of the school. Soon after his funeral the statuary was delivered at his home, and the widowed mother, beholding it, decided that only a school would be large enough to house it.

The school was therefore built, and, having succumbed to

the statuary craze, the mother added a set-piece on her own account. When distinguished visitors, inspecting the school, used to express mild surprise at this rather morbid collection, my father would reply: "You cannot have it both ways. But for the statues there would have been no Spier's."

In my infancy this cold, white marble statuary had an awe-inspiring effect on my mind. The main piece was in the tower, an eerie place full of darkness and nesting birds, and was shut off from the rest of the house by an iron grille. I never approached it without a feeling of trepidation and yet was drawn to it by the irresistible force of morbid curiosity.

When I revisited the school in 1937, I asked to see the statuary. I was taken up to the tower, now sadly smaller than I had photographed it in my memory. A heavy bookcase barred the entrance. With the aid of the headmaster and a schoolmistress I helped to move it, but it slipped from our grasp and fell, barking my shin in its descent. The grille was locked, but with a long stretch the tall headmaster, who stands six feet five in his socks, was able to reach and switch away the white sheet which draped the figures. And there before my eyes lay a marble Spier on his marble death-bed with angels from Italy hovering round and a marble widow and mother holding the dead man's hand and weeping for her departed husband and children. One day I shall write a book with the title *Never Go Back*, which, incidentally, was the original title chosen by Negley Farson for his *Way of a Transgressor*. This touching death-bed scene, which had stamped itself so clearly on my youthful mind, had lost its enthralling terrors.

Beith, a little manufacturing town in the north-east corner of Ayrshire, has little to commend it either for beauty or for local interest. Some years ago I wrote to a Scottish librarian to ask him to supply me with a history of the town. His answer was laconic: "I have been unable to find anything. Knowing the place, I am not surprised." As it is situated in a cleft between two hills, it first presents itself to the approaching traveller as a series of chimney stacks standing out of the valley and belching forth black smoke as though from some subterranean hell. Ayrshire and Lanarkshire were then full of self-made men who, having made fortunes in the industrial revolution, were striving to acquire the culture which would open the road to titles and to peerages. In miniature Beith reflected both the spirit of that revolution and the type of man whom it had brought to the front.

There was a local cabinetmaker who, having acquired wealth, thought it necessary to his new dignity to instal a library in his house. As he wished to have his books specially bound, he sent for a Glasgow expert. "Well, sir," said the bookbinder, "what about these bindings? Would you like them done in russia or in morocco?" "Na, na," said the local magnate, "a'am Scottish born and bred and Scotland's good enough for me. We'll just ha'e them done in Glesca (Glasgow)."

Cabinet-making, together with rope-making and tanning, is still the chief industry of the town, and close by at Kilbirnie are the great thread mills of the Knoxes, two of whom were at school with me at Fettes. Kilbirnie itself I best remember for its loch where the tragedy of a boy who was drowned while skating was recounted to me at great length by my nurse in order to give me proper warning of the dangers of water.

Nevertheless, Beith was the home of my first conscious memories, and I retain a sentimental interest in its fortunes. Here I formed my first impressions of my paternal grandfather and of my maternal grandmother. Both were strong, forceful characters with many of the national virtues and faults which have made the Scottish people what they are. My mother was a Macgregor and Highland through and through, with a warm, generous nature, an immense pride in her children, and a profound and sometimes misplaced belief in her own powers of second sight. The Lockharts were Lowlanders, and from an early age I was conscious of the different outlook on life which divides the Highlander from the Lowlander, or, to make a rough generalisation, the Celt from the Anglo-Saxon.

The Lockharts were by nature and upbringing provident and imbued with the spirit of self-denial. The Macgregors were and, as long as they run true to type, always will be reckless to excess, self-indulgent, and generous to a fault.

Both sides of my family sprang from the soil. In the eighteenth century my great-great-grandfather went from Kippen, a small village not far from Bannockburn, in Stirlingshire. At that time there were a hundred Lockharts in Kippen living on and by the land. To-day, there is not one. Presumably the Kippen Lockharts have followed the example of my great-great-grandfather, who left home in order to better himself. In Glasgow he established a tailoring business and in course of time became the leading tailor in Scotland. His son, my great-grandfather, carried on the business with even greater success and made clothes for King George IV and a respectable fortune for himself. His business premises were at 60 St. Vincent Street, one of the leading thoroughfares of Glasgow. He owned other property in the same street and in a house just opposite his own premises he had at one time as a tenant MacLehose, the bookseller and an ancestor of the well-known firm of Scottish printers, who, incidentally, print my books. Long before his death my great-grandfather sold his business, became a gentleman of leisure, and had his portrait painted by Sir Daniel McNee. The Glasgow tailoring business was carried on until 1931 by his successors. The premises are now the Glasgow headquarters of Messrs. Spalding, the well-known sporting outfitters.

From my direct Lockhart ancestors I ought to have inherited both sound business instincts and stubbornness of character, two virtues which I lack. My tailor great-grandfather had a brother Tom, who, being jilted by a girl, went off to New Orleans. He prospered there exceedingly, made a fortune in cotton, and came back to Scotland. He settled in

Glasgow where he had a large house and a fine collection of plate, but, as far as women are concerned, the iron in his heart never melted. To the end of his life, except on New Year's Day when his male relations were permitted to bring their wives, no woman was ever allowed to cross his threshold. Bachelors may note that he lived until he was ninety-six. He died in the year after I was born and left to his nephews the sum of £150,000 after having given away half as much again during his lifetime.

Part of this money came to my grandfather, and, as he also inherited a considerable sum from his father, he was, for those days at any rate, a comparatively rich man. In his youth he was interested in business, but in his later years he devoted his life to politics and to public work. He stood once as a Liberal Unionist Parliamentary candidate for Montrose Burghs and during the campaign stayed at Glamis Castle, the ancestral home of our reigning Queen. He was defeated and turned his attention to municipal politics in which he achieved considerable success. Well-read, a good French scholar, and a traveller who even in those days had visited the Dominions, he was, undoubtedly, a man of parts. He was a rigid Presbyterian, and as such, stern and strict both as a father and as a grandfather. He always kept my father on tight rations, and, although he was not a figure who compelled youthful affection, I regarded him with some admiration and considerable respect.

The early history of my Macgregor ancestors was equally humble, but more romantic. My mother's relations came from a sept of the Macgregors of Balquhidder who had been sent by Rob Roy to Rothiemurchus in Inverness-shire in order to assist the Grants in a feud against the Shaws. After a peace had been patched up, the Macgregors settled in Inverness-shire, inter-married with both the Grants and the Cummings, and at the time of the "Forty-Five" were living in Glenmore. A decade or two later, the then Duke of Gordon wished to turn Glenmore into a deer-forest. He therefore transferred the local population, including the Macgregors, to other parts of his vast estates. Some were settled on Deeside in Aberdeenshire. The Macgregors were moved to Tomintoul, the highest village in the Highlands, on the banks of the beautiful River Aven and not far from Glenlivet, the home of Highland whisky celebrated in the old jingle:

> "Glenlivet it has castles three,
> Drumin, Blairfindy, and Deskie,
> And also one distillery
> More famous than the castles three."

The rhyme states no more than the truth. The castles are now neglected ruins. The distillery still flourishes. Its buildings cover an area of more than ten acres with not a square foot of ground wasted, and the fame of its whisky has spread over the whole world.

In Tomintoul my ancestors learnt the art of distilling whisky and, doubtless, they learnt it as smugglers. Nor does the story do them discredit. For centuries the private distilling of whisky had proceeded in Scotland without disturbance, but after the "Forty-Five" the English put thumbscrews on the Highlands. One of their first acts was to abolish private distilling, and the new law at once converted what were legitimate stills into private stills and the honest men who worked them into smugglers. A period of whisky warfare ensued which in its lawless excitements was not unlike the Prohibition period during the post-war years in the United States. For this warfare Glenlivet and Tomintoul were well adapted, not merely because they possessed the three essential ingredients of the best whisky: good barley, good peat and good water, but also because their lonely glens were inaccessible to the forces of so-called civilisation. The crofters, furious at this English interference with their livelihood, banded themselves together and, organising trains of pack-horses, carried their whisky, already prized above all others, across the hills to the markets of the South. Armed and prepared to defend themselves, they struck terror into the hearts of the preventive officers or "gaugers" who were appointed to enforce the law. On several occasions the military had to be called out, and there were frequent clashes. For about fifty years the smugglers more than held their own, and an old record dating from the beginning of the nineteenth century states that in Tomintoul "everybody makes whisky and everybody drinks it".

When my great-grandfather, James Macgregor, who was born in Tomintoul, walked across the hills with his two brothers and his sister in order to start a farm in Cromdale in Strathspey, he knew everything about distilling. For many years it had been the practice of the numerous Macgregors established in Tomintoul to give to their women-folk a specified amount of barley for the making of whisky. After the woman of the house had supplied the family wants, she was allowed to sell the surplus to outsiders. This perquisite was regarded as the woman's pin-money. When my Macgregor great-grandfather made his big "trek" to Cromdale at the end of the eighteenth century, his sister continued to exercise her privilege. As Cromdale water and Cromdale peat were as good as or better than Glenlivet peat and water, the surplus whisky soon found a ready market in the neighbouring district. Very soon James Macgregor realised that the manufacture of surplus whisky could yield profits far beyond the range of a sister's pin-money and gradually he established a prosperous but illicit trade.

Then one day he received a visit from the local preventive officer. The conversation which took place made local history. After an introductory dram of whisky, the "gauger" asked to be shown over the farm buildings. He saw a long shed which looked suspiciously like a warehouse. "What will that be, Mr. Macgregor?" asked the "gauger". "Oh," replied my great-grandfather, "that's just the cow-byres." The malt barn was dismissed in similar fashion as a hay loft, and then the two men came to the still, which was more difficult to explain. "Now, Mr. Macgregor, what'll that be?" And the Macgregor replied blandly: "Why, that's the peat shed." The "gauger" said nothing, and the two men went into the house for a final dram. Then, as he was taking his leave, the preventive officer turned to my great-grandfather. "Mr. Macgregor," he said, "we live in hard times. If I were in your shoes, I'd take out a licence for yon peat shed." The "gauger's" tact won the day. My great-grandfather saw the wisdom of the hint and took out his licence.

This was the beginning of the Balmenach Distillery, which, licensed in 1824, in the same year as Glenlivet, ranks with that renowned distillery as the oldest licensed distillery in the north of Scotland.

My great-grandfather was a remarkable personification of the progressive Highlander. When he came to Balmenach there were only fifteen acres of cultivated land. By his industry and enterprise he brought many hundreds of acres of moorland into bearing, adding nine farms to his original holding. Undoubtedly whisky aided his farming, for the waste products of the distillery helped to fatten the cattle which he reared. But he was the great pioneer of the Cromdale district, and on one occasion the Earl of Seafield of those days declared publicly that James Macgregor had done more for Strathspey than any Seafield.

My great-grandfather's only reward from the Seafields was to have his rent raised by ten times. But he had little reason to complain. At Balmenach he brought up a family of sixteen of whom six sons and six daughters survived the period of early youth. His son John, who emigrated to New Zealand, made money and came back to Balmenach to take over the distillery, had nine children. When John died in 1888, his widow—my grandmother—carried on the business and sent her sons and daughters to good schools. In this manner, for over a hundred years, the distillery kept, in good times and in bad, the huge army of my Macgregor relations.

In 1897 it was formed into a limited liability company and a few years ago was taken over by Distillers Limited. It is now one of the properties of the huge trust which to-day controls the production of Scotch whisky. Only three years ago, my uncle Jim, my grandmother's eldest son and the last Macgregor link with the old still, moved out of the family house which has stood for over a century.

Although in their origin both the Lockharts and the Macgregors were essentially sons of the soil, there was a world of difference in the characteristics and natural instincts of the two families. The Lockharts were frugal; the Macgregors, like most Highlanders, kept open house to all and sundry whether they were barons or beggars. Indeed, in this respect, as in many others, I have often been struck by the similarity and kinship between the Highlander and the Slav. Both have the same generous instincts, which the Russians call "shirokaya natura" and which is best translated as "generous expansiveness". Both have the same spasmodic energy and the same lack of fixity of purpose. Both have the same uncertain temper and the same capacity for quarrelling with their own folk. To-day, the old feuds of the Highland clans have their counterpart in the never dormant hostility between the Slav tribes—between Serb and Croat, Czech and Slovak, Pole and Russian. And as for hospitality, I am reluctantly compelled to admit that its virtue is greatest among the races which are furthest removed from the influences of civilisation. At all events, the Serbs, who are the least civilised of the Slavs, are by far the most hospitable, and the theory can be further justified, without offence to either race, by the infinitely greater hospitality of the American as compared with the Englishman.

Admittedly, the Macgregors had other characteristics which are not shared by the Slavs. Chief of these were their indifference to intellectual culture and their superabundant share of Highland pride. In a remarkable comparative study of the Highlander and the Lowlander, Miss Ramsay has attempted with considerable success to destroy the sentimental conception of the Highlander as a mystic dreamer and a romantic poet as opposed to the shrewd, material, and essentially practical Lowlander, and to prove that the truth is exactly the reverse. It is a truism that the Lowlands have provided Scotland with her great poets. And, as far as my Macgregor relations were concerned, their innate hospitality and generosity were accompanied by a solid regard for the advantages of money. Their Highland pride, stimulated by intermarriage with the Cummings, who belonged to the ancient family of Comyn and who had some claim to the lands of the Earls of Seafield, made them look down on Lowlanders by tradition. In prosperous times this slightly superior attitude was also extended towards my father, because, although a scholar and a prizeman of two universities, he was a schoolmaster.

In point of fact, my father, through his grandmother, can point to a Stuart descent with far stronger proofs than can the Macgregors, who as sons of Alpin also claim to be descended from kings. In the case of the Lockharts the descent comes, not from my Bruce ancestor, whose birth like that of Alan Breck was, I imagine, not wholly regular, but from the Ronalds, who were direct descendants of James III of Scotland. A passion for royal ancestry is a weakness of many Scots. My old friend Lord Rosslyn has, in his house, a weirdly painted genealogical tree showing his descent from an early Scottish king. On one occasion an American visitor mistook it for a plan of the house drains.

My father set no store by these foolish vanities. As small boys my brothers and I suffered perhaps from the nature of his profession and from the fact that for a time we were both his pupils and his sons. He was a truly great teacher, but as a boy I found it hard to separate the father from the schoolmaster and never approached him without a slight feeling of awe. Since I grew up, I have come to know him better, and to-day there is no secret that I withhold from him, no subject which I am afraid to discuss with him. Frugal in his wants and Spartan in his self-denial, he has always been generous almost to a fault of weakness in his treatment of others. I have met no man who has so profound and so tolerant an understanding of the problems and difficulties of life and I can recall no occasion when he has ever failed one of his family in supplying in the hour of crisis both wise counsel and also the generous help which alas! is what one requires most in a scrape. To-day, at the age of eighty, he is a marvellous old man, a little lonely perhaps since my mother's death, but still wonderfully vigorous and young both in body and mind. He still plays his daily round of golf, still travels hundreds of miles to see a "rugger" international, and still takes the keenest interest in politics, new books, and, above all, in young people. He carries on a vast correspondence with his old pupils in every part of the world, is an inveterate writer of letters to *The Times* and is as pleased as a schoolboy when one from himself is published. In a sentence, he is reaping the reward of a life devoted to plain living and high thinking, and I hope that he is as happy as he seems to be.

My mother had a totally different character. Warmhearted, impulsive and extravagantly generous, she was perhaps not best fitted to be a schoolmaster's wife, for she was fond of social life, played every game with the natural ability of the born athlete, and, beyond seeing that the boys were well fed, took little interest in those details of domestic economy which in Britain so affect a schoolmaster's life that his success is frequently measured more by his business acumen as a hotel-keeper than by his ability as a teacher. She was, too, difficult with strangers, and her Highland pride made her resent sometimes too openly the imperative speech of vulgar parents. Her heart was in the Highlands, and when we migrated to England in 1906 she never took kindly to the country, living only for the annual return to Strathspey, where for over thirty years, at her insistence, we spent every summer holiday.

When my fourth brother, Norman, was killed at Loos, she changed completely, withdrawing into herself and refusing to be comforted. Her pride in her children was immense and unreasonable. My father, a keen student of history, took a broad view of such things as wars and peace treaties, but my mother's hate of the Germans and even of General French, whom she held responsible for the failure of Loos, was personal and unforgiving.

To us children, however, she was a wonderful mother, holding our affections until her death. She was ambitious for our success, and I remember vividly her words, constantly repeated to me as a small boy: "Every man can be what he wants to be if only he tries hard enough; you can be Prime Minister if you like." In a sense she was strict and whacked me more than once when I was old enough to resent the beating as an indignity. Her sense of justice was not the same as my father's, and one spanking, applied because I had gone off to a football match without permission and had returned with my feet soaking and my clothes splashed with mud, I remember to this day for my burning tears caused more by righteous indignation than by any physical pain. On that occasion my father, always indulgent where football was concerned, took my side, comforting me with such hackneyed reflections as "Never mind, you'll be a man before your mother".

But a sentimental appeal could always melt my mother's anger, and it was to her that I went in my scrapes when I was afraid to approach my father. Her intervention, which always followed my appeal, was almost invariably successful. There was almost no sacrifice which she was not prepared to make for her children, and to her we owe our love of the Highlands and many years of the happiest home life unbroken by the quarrels and jealousies which disturb the harmony of so many families. She died in 1928 when my fortunes were at a very low ebb. I was a sore disappointment to her, causing her sleepless nights of grief and anxiety. But as her first-born she loved me best and in the hours of my greatest failures never failed to tell me so.

My own character bears little resemblance to my father's, and, although I lack her virtues and graces, I get my impulsive temperament from my mother. There is, in fact, only one characteristic which I inherit from both my parents. In both sides of my family the travel-lust has always been strong. It is therefore small wonder that all my life I have been a wanderer.

Nevertheless, we Scots are a curiously clannish folk. In 1934 I crossed from the United States into Canada for one day in order to deliver a lecture in Toronto, the Presbyterian and Scottish stronghold of the Dominion. The chairman who introduced me was a Scottish minister, and in his prefatory remarks he said kindly but rather patronisingly that, although he had been only fifteen years in Canada, he must say as a Canadian that it was absurd for me to come to Canada for one day and that I could claim no knowledge of Toronto until I had seen it in the fall. In my reply I admitted the indiscretion of my one-day visit, but pointed out that I had been in Canada before, that I had seen Toronto in the fall, and that my connection with Canada went back far farther than the minister's, for my father was born in Montreal in 1858. I added that, while they called themselves Scots-Canadians, my father was probably the oldest living Canadian-born Scot. My lecture did not matter. The reference to the Canadian-born Scot did the trick. The local Press gave full prominence to my statement, and on the strength of it a Toronto newspaper bought the serial rights of my next book.

My father was born in Montreal during my paternal grandfather's first and longest visit to Canada. By a curious coincidence my mother was also born in a Dominion. Her father, John Macgregor, made a marriage which displeased his proud Cumming mother. He emigrated at once to New Zealand, leaving on the day after his wedding and suffering great hardships on the voyage because his ship was delayed by a mutiny among the sailors. In New Zealand he prospered, acquiring a station of his own and laying the foundations of the wealth which, on his return to Scotland, was to restore the fortunes of the Balmenach Distillery. In this way most of his family, including my mother, were born in New Zealand; and, when I complete my world travels with a visit to that angler's paradise, I hope that a reference to my mother's birth-place will stand me in as good stead with New Zealanders as did my reference to my father's with the good people of Toronto.

CHAPTER THREE

RECOLLECTIONS OF EARLY childhood are dangerous and unconvincing. It is so easy for anyone possessed of a vivid imagination to embroider and to credit to memory what has been told to one by others at a later period. The truth is that it is not the great events which impress themselves on a child's mind. While certain recollections are very clear, they are nearly always trivial, and even with the help of one's parents their date is difficult to place. In writing this chapter I have before me a warning in another Fife proverb:

"Lundie Mill and Largo, the Kirkton and the Keirs,
    Pittenweem and Anster are all big Leears (liars)."

My first distinct impression is of a tremendous gale which nearly blew me away. I can still see myself in my white-belted dark blue jumper, and the young fir trees in the plantation bending almost to the ground before the wind. It was Christmas time, and the house was full of my parents' friends. They were standing by the front door, and, as I struggled in vain to reach the steps, I was rescued by the "K.K.", one of the strongest men who ever played rugby football for Scotland. His name was W. A. Macdonald, but for some reason which I do not remember we always called him the "K.K.", which stood for "Kinquering Kong". He was a very old friend of the family and, as long as we remained in Scotland, always came to us for Christmas. Later, when we were older and wore the kilt, my second brother Rufus and I fought terrific battles with him. We were encouraged to use our fists, to hit as hard as we liked, and to tackle him by the ankles. But soon the grip which had laid low many an English forward held us as in an iron vice, and the muscles of our bare legs were hardened by resounding slaps which at other times would have brought tears but which in the heat of the struggle scarcely seemed to hurt. Dear "K.K." You are still alive and now live, where I would fain live, in the north of Scotland. But you are an old man, nearly as old as my father. Your grizzled hair is snow-white, and your massive frame which enabled you to hurl the cannon-ball prodigious distances is shrunk. I must now be as heavy as you are, and against the combined forces of my brother and myself you would not stand a chance.

I remember, too, very clearly a formidable nurse called Lena. Her instrument of torture was a red slipper which she used frequently, especially when I succeeded in opening the wicket-gate which barred the upstairs nursery from the staircase. My earliest recollections are mostly painful, for from an early age corporal punishment was the penalty for nearly all my transgressions. At Beith were born three of my four brothers: J. H. B., the Cambridge double Blue and Scottish "rugger" and cricket international and now headmaster of Sedbergh; Rob, now a colonel in the Indian Army, and Norman, who was killed at Loos. "J. H. B." was my junior by only a year-and-a-half and at an early age was called Rufus on account of his red hair. Later I christened him "K", which is the phonetic abbreviation of "Carrots". By the time I was six we always had two nurses. Lena was rigidly strict, but Susie, the younger nurse, who was then only a girl, was tender-hearted. On one occasion I was being beaten by my father for some unremembered offence. As my screams rent the air, Susie rushed to my mother and shouted: "For the Lord's sake, come quickly, madam. The headmaster is killing the child." My father stopped. From that moment Susie won my lasting affection. She remained with us for many years and was always a firm friend and ally. Her brother John won a bursary or scholarship at Spier's and was one of my father's best pupils.

On a similar occasion I played a less generous part. As a child, my second brother Rufus had a fiery temper. One day, while the nurses were out of the room, we quarrelled at dinner, and my brother seized the carving knife and threw it at me. It missed, but was promptly followed by a bottle which hit me on the head and made a deep gash behind my ear. The howl which I raised brought the whole household to the nursery. While my mother bandaged my head, my brother was taken to my father's dressing-room next door and was dealt with sternly. His yells seemed to me like the most soothing music and had an immediate effect in calming my own sobs.

This incident was of double benefit to my brother. His unerring aim with the bottle justified itself afterwards in several prizes won for throwing the cricket ball. The thrashing which he received had a permanent effect on his character, for to-day he has the self-discipline which every good schoolmaster requires, and his patience in face of irritation is almost saint-like.

Another faithful friend of those years of childhood was Bessie, the cook. She came from Islay, the most southerly of the Hebridean islands and famed the world over for its whisky. To citizens of the United States the island recalls a tragic memory of the Great War, for off its unfriendly coast two liners, carrying American troops, were sunk, one by a torpedo and the other as the result of a collision, with the loss of hundreds of lives.

Bessie lives in my memory for the presents of tartan plaids which she always brought us after her annual holiday in her island home. She was, too, the queen of scone-makers. When she was baking, we always seemed to know, and a visit to the kitchen was always rewarded with scones hot from the oven and thickly spread with butter and black-currant jam. These orgies generally had a painful ending in which "Gregory's Mixture", to me far more obnoxious than castor oil, provided the pain as well as the necessary corrective. We were very simply brought up. Very rarely were we given sweets to ruin our digestions, and for years we were never allowed to have both butter and jam on our daily bread. Bessie is still alive and I saw her when, after an absence of forty years, I revisited Beith in 1937.

I met her in a manner which throws an interesting light on the democratic virtues of Scottish education. I was being shown over the school by the headmaster, and in one class was introduced as an old boy who had achieved some distinction. As we were leaving the room, the schoolmistress came up to me. "You will not remember Bessie Lachlan, your old cook?" she said. "Her daughter is a friend of mine and a school teacher like me." She gave me Bessie's address, and I went straight off to see the old lady. I found her fully versed, though goodness knows how, in our family history and more than proud of her own. She had married a cabinet-maker, and, in addition to her schoolmistress daughter, she had a son who taught cabinet-designing at a technical college and another daughter married to a brilliant young Scot who is to-day a professor of Roman law at an English university.

At an early age we were taught to read and write, both our parents taking a keen interest in our education and visiting any slackness or evasion of lessons with appropriate sternness. When we were good, we were rewarded by being allowed to play in my father's study—a rather grim room with a large desk, a huge bookcase, and plain-papered walls decorated with numerous pictures of heavily moustached and sometimes bearded athletes who I afterwards discovered were Cambridge undergraduates. It had an atmosphere of awe, and we were always very quiet, curling up on the rug before the fire with a picture-book and scarcely daring to ask even the most exciting question, for my father always seemed to be working. Occasionally there would be a timid knock at the door. A stern look would come over my father's face, and we would be sent away to play with my mother. As we left the room, a boy with downcast face would be waiting outside. The door we had left open would close behind him. Then from the drawing-room across the hall we would hear the sound of the tawse, a long, thick leather strap with three thongs, as it descended on the victim's hand. The noise sounded terrifying, and in order to hear it better, we would steal into the hall. In a few minutes the study door would open, and the boy would slink away, rubbing his eyes with his coat-sleeve.

These scenes made an indelible impression on my youthful mind. Some years later, when I went to a real school, I was to have practical experience enough of knocking at study doors. Without exaggeration I can say that it required more courage than any experiences of my manhood, and from them I do not exclude my arrest and imprisonment by the Bolsheviks in 1918. Even to this day I never enter a school-master's study without feeling some twinge of self-conscious fear or without glancing round the room to spot the chair which serves as the throne of execution.

Fear, indeed, dominated my childhood more than any other emotion. My father, a great believer in the combination of a healthy body and a healthy mind, saw to it that we went out in all weathers. Nor was he in favour of too much supervision out of doors, holding that woman's sphere was in the house and the realm of nurses in the nursery. As the grounds of Spier's were extensive, they provided for us a new world which we were allowed to explore almost without restraint. There was a large plantation of young firs, and here we wandered at will, playing delicious games against Indians who had entered into my brother Rufus's life at an absurdly early age. For many years I do not think he ever read any other books than Kingston's *Adventures in the Far West* and *With Axe and Rifle*. Those two he knew by heart. In this plantation I found my first nest, and the discovery, since there was no one to put a check on our predatoriness, led to much subsequent and unnecessary cruelty.

In those early days Spier's, being new, always seemed un-finished, and, after reading *Kidnapped*, which I read and re-read by the time I was six, I succeeded in frightening myself with the thought that the house was the original House of Shaws; and, strangely enough, the picture of the House of Shaws in my edition of *Kidnapped* did bear some resemblance to Spier's. To be accurate, the house which Stevenson included in his story was at Cramond near Cargilfield, the well-known Scottish preparatory school of which my brother was subsequently headmaster before going to Sedbergh. Cramond was near Edinburgh, and we were living on the other side of Scotland. But in those days geographical distances meant nothing to me, and, if I ventured out on to the road near dusk and saw an old tramp woman approaching, I was convinced that she was Janet Clouston and that she was coming to call down "twelve hunner and nineteen" curses on our house and home.

From that period dates my nervous fear of tramps—a nervousness which in my Beith days amounted almost to an obsession. On one occasion both my brother and I had been given new shillings by a banker friend of the family. Immediately afterwards we met a tramp begging at the back door, and I promptly gave him my shilling. My good deed was recounted to my parents by my brother and did my credit in their eyes much good. Their confidence in me was misplaced. The impulse which induced me to part with my shilling was prompted neither by generosity nor yet by inherited Macgregor extravagance but by fear mingled with the hope that my offering would avert from me the effect of the tramp's evil eye.

My early dread of tramps had been greatly increased by a burglary which took place at Spier's about this time. Thieves broke into the cellars one night, and, although they removed nothing more valuable than a big load of potatoes, the incident assumed terrifying proportions in my mind. Doubtless my youthful imagination had been fired unhealthily by the story of the Arran murder which took place a few weeks before we went to Beith and which I had frequently heard discussed by John Wilson, the well-known Scottish advocate, who with Comrie Thomson defended Monson in the famous shooting case, and by other barrister friends of my father and mother.

The murder took place on Goatfell, the noblest peak in an island of noble mountains, and for a series of reasons at once stirred the imagination of the public in a remarkable degree. People were "jumpy" and nervous, thanks to Jack-the-Ripper, who was then at the height of his notoriety, and the public had murders very much in its mind. Moreover, Arran itself had a romantic appeal, for the island has a special niche in Scottish history as the place from which Robert the Bruce, encouraged by the example of the famous spider, set out on that last desperate expedition against the English which ended at Bannockburn. To those who like to sentimentalise over murders, what setting could be more morbidly exciting than Goatfell with all the scenic splendour of its lonely glens and corries. Add to this the fact that the murder took place in July, that the island, then as now, was a favourite holiday resort for Glasgow tourists, and that for nearly three weeks holidaymakers took part in the search for the murdered man's body, and you have the elements of a first-class murder drama.

Yet, stripped of its romantic trappings, the murder was a sordid one, for the only motive was robbery, and in the circumstances the gain to be expected could be, and indeed was, trifling. Two young men, an English clerk called Rose and a Scottish artisan named Laurie, met as holidaymakers on a steamer during Glasgow Fair week and decided to climb Goatfell together. From that climb Rose never came back, but it was not until he was expected in London at the end of his holiday and failed to return home that any fears were entertained for his safety. Even then no suspicion fell on Laurie, and it was only when Rose's body was at last found buried under a pile of stones in a lonely gully whose Gaelic name means "The Glen of Fire" that a hue and cry was started for his missing companion. A month after the discovery of Rose's body Laurie was captured. With commendable despatch he was taken to Edinburgh for trial.

Although the trial itself still ranks as one of the most notable in the long history of Scottish murder trials, it lasted only two days. Laurie was sentenced to death, and in the streets excited crowds fought for the special editions of the newspapers announcing the verdict. The excitement, however, was mild compared with the intense dissatisfaction when Laurie was subsequently reprieved on the ground of insanity, his sentence being commuted into one of penal servitude for life. Although public opinion was divided, the newspapers published caustic leaders, and questions were asked in Parliament. Nevertheless, the Secretary for Scotland seems to have acted with proper clemency, for of the forty-one years which Laurie endured in prison nearly the whole portion was passed in the lunacy department.

As a child of two or three I myself had spent a holiday under the shadow of Goatfell, and, although I remembered nothing about it, the fact that I was told I had been there gave me almost a personal connection with the murder, and my commonest form of nightmare was a kinematic picture of Laurie escaping from prison and, knife in hand, coming up the drive at Spier's. This story of the Arran murder, combined with the burglary which took place at home, so acted on my nerves that for several years I was terrified of the dark and was afraid to sleep alone. It is fortunate for me that these youthful fears left me as soon as I attained puberty. In Malaya, where I was the only white man within a radius of ten miles, I never felt a qualm, and to-day I would rather sleep alone in the jungle than share a room with my best friend.

I had other fears which are less easily explained. One was of my South African uncle, who with my aunt came to stay with us during one of their rare visits to Europe. His name was Marchand. He had been a South African student at Edinburgh University with my father. The two men had been friends. My father had brought him home, and the visit had ended with Marchand marrying my father's sister. He was of Huguenot descent, being, in fact, a grandson of the Marchand who as chamberlain accompanied Napoleon to St. Helena. When Napoleon died, the chamberlain settled in South Africa. And there my uncle was born. Although he was a Frenchman and, with his neat black beard and piercing black eyes, looked like one, he was an Afrikander through and through, spoke Afrikaans, was an ardent pro-Boer, and ended his career as one of the leaders of the Dutch Church in South Africa.

I can explain my fear of him only by two reasons. He was the first foreigner that I ever saw. He was a Calvinist minister, and I was even more afraid of ministers than of schoolmasters. The fear was wholly unreasonable, for, although grave and serious in all things, he was a kind and upright man incapable of any mean action. Indeed, whenever I see General Smuts, he always refers to this uncle in terms of admiration and respect. I think it must have been his strength of character which made me feel even smaller than I was. Perhaps my wayward soul realised instinctively that those piercing eyes could see through it, and that by such an inquisitor my own character would be weighed in the balance and found wanting.

I do not wish to create the impression that I was a nervous, timid child. My fears were kept to myself, and, if they loom large to-day, they troubled my thoughts only at long intervals. Children, in fact, are very like puppies. They jump about when they are amused and they slink away when they know that they have done wrong. Reasoning scarcely enters into these instinctive reactions, and both the joys and the fears are transient. In any case, even if I had possessed the faculty, I had little time for introspection. I went to school at Spier's at the age of six, and my brother Rufus, who was only four-and-a-half, went with me. As there were also boys of seventeen in the school, there was a considerable gap between the ages of the oldest and the youngest pupils.

I have no recollection of my first day. We were in the bottom form—a very juvenile class of girls and boys taught by a schoolmistress called Miss Rose. She was very kind and gentle, and, while the novelty lasted, I enjoyed the work better than play. The form was little more than a Kindergarten, and, while we learnt reading and spelling, struggled with sums, and wrote laborious copybooks with such inspiring texts as "Example is better than precept", the chief fun was the handiwork which occupied a large part of our time. We made plates for tea-cakes with string bound in neat designs round firm pieces of cardboard. Very insanitary plates they must have been, for they were of course unwashable, and we licked the string and pressed it down with dirty fingers in order to make it bind more closely. We also practised crewel work, if the name of that art can be applied to our designs made with coloured worsted on thin, perforated canvas. The first present that I ever gave to my mother was a kettle-holder with the words "Polly Put The Kettle On" blazoned in green, blue and yellow worsted. Miss Rose supplied me with the text, and, as my mother was christened Florence, I was a little puzzled by the "Polly".

But more important by far than school were the games which were organised for us. Since his own childhood my father's devotion to rugby football and cricket has been whole-hearted and single-minded. Although a good cricket coach, he was never much of a cricketer. His own football career was spoilt by pneumonia which wrecked his chances of a Blue and an International cap. But this misfortune has never chilled his ardour for the game, and his contemporaries have often told me of his prowess both as a player and as a pioneer. He took the first Cambridge college team to Scotland. He was at different periods of his life a member of the Scottish Rugby Union, that privileged body which selects Scotland's international teams. He introduced rugby football at Spier's in a district where rugby was almost unknown, and the fact that to-day the schools of the south-west play "rugger" is in a large measure the result of his early efforts.

Of that pioneer work we ourselves were a small but important part, and before we went to the Kindergarten and, indeed, almost as soon as we could walk we were carefully initiated into the mysteries of the game of games. My father had a special small size of "rugger" ball made for us. A small level piece of grass with baby goal-posts was reserved for our exclusive use. And here at the combined age of ten my brother and I learnt to punt and drop-kick, to tackle, to scrum, to dribble, to pass, and finally to indulge in terrific battles of one-a-side. Many of my father's friends were well-known footballers, and frequently we were urged to that extra ferocity which is the key-note of rugby football by the cheers and exhortations of famous internationals. Tears and sobs, more often the concomitants of violent rage than of physical pain, were frequent, but were never allowed to interfere with the rigour of the game.

Occasionally, too, my father and one of his friends or my two uncles would take part in the game, and then our excitement became hectic. If my uncles played, my brother and I had to play forward and "scrum" against each other. Then, as we pushed and swayed violently, an uncle would creep forward and give one of us a sly hack on the shin, so that each of us would think the kick came from the other, thus imparting more "ginger" to the struggle. Then tempers were unchained, and the "scrum" finished with a battle of flying fists. No doubt it was good fun for my uncles and the spectators, but to us it was grim and deadly earnest. We were almost as keen on cricket, and I have already told in *British Agent* how, when my brother Rob was born, I stole a raw beefsteak from the kitchen and placed it in his cradle so that he might grow strong and big very quickly and we could then have one to bat, one to bowl, and one to keep wicket.

I hate to think that there is anyone responsible for my actions except myself, but there is, undoubtedly, something in heredity. Thirty years after these stirring contests, I went to Rugby to stay with my brother Rufus, who was then a housemaster at the school which owes part of its renown to the fact that it was the original cradle of the particular type of football which bears its name. My brother's boys, John and Rab, were then about the same age as we were at Beith, and rather foolishly, for I was dressed in my best London suit, we renewed the old family game with Rufus and myself in the rôle of the grown-ups. I remember it painfully. The ground was just such a strip of grass beside the house as our old playing-field at Beith. But my brother bred Irish wolfhounds, and at a critical moment in the game I dashed across the ground to tackle my young nephew. A lusty wolfhound, thinking that I was attacking the child, made one bound at me. His snap was fortunately short of the flesh, but he caught my trousers just at the top of my posterior and ripped the back of one trouser-leg clean off, to the vast amusement of my brother, my nephews and a large group of Rugby boys who were looking on.

Although my own early passion for rugby football has declined in the more arduous struggle for life, my father's zeal remains unstaled by age or custom, and I doubt if there is any man living who knows so well the history of Scotland's international matches and of every man who has played in them.

Of his enthusiasm I shall give only one personal instance. I spent the first week-end of December 1936 with him. The Abdication crisis was then at its height. My book, *Return to Malaya*, had just been published and was reviewed at some length in the Sunday newspapers. Did he refer to the crisis or as much as mention my book? He did not. The newspapers also printed on that day the names of the Cambridge "rugger" fifteen who were to play against Oxford, and that of my young nephew, Rab, then in his first term, had been omitted. During the whole week-end, my father could talk of nothing but this family calamity.

Since then Rab has won a cap for Scotland, and my father's faith in a righteous world has been restored. He has been the best of fathers to me, but I cannot help feeling that his generosity, already more than ample, would have overflowed had I but worn the royal blue jersey of my country at

Murrayfield or Inverleith. As it is, this honour went to my brother Rufus, but I make bold to claim that he owes much of his skill at games and some of his sterling character to me. We were inseparable companions, and he, at least, was not spoilt. From an early age I kept him severely in order. In our football games he had to play to my whistle. At cricket he had to bowl to me, and my l.b.w. decisions were final. When we fished, I had first choice of pools, and he had to follow behind, taking what trout I had missed. He had to wear my cast-off clothes and shoes, and the rigorous training which I imposed bore its fruit in due season.

I am convinced that the right of primogeniture, not recognised in Scotland, has something to be said for it. Younger brothers have all the benefit of the eldest brother's discipline and experience. An eldest son has no one to guide him past the pitfalls of youth.

Of my parents and relations I have only one complaint to make, and that is their partiality for the Christian name of Robert and its various Scottish abbreviations. I myself was christened Robert after my father and my paternal grandfather. But I had also a Macgregor uncle called Rob, who was my mother's favourite brother. I have therefore both a brother and a cousin called Rob, and a nephew who was christened and is called Rab. This profusion of "R's" in one family is bewildering both to our friends and to ourselves and frequently results in the muddling of our bank accounts and correspondence. The temporary advantages which I have sometimes derived from the despatch of my bills to my brother's address are no real compensation for this irritating confusion, and I am strongly in favour of children being allowed to choose their own names as soon as they come of age. I should add that this criticism applies even more aptly to myself than to my parents. I christened my own son Robert.

CHAPTER FOUR

IT WOULD BE unjust as well as ungenerous if I were to create the impression that my father is a games-fanatic. At Beith he was a man of simple habits but catholic tastes and of far more tolerant views than most schoolmasters. He was, too, a Balfourian in the sense that he could always see every side of a question, and in those days his two heroes in history were Cromwell and Prince Rupert, a truly strange combination for a man who was brought up in the Presbyterian tradition and who has never shared my romantic enthusiasm for the Jacobite cause. Although his delivery is nervous and halting, he would have made a great preacher, for there was conviction and the power to transmit it to others in all that he said. Many years afterwards, when I heard him preach in the school chapel at Sandhurst, I used to feel a lump rise in my throat, caused partly by the emotional atmosphere which he could create and partly, I admit, by fear lest he might break down altogether. Some part of his rhetorical ability has been inherited by my second brother, who in recent years has made a considerable reputation as a school preacher.

In those Beith days my father stands out in my memory as a tremendous worker and as a man who, whatever he was doing, never relaxed. By more ways than mere example he was able to impose his own capacity for industry on his children. Under his influence I developed an early taste for history, and one of my favourite books was Peter Parley's *Universal History*, given to me on my seventh birthday. I have it still—a thick brown book of 568 pages with my father's bold handwriting on the title page.

Curiously enough, the author of the Peter Parley series was an American, to wit, Samuel Griswold Goodrich of Boston. Apart from his children's books he has a permanent place in American literary history as the editor of *The Token*, the periodical in which Nathaniel Hawthorne's first literary efforts were published. If in my case a Scot owes something to America, many Americans also owe much to a Scot, for McGuffy, the author of the once famous American school-readers, was, like Washington Irving, Herman Melville and many other American writers, of Scottish origin.

Peter Parley's *Universal History* became my Bible, and in a short time I could answer all or most of the questions which formed the appendix to every chapter. It was a great book, and to-day I would give much to know all that it contains. In my early youth I was a precocious child. To-day, I realise that this was a misfortune and a handicap, for all too often precocity burns itself out, and nearly always it is the plodder, like my brother Rufus, who reaches the fuller development.

In my Peter Parley stage my precocity or, perhaps I should say, my good memory soon led me into trouble. Our Kindergarten classes occupied only the morning, but at the age of seven I was made to attend the history class of a higher form during the afternoons. Here I sat at a desk by myself in my brown tweed coat and kilt of Macgregor tartan among boys who were twice my age. The master, Peter Harrower, had an unpleasant habit of asking me to supply the answer—generally a date or a name—whenever one of the bigger boys failed. If my answer was right, out would come the tawse, and the bigger boy was made to come up to the desk and hold out his hand. I must have been a hateful and un-popular child, for I was neither humane nor wise enough to learn the trick of answering incorrectly on purpose. On the contrary, I was all eagerness to raise my voice, holding up my hand and jumping about in my seat if I thought I knew the correct reply and feeling very crestfallen if, as sometimes happened, it was wrong. Later, I was to pay dearly for this early bumptiousness, but at that time I was serenely innocent of the enormity of my offence, and, of course, both on ac-count of my tender age and because I was the headmaster's son I was immune from all punishment.

To the credit of my better nature, I did not gloat over the thrashings. On the contrary, they filled me with a dread of corporal punishment, and, although I believe in this form of penalty for the normal boy and remember more with pride than with any other sentiment the numerous beatings I myself have received, I have never laid a hand or a cane on my own son. What the tawse did inspire me with was a feeling of immense admiration for the courage of the boys of Spier's School. The tough strips of leather made their hands red and swollen, but very few of them cried. When a boy called Glen burned the instrument of torture, I was so proud of him that at afternoon tea, at which my brother and I always appeared, I recounted this deed of daring in all innocence to my father and mother. The incident provided a salutary lesson to me and a happy conclusion to the pending troubles of Glen, for I was reproved once and for all for tale-bearing, and Glen, who had been reported to my father, was spared the castigation which would otherwise have been his inevitable fate.

Scottish education was a great force in those days, and greater still was the urge of poorer families to acquire it. Many of the pupils at Spier's School were poor boys who had won scholarships. Some of them did brilliantly, and by their subsequent success in life supplied further proof of the theory that, whatever money may do for breeding—and in two generations it can achieve miracles—brains are the real source of culture. During my father's time the best scholar was the son of the local blacksmith. From Spier's School he went with a succession of scholarships, first to Glasgow University and then to Balliol, Oxford. He is to-day Dr. W. K. Gillies, Rector of the Royal High School, Edinburgh, where Edward VII was once a pupil. But my own hero among the bigger boys was Alec Frew, now a leading doctor in South Africa and the first Scottish "rugger" international ever produced by Spier's School. If my admiration was inspired by games-prowess, it was not misplaced. Frew was a boy of

outstanding character and was one of the small band of tee-
totallers in the invincible Scottish side of 1901.

Going to school made one great difference in my life. It
enabled me to distinguish between lessons and holidays. Although most schoolmasters would disagree, I am convinced
that holidays have more influence on a boy's character and
imagination than his schooldays. This theory applies with
special force to the sons of schoolmasters who, themselves
having long holidays, are able to share them with their children. Certainly in my own case the holidays stand out as the
clearest landmark in my memories of my childhood.

Even as a baby I travelled far afield. I am told that, with
the exception of one summer in Arran, I spent every August
and September, from my birth to my sixth year, at Balmenach, my mother's old home in the Highlands. I accept this
testimony as correct, but it would be stretching my imagination to the limits of exaggeration to say that I have anything
more than the vaguest recollections of these early visits to the
north. It might have been different had I gone there only
once. But these returns to the north were to be recurring
until my mother's death, and my first visits are now shroud-
ed in the accumulation of subsequent and clearer memories.
I have, too, only a foggy recollection of an early visit to my
father's relations at Prestwick and of a bent old man with a
black coat and a large gold watch who I was told was my
grand-uncle. His name was John Wilson, and he and his father before him had been factors to the Scottish estates of the
Duke of Portland and in this capacity had superintended the
building of the first private railway in Scotland. I remember
faintly the green, sandy turf of the golf course and the famous Pow burn.

My first conscious memory of an outing was a trip to
Glasgow in the spring of 1894. My brother and I were taken
by Colonel Faulds, a friend of my father. We went by train
and were alone in his charge. The event of the afternoon was
a visit to Bostock and Wombwell's circus and menagerie. We

rode on the elephant and on camels and were both awed and thrilled. It is not for these reasons that this treat is so clearly impressed on my memory. For the occasion we had been dressed in new sailor suits. We had been told to be very careful of them. And so we were until we became fascinated by the lions. A considerable crowd was watching them as they circled restlessly round their cage. Holding my brother's hand I pressed forward to get a better view. At this moment an old lioness chose to turn her back on her audience and to make her water through the bars. Unable to retreat, we were drenched. We cried bitter tears of discomfort and mortification. And the Colonel, a nervous, orderly man unused to children, was so embarrassed that he took us straight to the station without giving us the scrumptious tea which we had been promised and to which we had looked forward with the healthy gluttony of childhood.

These, however, were only minor incidents in a life of uneventful domesticity, and the first great adventure in my career begins with the summer of 1894 when for the only occasion in the conscious memory of my lifetime the family did not go to the Highlands. I suppose that every family has its foibles known to all its members. In our case the recurring weakness was the annual discussion where to spend the summer holidays. The discussion began in the spring and lasted until July. It always took the same course. My mother's answer was unchanging and, indeed, unchangeable. Strathspey was in her blood. But my father always wanted to break fresh ground. He would produce maps, guide-books and house-agents' prospectuses and leave them lying about the house for my mother to see. Then at luncheon he would say with affected heartiness: "What about the West Coast for this summer? I've heard this morning of a suitable house at Machrihanish." Machrihanish meant golf, which my father liked. Except for a mild interest in the crudest form of sea-fishing he was no angler. My mother would ask to see the prospectus of the house. With feminine diplomacy she would make no opposition to Machrihanish as a holiday choice, but before the evening she would be sure to find a hundred objections, sanitary or domestic, to the house. And so it went on until in the end my father surrendered to the inevitable. And such is the force of habit in the lives of good fathers and good husbands that since my mother's death my father, alone, without wife and without children, always spends August in Strathspey.

But in this summer of 1894 my father's will triumphed, and we went to Strachur, a little fishing village on the east shore of Loch Fyne, that long, narrow inlet of the sea which is famous the world over for its herrings. My mother, bringing her gift of second sight into play, was gloomy with forebodings, and, in truth, the venture began with a minor tragedy. For these summer jaunts we had a general's baggage-train, taking with us servants, plate, linen, and other household impedimenta. On the day fixed for our departure the luggage went off first in a huge cart. My mother, my brother Rufus and myself, and the nurse with my brother Rob, followed in one of Beith's few four-wheelers. My father was to come later in the family dog-cart. In her attitude towards transport my mother suffered temperamentally from train-fever and always arrived at the station half an hour before the train was due to start. In those days my father was never known to catch a train until it was leaving the platform. On this occasion parental characteristics ran true to form. My father was late and arrived just as the train was entering the station. But the luggage was later still. A wheel had come off the cart. The driver did his best and was seen cresting the station hill just as the guard blew his whistle. "Please keep the train back," said my mother imperiously, but the stationmaster was inexorable, and, as there was only one steamer a day to Strachur, there was nothing left for us to do but to go home and try our luck on the following morning.

My mother's rage was epic, but the heat of it was diverted

from my father to the unfortunate stationmaster who had refused to hold back the train. From that day I have inherited my mother's train-fever, and in a long life of travel have never missed either a train or a steamer. My brother Rufus, a man of nearly all the virtues, takes after my father in his razor-edge economy of time.

For us boys the accident to the luggage was a happy one, for during the whole of that day the rain fell relentlessly, and the next morning was gloriously fine. We went to Glasgow and embarked in the *Lord of the Isles*, a Clyde paddle-steamer on the Inveraray service and the second of her name. She maintained that service until 1912 when she was beaten by the turbine engine and replaced by a more modern steamer. But she was still employed on excursion traffic until she was broken up a few years ago and during her long life must have carried hundreds of thousands of Glaswegians. She is now honoured by a beautiful model in the Glasgow Art Galleries.

In 1894 she was almost a new steamer, being barely three years old, and as this was the first time, to my knowledge, that I had been on the sea, the details of that first voyage are far clearer in my memory than those of subsequent voyages now blurred by the mists of multiplicity. Perhaps because never again have I sailed from Glasgow, I can still see the grimy water at Port Glasgow gradually melting into the blue of the Firth of Clyde. I can still visualise Dunoon and Rothesay, where we called on our way, and in spite of all changes would know them again to-day. And without effort I recall our excitement when we passed our sister-ship, the *Iona*. *Wee Macgreegor* was not then written, and there was no Aunt Purdie to say don't do this and don't do that. My fourth brother, Norman, was then five months on his way into the world, and my mother was far from well. My father, never a stern disciplinarian out of school except on Sundays, spent most of his time by her side, and we were free to roam the ship as we pleased and even to penetrate into the engine-room where the engineer, kind to children whatever he was to grown-ups, lifted us with his oily hands and let us see and smell the piston and the other arcana of his mechanical temple.

Since then I have met Glasgow engineers and seen Glasgow engines on scores of ships, from cargo steamers in the East Indies and coasting steamers in the Adriatic to the *Queen Mary* and the other giant liners of the trans-Atlantic service, but no engineer and no engine-room have ever given or will ever give me quite the same thrill as those primitive engines of the *Lord of the Isles* and the sweating, grizzly-moustached Clydesider who was so proud of them. Better even than the engine-room was our point of vantage behind the paddle-box from which we watched for hours the kaleidoscopic changes in the colour of the water as the paddles churned it into delicious eddying circles of every shade of green and blue.

When we arrived at Strachur, we were far too excited to want to go to bed, and I remember exploring with all the enthusiasm of a gold-hunter the secrets of our temporary home, probably the most primitive and ill-furnished of all the many houses which we leased for the summer holidays. But it was close to the sea and had a little stone jetty of its own. There was an orchard behind it, and the nursery had a plain, white-wood table which on wet days could be turned upside down and converted with the aid of napkins into a schooner in which we sailed imaginary and hitherto uncharted seas.

This was the prelude to an enchanting holiday which had no dull moments and only one minor tragedy. The tragedy had its opening scene in the orchard. The apples were far from ripe, and we had been warned not to touch them. Here, however, was a new temptation, and I yielded to it, playing Eve's part by giving some of my stolen fruit to my brother. The results were painful. We were very ill and in our distress were forced to confess. My mother, a severely practical woman in big issues, had reduced medicine to the simplest science: Parrish's Food, a delicious concoction, to give strength to good children, Gregory's Mixture for the disordered stomachs of naughty boys. On this occasion we had Gregory's Mixture, early bed, and a disturbed night.

Dr. Gregory was something more than a family remedy. He was, I believe, a relation. At least he was a Macgregor, although this knowledge did not make us alter our dislike of him. Like many Macgregors, his parents had been forced to change their name. Dr. Parrish still obtrudes himself pleasantly on my memory. He was the great-uncle of my publisher's wife and, true to the highest professional standards, never made a penny out of his famous prescription.

Our orchard disaster was soon forgotten in the compensations which Strachur afforded us. Sunsets and scenery then meant little to me, but every day brought a new discovery in that children's world which our natural curiosity was given free rein to explore. Of these early discoveries fishing was the first, and it has been the most lasting. To-day, one of the least harmful of my vanities is my pride in my skill as an angler. I should dearly like to say that the first fish I ever caught was a trout. But the truth compels me to admit that the first fish was, in fact, a crab caught from our Strachur jetty with the faithful Susie shouting warnings to us from the shore as we slithered on the seaweed-covered, slippery stones. No hook was employed in this capture, for the lure was merely a limpet securely attached to a stout piece of string. It was the gardener's boy who showed us the trick, and very grateful we were to him.

After this first triumph we regularly went sea-fishing with my father in a boat and caught lots of whiting and small cod. When it was calm we were allowed to hold on to our father's or the boatman's oar and to pretend that we were rowing. But of course we were forbidden to go out in the boat alone, nor, indeed, had we any chance of doing so, for it was always securely padlocked. This greater fishing, therefore, was less attractive than our own mass slaughter of crabs, and, since in the boat the boatman baited our lines and told us when a fish was on so that we had merely to pull it in, we speedily learnt that the true joy of fishing lies in fishing alone and in doing things by one's self.

Sometimes the boatman was left behind, and I remember our early fears when my father, a very keen swimmer who to-day still bathes in the open air and until his seventieth year terrified us all by continuing his daily swim right up to Christmas, used to undress and plunge into the middle of the sea-loch, leaving us alone in the open boat. On one occasion a small whale came up at what seemed an alarmingly close distance, and we howled with fright until my father clambered back into the boat. This whale made a tremendous impression on our minds. Doubtless my father would have preferred us to say nothing about the incident, but he had far too fine a sense of loyalty even to hint that it would be wiser not to alarm my mother. As it was, the story was faithfully narrated at luncheon and with the many "ohs" of childish exaggeration lost nothing in the telling. My mother, properly frightened, was angry, and my father received a scolding.

Just opposite Strachur there was a tiny fishing village on the other side of the loch to which my father often rowed us. The cottages were indescribably poor, and the villagers were queer, dark folk who looked more like gipsies than fishers.

During those holidays my father read to us Samuel Baker's *Cast Up By The Tide*, a splendid boys' thriller of smuggling and deliberate wrecking. The chief character was a horrible old woman who during storms used to light beacons on dangerous points of the coast in order to entice ships to their doom so that she and her friends could plunder the wreck. In the end, in her excitement, the old hag with her tar-stained clothes drew too near to her own hell-fire and was burnt to death.

My juvenile taste for the macabre made me connect this story with the village opposite. The fishers were dour and to our minds suspect, and there was an old woman who sold mussels and who looked the very incarnation of the old witch in Baker's book. I did not like going through that village and was always very silent and kept very close to my father. I think that in those days I subconsciously enjoyed giving myself the creeps. At any rate it is a form of excitement in which I still indulge.

Even in holiday time our education was not entirely neglected, and we were encouraged to draw and to write. I liked writing stories with a plentiful sprinkling of terrorising adjectives. My handwriting was atrocious and is worse to-day. My brother Rufus preferred drawing and playing with water-colours. To-day he spends most of his holidays in painting, and, almost without a lesson, has carried the art so far that he has been "hung" both in the English and Scottish Academies.

On wet days my father, a great believer in learning poetry by heart, used to give us a piece of verse to master. From those Strachur days dates my knowledge of *Lord Ullin's Daughter*. In my youth this ballad figured in every Scottish school anthology—goodness knows why, for it must be the worst poem that Campbell ever wrote, and to-day even a Fourth Form schoolboy would be ashamed to show up as original verse these last four lines:

> "Twas vain: the loud waves lashed the shore,
>   Return or aid preventing;
> The waters wild went o'er his child,
> And he was left lamenting."

But at that time it was as much a story to me as an Edgar Wallace thriller is to the modern boy, and, although Loch Gyle, the scene of this treacly tragedy, was far away in Mull, with my passion for adapting everything to my own environment I was easily able to visualise it as Loch Fyne.

Rain or no rain there was one delight which we never missed and of which we never tired. This was the arrival of the daily steamer. When it came in sight, we would clamber out on to our little stone jetty and, standing there in our short blue mackintosh capes, wait patiently until the waves from the steamer's wash broke in foam against the tiny wall and wet our feet.

Assuredly, the simple joys of poor children are more lasting than the transient pleasure of the most expensive toys, for they endure far beyond the age of childhood and retain their full charm in retrospect. They have the additional merit of providing a better training for the battle of life.

CHAPTER FIVE

THE GREAT EVENT of those Strachur holidays was the trip with our father to Inveraray, the royal burgh of Argyllshire and the ancestral abode of the Dukes of Argyll and the Clan Campbell. To my father as a Lowlander the Campbells are honest, God-fearing patriots who saved Scotland for Presbyterianism. To my mother they were pirates and robbers who deprived the Macgregors of their rightful lands. In her opinion they were not to be trusted even to this day; and she was inordinately proud of a Stewart ancestor, who after the Forty-Five lived as a refugee in the forests near her Highland home and spent his time in adapting the Psalms to his own anti-Campbell liking. One began somewhat in this fashion:

> "The Lord's my shield; I shall be stout
>   With targe and trusty blade.
>   Though Campbells come in droves about,
>   I shall not be afraid."

On the occasion of my first and only visit to this Campbell stronghold my mother stayed at home. My father, who knows his Scottish history well, was an inspiring guide. While we visited the castle, he told us the story of *Catriona*, the sequel to my already well-thumbed *Kidnapped*, and of the famous trial—or rather of the judicial murder, for the jury was composed exclusively of Campbell men—of James of the Glens for the shooting of the "Red Fox", the Campbell factor who collected the rents from the unfortunate Jacobites. Stevenson has popularised the story of the Appin murder far beyond the confines of Scotland, and even to-day the hanging of a man, well-known to be innocent, for political revenge has an interest to law-students far excelling that of the most exciting modern murder trial and has supplied a subsidiary theme to more than one modern Scottish historical novel.

On me the story had an immediate effect, and I think that my Highland blood must have asserted itself from that moment. At any rate ever since then I have never taken kindly to those Scottish chieftains who owe their lands and such wealth as they still possess to their having taken the side of the Hanoverians against the Stuarts. This instinctive antipathy is the most biased historical sentiment and is purely impersonal. I have played billiards with the present Duke of Argyll's heir, without being conscious of instinctive hate and without even feeling my temper rise when I was soundly beaten. Nevertheless, the anti-Campbell instinct is there, and there is no accounting for it except by those traditional impulses which are bred in our mothers' wombs and which constitute and will continue to constitute the chief bar to the realisation of an international Utopia.

In the Highlands themselves this hate of the Campbells is now dead, but it lasted for over two hundred years. I remember being told by a Highland peer how, when he was a boy, he wished to bring a school friend home for the holidays. He asked his mother's permission, and of course it was given at once. Later, she asked casually what the boy's name was. Her son said—Campbell, and at once the mother's face lengthened. "I'm afraid you will have to put him off," she said. "Surely you know that your father will not have a Campbell under his roof." In more recent times I came across a book on the Highlands by the most tolerant of Catholic bishops. It is a charming book devoted to history, folklore and old legends. Politics have no place in it, but in one reference to the persecution of the Clan Gregor by the Campbells, the prelate could not help adding the epithet, "a name for ever odious in the Highlands." And child as I was at the time of this first visit to Inveraray, I felt a shudder of resentment when my father pointed out the place where scores of Macgregors had been hanged to satisfy the Campbell lust for power and possessions.

To-day, Inveraray is chiefly associated in my mind as the

home of that great writer and great Highland gentleman, Neil Munro. Several of his novels, notably *John Splendid* and *Doom Castle*, have an Inveraray setting, but, although I believe that Munro had Campbell blood in him, most of his heroes belonged to those minor septs who served their masters well and whose loyalty to their chieftains rightly provides the romantic appeal of the Jacobite cause and, incidentally, the chief attraction of the Highlander.

It always shocks me when my English and American literary friends raise their eyebrows when I mention Munro. "Neil Munro," they say with a querying smile, "not Harold? Ah yes, I remember. I read him as a boy. An excellent Scottish Weyman."

And these are not only the highbrows, but also the middlebrows who rightly delight in John Buchan!

Perhaps there is too much dialect in Munro for Anglo-American tastes, but he is, I am glad to say, becoming an increasingly important figure in his own country, and, more than any other Scottish writer, is the spiritual father of the post-war school of Scottish writers who have already done so much to revive Scottish letters. Munro brought back to Scottish literature the national spirit and the Gaelic poetry which had too long been absent, and his place in the national temple of heroes is secure.

That I never even saw Stevenson was no fault of mine. But I was offered many opportunities of meeting Munro, and my neglect of them ranks high among the regretted things which I have left undone. As a poet he makes an even stronger appeal to Scottish exiles than does Stevenson, and there is one verse of his which has become interwoven in the texture of my philosophy of life:

> "I must be rising and I must be going
>   On the roads of magic that stretch afar,
>   By the random rivers so finely flowing,
>   And under the restless star.

I must be roaming on the roads of glory,
So, I'll up and shoe me with red-deer hide,
For Youth must be learning the ancient story—
Let the wearied oldsters bide."

To my father this Inveraray trip was to afford no road of magic, although it involved a vast usage of shoe-leather if not of red-deer hide. I have already referred to my mother's delicate state of health, and one of the objects of our journey to Inveraray was to buy some medicine for her. The medicine was duly purchased, and we were already half-way down the loch on our way home when suddenly my father clapped his hand to his pocket. A look of dismay came over his face. He had left the bottle of medicine in the little hotel where we had had tea.

There was only one steamer a day and, therefore, only one thing to do. After bringing us home, my father took the rowing boat, rowed across the loch to the village opposite, walked the twelve miles to Inveraray and back to get the medicine, and then rowed home again. My father is sometimes a rather forgetful man, but in self-denial and in doing the right thing he has always been heroic.

To my father and mother that Strachur holiday was purgatory, for it rained every day of the six weeks that we were there. The experiment was therefore never repeated, and henceforth my mother had her own way about Strathspey. True, I remember many holidays in that delectable valley when it rained incessantly, but to my mother there was all the difference of two worlds between Strachur rain and Strathspey rain. As far as we children were concerned, rain never interfered with our lives and a little later was prayed for and welcomed for the "spates" which it brought to the burns in which we served our trout-fishing apprenticeship.

For my own part I have no recollection of a rain-sodden Strachur, and to-day I see the little village under blue skies with the loch shimmering in the sunlight. When, at the end of the holidays, I arrived at the station hotel in Glasgow where we spent the night, I felt a good two inches taller. I had advanced a long mile on the road to the knowledge of life. I had discovered the new world of sea and boats.

I was not to revisit Glasgow again until I came back in 1919, soon after my release from the Kremlin and my exchange for Litvinoff, in order to address the Scottish-Russian Society and to be entertained to luncheon by the City Corporation. Although the city itself contains a quarter, and the whole area more than half, of the total population of Scotland, I know Glasgow less than any other Scottish city. Nevertheless, although I am always appalled by the stunted growth of its working-classes, I have a warm affection for the place, and especially for its people. Between Glasgow and Edinburgh there is something of the same rivalry that exists between New York and Chicago and between St. Petersburg and Moscow. My own preferences were for Moscow and Chicago because their inhabitants are, or were, free from the taint of official snobbishness and because their hospitality is spontaneous. I feel that, for all my love of Edinburgh as the most beautiful capital in Europe, I should, for the same reasons, give my vote to Glasgow if ever I were asked, which God forfend, to make the choice. Certainly no lecturer would hesitate to choose a Glasgow audience in preference to an Edinburgh one. An Edinburgh audience is coldly critical, sizes up a man by the substance rather than by the fireworks of his address, and reserves its judgment until the end. Glasgow's emotions are nearer the surface, and it gives its heart generously to those who can touch it. I hope that I am not ungracious to a city in which I have spent many happy years and which I come back to again and again. Perhaps it is the climate which influences my judgment. The west wind is softer than the east.

The autumn term after our Strachur holiday was the beginning of my last school year at Beith. Certain events of that year are photographed for ever in my memory. First, there was an exceptionally severe winter, when six weeks of continual frost gave me my first experience of skating. My father "curled" nearly every day at Loch Winnoch, making by train what to-day is a very short journey by motor car. But my mother skated nearer home, and took me with her to the private pond of an old gentleman who had a place with charming grounds called Morrishill. We drove there every day in the dog-cart, my knees being covered by a lion-skin rug, a gift from my aunt in South Africa. My first pair of skates were Acmes and were very difficult to put on. Frequently, too, a skate would come off just as one was gaining speed, and the results were painful to the skater. To-day, after my life in the tropics, I cannot stand the cold and during my eight years in Russia I skated only once. But in those Beith days I was hardy enough. I skated in a kilt, with very short trews, and suffered nothing worse from the winter than chapped knees.

Skating increased the circle of my youthful acquaintances, and at Morrishill I made firm friends with the Sneddon boys and girl, the children of the doctor who brought three of my brothers into the world. Robert Sneddon, the elder son, was rather too old for us and was already one of the bigger boys at Spier's School. In later life he took to writing and was, I think, the first author that Spier's produced. When I was a young man, one of his books, *Alphonse in the Land of Cakes*— a humorous description of a Frenchman's sporting adventures in Scotland, was serialised in a Scottish newspaper and gave me a vast amount of amusement.

The second son and the daughter Jean became our constant companions, and in the spring, eager to put our Strachur fishing experiences to a further test, we made many angling expeditions together. Our first attempts were made in the Marshland burn which ran close to the school football ground. It contained a few small but very wily trout, and alas! we never succeeded in making a single capture. A happier hunting-ground was an old disused quarry full of water.

It was deep, and we could not swim. Doubtless, to-day, the modern mother would be aghast at the idea of allowing young children to fish in such dangerous holes, but, as far as we were concerned, the permission was never refused for the simple reason that it was never sought. Armed with tiny shilling rods and carrying old tin cans which served as pails, we marched off every day to the quarry, and here with small hooks baited with worms we caught hundreds of sticklebacks.

Brought up in the competitive games spirit, we formed ourselves into teams and backed one catch against the other. My team-mate was Jean Sneddon, and it would be easy to exaggerate this association into the first idyll of my youthful life. But I do not think that my affection ever progressed beyond the stage of baiting her hook and championing her in the frequent disputes which arose over the legitimacy of a capture or the size of the biggest stickleback.

In due course these fishing expeditions produced the inevitable accident. One day the Sneddon boy was baiting his hook with the line lying on the ground. My brother tripped over the line, and the hook went deep into the Sneddon forefinger. We tried a little amateur surgery, but it was soon stopped by the patient's screams. Mournfully we formed a procession and in Indian file, with me carrying the rod, my brother and Jean holding the line, and the Sneddon boy with the hook in his finger, trooped off to the doctor's surgery. The finger had to be lanced, but the mishap did not damp our angling enthusiasm, and the next day the victim, with his finger bandaged, was back in his place.

A few weeks later I landed my first trout. It was a big fish, far bigger than any that I was to catch for several years, but the method of its capture was inglorious. As a reward for our keenness we were taken by Smith, the Beith joiner, to the local reservoir. He had with him three large rods. They were baited with worms. Then, with a prodigious cast, he hurled the baits far out into the reservoir and laid the rods down, labelling one "Master Bertie's" and another "Master Rufie's" and keeping one for himself. Then we sat down and waited. The waiting was tedious, for sport was slow, and, after eating the scones which Bessie had made for us, we lost interest and deserted the water's edge for the mysteries of the wood beside it. At last, a shout from Smith brought us scurrying back. Fortune had favoured my rod. Far out in the water we saw a commotion. It was undoubtedly a fish, and it was at the end of my line. Smith played the trout until it was exhausted. Then he handed the rod to me and allowed me to reel it in. It was a fish of nearly a pound and a half, and, triumphant, I bore it home to exhibit it and to recount its capture to my father and mother and to the more appreciative audience of the servants' quarters.

During my last summer term at Beith I widened my horizon by a visit to Largs, a pleasant town on the Ayrshire coast, which to-day serves as a kind of Margate for Glasgow. From its shores Clyde-built vessels, from the *Queen Mary* to the smallest motor-boat, may be seen testing their engines on a measured mile between the town and Wemyss Bay. Largs, too, has an honoured place in Scottish history as the birthplace of Sir Thomas Brisbane, one of many Scots who have given their names to cities of the British Empire, and as the site of the great battle in which Alexander III of Scotland defeated King Hakon of Norway, thus adding to the Kingdom of Scotland the Hebrides and the Isle of Man which had been held by the Norsemen for more than four centuries.

My visit to Largs was not educational. I went as the reserve for the Spier's School junior cricket team. I was not worthy of my place even as a reserve and had been given it by a gross piece of favouritism as the headmaster's son. The school that we were playing against was Routenburn, one of the first preparatory schools in Scotland. It was founded by Norman MacLachlan, an Old Lorettonian and one of the few Scottish schoolboys to win a cricket Blue at Oxford, and by E. P. Frederick, a former Loretto master and a lifelong friend of my father. The school was run on Loretto lines, and here for the first time I saw the scarlet blazer, the scarlet stockings, cricket shirt and white shorts which form the neat and distinctive uniform of that famous school, whose brilliant company of "rugger" Blues and Internationals was trained on Pinkie, a football ground which as a boy I always believed was the actual site of the great battle. Later, I myself was to do battle both at cricket and football against Loretto, and, as I did better in those matches than in any others, I have a natural admiration for the school. But of my first experience of Routenburn, its nursery, I have only vague memories: a feeling of awe at lunching in a big hall with strange boys and a dim recollection of a dismal afternoon's cricket during which we were soundly beaten. The truth is that the day was too tiring for me, and long before its end the youthful reserve was sleeping in his father's arms.

Infinitely more vivid are my memories of the great crisis which led to my father's leaving Beith. I have already said that the founder's wishes had not been clearly expressed in his will, and from the first my father had difficulties with the governing body, or, to be accurate, with one member of it. This school council was composed of members of the local gentry including a Cochrane Patrick, a Dalrymple Hay and a Macdougall of Garthland, and an equal number of representatives of the town of whom the chief was the local parish minister. My father wanted to run the school as far as possible on public school lines, and in this effort he received the support of the aristocrats. The town governors, however, were Radicals and advocates of cheap education. They insisted that the founder's intentions were to provide a school for the poor boys of Beith.

The difference of opinion between the parish minister and my father developed into a personal quarrel, and soon the situation assumed all the elements of those Scottish parochial comedies of which James Bridie, the Glasgow dramatist, is such a successful exponent. The friction was extended to, and amplified by, the wives. My mother, young and full of

Highland pride, hunted; worse still, she was fond of dancing. An even graver offence was the fact that she was on friendly relations with the three Patrick families, and it was on the small private course of one of their Ayrshire homes that I played, or rather tried to play, my first game of golf. In those days hunting, dancing, and even golf, whatever their virtues may be, were vices in a schoolmaster's wife, and Mrs. Parish Minister made little attempt to disguise her disapproval. My mother was not given to wrangling, but her freezing attitude could say more than words. The personal antipathy became so marked that my father left the parish church and transferred his religious allegiance to the United Presbyterian whose minister was Mr. Glen, the father of the boy who burned the tawse. This old gentleman with grey beard, wistful, kindly eyes, and a broad Ayrshire accent is the first of many Scottish Presbyterian ministers whose portraits I shall remember until the grave. He was fond of children, carried a poke of sweeties in his coat-tails, and was one of the few ministers of any church of whom I stood in no awe.

Although my father had strong backing, he was in a weaker position than that of the parish minister. The landowners were irregular in their attendance at the governing body's meetings; the town representatives, having the advantage of proximity as well as the greater zeal, never missed a sitting. The climax came when a school board election, fought on the issue of free books, ended in a victory for the parish minister. This would have given him a dominant position in the council, and my father, whom without prejudice I should have considered the most difficult man to quarrel with in the world, gave up a struggle, as unequal as it was undignified, and sent in his resignation which was to take effect at the end of the term. He had long been considering purchasing a private school in which he could carry out his own ideas, and shortly after his resignation he made a trip south in order to inspect possible properties in England. His absence made the story of his resignation public, and the first rumour of it came to me through that recognised news medium for children, the servants' hall.

My father's business trip did not result in our immediate transfer to England. While staying at Clifton with an old schoolmaster friend he met Otto Siepmann, the well-known modern languages expert, and the father of my friend Harry Siepmann, who under the aegis of Mr. Montagu Norman now controls the Equalisation Fund of the Bank of England and, incidentally, the purchasing power of your pounds and mine. This meeting was accidental, but it altered the family destiny, for Siepmann had recently been approached by some prominent citizens of Dundee with a view to finding a man who would be prepared to start a preparatory school on English lines in Forfarshire. As a result of their meeting Siepmann recommended my father and gave him letters of introduction to the interested parties in Dundee. With surprising quickness, for my father has always been a man of deliberation, the deal was concluded, and for his new venture he purchased, with the aid of his own father, Seafield House in Broughty Ferry.

When the news of this purchase became public, the local quarrel collapsed like a pricked balloon. With characteristic parochial sentiment the governing body, now almost unanimous, invited my father to withdraw his resignation. But it was too late, and instead of what would have been inevitably a return to the former state of affairs there were emotional scenes of farewell. I assisted at one of these when the whole school assembled in the big hall beside Spier's statue to present a gold watch to my father. As usual, he spoke nervously but with an emotional effect which made a deep impression on the boys, including his eldest son.

His pending departure produced no relaxation of my father's industry. Indeed, I think he would go on working even if he were under sentence of death and would be writing notes and preparing school timetables up to the moment of his execution. Part of his industry was devoted to supervision of our homework, and, thanks to his vigilance, I had a successful term. Pride in my own efforts, however, provided the usual pitfall. The summer term, as the end of the scholastic year, had a prize-giving ceremony. A special school list was published by the local printer, and under the heading of Junior School I found my name mentioned twice: once as first in history and again as "prox. acc." for geography. I had been told that all the "mentions" in the school list would receive prizes, and I had been duly warned by Miss Rose, our schoolmistress, to walk up promptly to the platform when my name was called out.

When the great day came, a large gathering of parents and boys assembled in the big hall. The proceedings opened with a short musical programme to which the Junior School contributed a sickly sentimental song, each verse beginning with a melancholy wail of:

> "Pitter patter, pitter patter,
> Pitter patter, goes the rain."

Then my father, dressed in his Cambridge B.A. gown with white rabbit fur and armed with a sheaf of notes and lists of marks, stood up on the platform. The prize-giving was about to begin. Impatiently I waited while the bigger boys received their prizes from the hands of the wife of one of the governors. At last my name was read out, and briskly I walked along the narrow lane to the platform. My father handed a book to the governor's wife who smiled graciously as she presented it to me. It was a boy's life of Cromwell.

I should have returned to my seat. Instead, I remained standing on the platform. I was not rooted there by nervous paralysis. I was waiting for my second prize. True, I had no idea what "proxime accessit" meant, but my faith in the printed word was immense. Had I not been told that every "mention" meant a prize? My father's face was buried in his lists, and there was an awkward pause. At last my father noticed me and, bending down, whispered to me to return to my seat at once. "But I want my second prize," I said in a voice that, squeaky with nervousness, carried to the end of the hall. This time my father, not understanding my dilemma, looked stern. He took me by the arm and turned me round. "There is no other prize," he said. "Go back to your seat immediately." With burning cheeks and tears welling up in my eyes I scurried past the sea of eyes to my place. This was my first acquaintance with the agonising terror of self-consciousness, and the mortification of that moment has pursued me throughout my life so that to-day, in spite of much public speaking and lecturing in various countries, I am still unable to conquer that trembling of the knees and blankness of mind which overcome me whenever I take my stand on a platform.

We children took no part in the final act of departure, for we were packed off under the charge of Barclay, the head nurse, some days before the general packing up began. But we had our farewells to make. They were mostly in the servants' hall where we had many friends and allies. Some of them, like Susie, were going with us to Forfarshire, but Bessie, the cook, was married or engaged to be married and was not prepared to abandon her man. She hugged us all in an emotional farewell in which her tears flowed more freely than our own.

My otherwise erratic life divides itself almost evenly into six periods of from seven to nine years: eight as a child at Beith, nine as a schoolboy at Broughty Ferry and at Fettes, seven as a student in Germany and France and as a planter in Malaya, seven in Russia as a consul, nine as a diplomat and banker in Central Europe and the Balkans, and nine as a journalist and author in London.

Beith was the first climacteric and marked the period of innocent childhood. When I left the little Ayrshire town, I was, for all my zest for games and open-air life, a quiet, studious boy whose presents, at his own request, were nearly always books.

BOOK II

KINDERGARTEN INTO SCHOOL

"We were little Christian children and had early been taught the value of forbidden fruit.—*Mark Twain.*

CHAPTER ONE

WHILE THE NECESSARY alterations were being made to convert Seafield House, our new home at Broughty Ferry, into a school, my brother Rufus and I were sent, after a short visit to the Highlands, to stay with our Macgregor grandmother in Edinburgh. This was not only the first and only summer holiday that we ever spent in a city; it was also our first introduction to the capital of our country.

Although I was afterwards to spend nearly five years at school at Fettes on the north-west side of Edinburgh, my earliest school associations were with another well-known Scottish public-school. This was Merchiston Castle, once the home of the Napiers, including the famous John Napier, the inventor of logarithms, and converted into a school in 1833 by Charles Chalmers, a younger brother of Thomas, my Anstruther hero.

My grandmother's Edinburgh home was within a stone's throw of the Castle and, indeed, later became one of the school houses. My paternal grandfather's house was just behind it. To this topographical accessibility must be added the proximity of personal association. Not only had my father been a master at Merchiston before his marriage, but my Macgregor uncles had been educated there, and Alister and Tom, both members of the football fifteen, had only recently left school. Moreover, I had met several of the masters including the famous Dr. Rogerson, whose portrait hung in the place of honour in my father's study. But the one whom I knew best was Burgess, the mathematical master. The son of a Grantown butcher, he had been at Cambridge with my father. It was he who organised the reading party at which my father first met my mother, and Burgess himself, who always spent his holidays in his native Strathspey, had been a figure of interest and wonder to us from our infancy. The wonder came from the fact that his ear had been bitten off—not by a football opponent but by a horse.

At Merchiston, Burgess, inspired by the shadow of Napier, was a great mathematician, but his real genius found its expression in coaching the school football team. He himself had never played rugby football. Yet by the force of his personality he continued, year after year, to turn out football teams which by their grit, courage and skill spread the fame of Merchiston far beyond the confines of Scotland. Several of the boys played for Scotland while still at school. The school's football prowess in those days may be gauged by the fact that until the war the fifteen played Sedbergh, to-day probably the best English "rugger" school, and were beaten, I think, only twice. Indeed, I believe that the Merchiston team of 1900–1901 was the best school side that I have ever seen, and I pay this tribute to Merchiston as a Fettesian who played in the Fettes side of 1904–1905 which many of my contemporaries consider "the best side ever".

In those days Merchiston provided a rough and Spartan training, but it produced a fine type of hardy Scot, and the tone was probably healthier than that of any other school in Scotland. Its two most famous alumni are Sir Eric Geddes and Lord Davies, Welsh coal magnate, teetotaller, and private secretary to Mr. Lloyd George during the war. Both were friends and contemporaries of my uncles.

In the autumn of 1895, my uncles took me over the Castle, then empty of boys, and also over the famous football ground off Colinton Road where later I was to experience the bitterness of defeat more often than the sweets of victory.

My grandmother, who, for all her knowledge of the Bible, could hardly be called an intellectual, was a great believer in keeping idle hands from mischief, and every day my brother Rufus and I were sent on long walks which provided a certain amount of permanent instruction. We visited Edinburgh Castle, travelling by horse-tram to the

Mound and then walking up the steep hill. If we were still too young to appreciate the aesthetic beauty of the site, we certainly entered a new and inspiring world when we passed through the outer gateway of the Castle itself. There was then no National War Memorial and no statue of Haig, but we were thrilled by Mons Meg, the comic old cannon presented to James II by the blacksmith who made it, by the sight of the spans of the Forth Bridge far away in the distance, and, most of all, by the crown of Bruce, although it is more than doubtful if he ever wore it. Even more awe-inspiring were the staterooms in the Palace of Holyroodhouse, where, in those days, the bloodstains of Rizzio, murdered almost in the sight of Mary Queen of Scots, were still shown and, indeed, were freshly painted in once a year. Already our minds were very busy with Scottish history, and Edinburgh, where, before the disfiguring post-war building, almost every stone told a story, was the place in which to acquire it. Even at that youthful age we were fierce patriots, glorying in Wallace and Bruce, whose exploits I was familiar with from reading Jane Porter's "Scottish Chiefs", Bonnie Prince Charlie and Mary Queen of Scots, and decrying Knox, whose lack of gallantry we disliked, much to the disgust of my grandmother who was a staunch champion of that rigid Calvinist and a bitter critic of Mary.

But the old lady was very patient with us. Almost every day we used to go out driving with her in her carriage, and almost daily, too, there was a fight between Rufus and myself to decide who should sit beside Forbes, the coach-man, this preference being dictated not by a desire to escape from our grandmother, but by a youthful ambition to hold the loose end of the reins and to imagine that we were driving. It was in this way that I came to pay my first visit to Roslin, the private chapel of the Earl of Rosslyn and perhaps the chief architectural glory of Scotland. More than twenty-five years later I was to become a great friend of the Rosslyns, and since then I have often visited the chapel, which, apart from its own sculptural beauties, lies in romantic surroundings in the rocky glen of the Esk with the Pentlands forming a superb background.

This chapel was the burial ground of the ancient family of the St. Clairs, of whom the present Earl of Rosslyn is the lineal descendant, and, according to legend, the barons, until 1650, were always buried in full armour. The story has gone down to history in Scott's poem:

> "There are twenty of Roslin's barons bold
> Lie buried within that proud chapelle;
> Each one the holy vault doth hold—
> But the sea holds lovely Rosabelle!"

Some forty years ago the present Earl, whose elder daughter is called Rosabelle, was temporarily hard up and was earning his living as an actor. Being then in Edinburgh, where he was playing Sir Walter Raleigh in *Kenilworth*, he remembered the poem and determined to dig up the barons, thinking that their armour would fetch a high price in the United States. As in another famous burial poem, the digging was carried out at dead of night. But the noble earl was too late. Some other baron in similar need had been there before him or perhaps the legend itself had been embroidered out of fancy. At any rate, the vault was bare of all but bones.

Roslin added its outline to the historical background which was now rapidly shaping itself in my mind during this first stay in Edinburgh. But the great attraction of our drives with my grandmother was the visits to the Princes Street shops. The old lady, as we called her afterwards and perhaps even then, was addicted to shopping for shopping's sake—a mania which I have inherited. Moreover, she was a generous shopper, and nearly always our patience, while she ordered yards of silk and lace for the black dresses and white caps that she wore, was rewarded with presents. Tin soldiers were then our chief delight, and soon we had huge armies. They were employed in the historic battles of the Anglo-Scottish conflicts, and, claiming the privilege of the elder brother, I always commanded the Scottish troops.

We were very militant in those days, and our martial ardour was whetted by the spectacle of a burnished sword which used to hang in the dining-room of my grandfather's house. In his black square-cut morning coat he did not look very like a soldier, but he had taken part as an officer in a great parade at the foot of Arthur's Seat when the Scottish volunteers were reviewed by Queen Victoria, and he cherished the sword as a memento of this occasion. We cherished it, too, and its presence in that rather cold room gave us a new respect for the man who had worn it.

There was also a more imposing military figure whom we often met on our walks. This was the eccentric Theodore Napier, who by his frequent appearances in the streets must have been well-known to every Edinburgh boy and girl of those days. Tall, erect, with long hair and flowing beard, he used to walk abroad, clad in kilt, plaid, and sporran, with tartan stockings and brogues of deer-hide. There was a fierce glint in his cold, blue eyes. He looked for all the world like Allan McAulay, the wild Highland seer, whose portrait adorned my first copy of Scott's *Legend of Montrose*. Napier was a Jacobite fanatic more ardent than any Stewart or Cameron of the "Forty-Five". His dress was of the period. An exhibitionist, he honoured demonstratively every commemoration date in the Jacobite calendar. Once a year, too, he sent a wreath of white roses to Mary of Modena, whom he regarded as the rightful Queen of Scotland and of the British Empire. When I remember that Mary's son is Prince Rupprecht of Bavaria and that this prince is to-day the "rightful king" of Britain, even my sentimental Jacobitism cannot make the jump from 1745 to 1937 but wisely stops short in the romantic glamour of the past.

To many Edinburgh people Napier was a figure of fun, but my brother and I regarded him with veneration mingled with fear and fitted him into the squares of our historical chessboard. Vaguely I used to connect him with the Napiers of Merchiston. He was, I believe, an Australian who by a curious process of atavism had reverted to the type of clansman of the Gladsmuir period.

I should create a false impression if I were to suggest that our time was wholly occupied by inspecting castles and in acquiring knowledge. My grandmother, an inveterate letter-writer and a slow mover, spent most of the day indoors in the high armchair from which she liked to deliver her *ex cathedra* addresses on the decadence of the modern world. The fairly spacious grounds of her house were therefore at our undisturbed disposal. Our uncles were kind to us, and from them we learnt in those few weeks more healthy mischief than I had assimilated during the whole of my time at Beith. They, too, were mildly football-mad, and on the lawn outside the house we had many battles of "rugger", this time with a full-sized ball which wrought ruinous havoc on the glass of the greenhouses.

My grandmother was a stern disciplinarian and, although a widow, was fully capable of keeping her sons in order. She kept a strict eye on their comings and goings and insisted on what used to be called "respectable hours". On one Saturday evening one of my uncles had been making a night of it. He was then a young apprentice in a bank and was not allowed a latch-key. Coming home very late, he was afraid to ring the bell and tried instead to crawl in by a window which he had managed to prise open. Unfortunately, he could open only the upper half. He reached the top safely, but, in clambering through, slipped and fell heavily inside the room, dragging down with him in his tumble a huge venetian mirror. In the silence of the night the crash was terrific. Almost before he could recover his senses and pick himself up, my grandmother, apprehensive but determined, her hair in paper-curls, her dressing gown tucked up to her knees, a candle in one hand and a poker in the other, opened the door. She saw the sheepish figure sitting on the floor. Her eye, stern and cold as an oyster, flashed round the room and rested on the ruins. With one glance she summed up the situation.

"Boy," she said sternly, "what have you been drinking?"

"Only sgin and sginger," was my uncle's reply.

For years afterwards he was always known as "Gin and Ginger".

Naturally, my brother Rufus and I were generally on our best behaviour in the imperious presence, and on the whole we were remarkably successful in avoiding the old lady's displeasure. On one occasion, however, we felt the full force of her disciplinary rigour. During that summer she suffered from asthma, and in order to obtain relief used to burn some kind of smoky powder which lived in a brown tin on the mantelpiece. It was always rather a mysterious performance to my brother and myself, for the powder made no flame, but, when lit, crackled very slowly, emitting a thick pungent smoke until it consumed itself and left a neat mountain-shaped pile of ash marvellously like a miniature Vesuvius. As a treat, we were occasionally allowed to prepare the powder and to light it, and, as the smoke was very like the vapours which used to exude from the magician's bowls in the booths at the Edinburgh Carnival, we could always imagine ourselves in the rôle of the professional wizard. Youthful imagination, when uncurbed, is the quickest slide to temptation that I know, and so it proved to be in this instance.

One wet morning my grandmother drove out to Colinton to lunch with a friend. Unable to go out and left to our own devices, my brother and I had grown tired of our tin soldiers when the devil entered the room in the shape of Maggie, the tablemaid. She had come in to place a new tin of my grandmother's asthma powder on the mantelpiece. The temptation was too much for us. To open the tin was to go three-quarters of the way to disaster. Taking a newspaper and spreading it on the floor, we poured out the whole contents of the tin until they formed a splendid mountain. Then we set fire to it. The effect was superb. The powder spluttered beautifully, and a glorious pillar of smoke ascended evenly to the ceiling. True, the smell was rather overpowering. But the newspaper did not catch fire, and all we had to do was to lift it and empty our extinct volcano into the fireplace. Alas! when we raised the newspaper, it came away in our hands, leaving the mountain of grey ash behind on the floor. Not merely had the powder consumed the newspaper below it, but it had burnt a large hole in my grandmother's best Turkey carpet.

As I inspected the results of our handiwork, a cold chill froze my heart. Vainly I tried with my shoes to rub out the charred blackness of that all too prominent patch. I spoke to my brother in a hushed whisper. Then with the consciousness of guilt heavy upon me I took his arm and drew him away to one of the greenhouses.

The rain still fell relentlessly, and the hour until my grandmother's return seemed like eternity. But after we heard her carriage draw up at the front door we had not long to wait. Presently Maggie came out to the side-door and began to call us. Sheepishly we emerged from our hiding-place to be greeted with a "My, you're in for it. Your grandmother wants you at once." The old lady was standing by the fireplace. She was tapping vigorously with her walking-stick on the black, bare hole in the carpet. She wasted no words. "Did you do this?" We hung our heads. "Into the store-room immediately!" Walking-stick in hand, she marched us across the passage into the dark store-room. She slammed the door behind us. We heard the key turn in the lock, and there we were left. It was not the end of our punishment. In the evening we were again summoned to the imperial presence and were favoured with a lecture on the enormity of our offence. Worse still, the homily was delivered in the presence of G. O. Turnbull, who was held up to us as the pattern on which we should model our wayward lives. G. O., a brother of Sir Hugh Turnbull, the Chief of the City of London Police, was then the star Sandhurst cadet, a "rugger" international, and our particular hero of the moment.

In these circumstances, my grandmother's lecture was an offence to my dignity and rankled more than my temporary imprisonment. But I bore the old lady no grudge. If the advice which she gave me had been as freely taken as it was freely offered, I should have avoided many an unnecessary scrape, and, as far as tipping and presents went, she was, until the day of her death in 1921, the queen of grandmothers.

During this Edinburgh period I had my first experience of the surgeon's knife, or rather, in this case, of the surgeon's scissors. Swollen tonsils were my trouble, and my grandmother, much against my wishes, wrote to my father and mother about their effect on my general health. My father was far too busy to do more than send a postcard recommending the Merchiston School doctor as the man who should be consulted. School doctors, in those days at any rate, did not enjoy a reputation for tenderness, and Dr. Burn-Murdoch, although not unkind, wasted no time over such trivial questions as the psychology of children's fears. I did not take kindly to him when he opened my mouth in a business-like manner. I disliked him still more when he pushed a long, bony finger into the back passage of my nose in a search for possible adenoids. I regarded him with intense hate when he announced tersely to my grandmother: "No adenoids, Mrs. Macgregor, but the tonsils should come out at once."

My parents were informed, and my mother came over from Broughty Ferry for the operation, which was performed in my grandmother's house. Enucleation was unknown in those days, and the operation, known as guillotining, was regarded as a simple affair. Dr. Burn-Murdoch and his assistant, Dr. Dowden, arrived punctually at eleven o'clock in the morning, and I was brought into my grand-mother's sitting-room—the same room in which we had ruined her Turkey carpet. There was a plain kitchen chair beside the window and another alongside it, with a basin of hot water. Without fuss or ado, I was planted on the vacant chair. Dr. Dowden, an old Merchistonian and a "rugger" player, pinioned my arms in a comprehensive tackle. With one gigantic hand Dr. Burn-Murdoch held my mouth open and with the other inserted his guillotine. I tried to kick, but my second yell had scarcely reached its highest note when suddenly I found myself released. The next thing that I remember was Dr. Burn-Murdoch picking up my tonsils out of the basin and showing them to my mother. "Useless things, Mrs. Lockhart," he said, "perfectly useless things."

My mother, overwrought perhaps by my screams, was shocked, but my father, when he heard the story, was delighted. He had curious ideas about doctors and dentists, judging their skill solely by the degree of torture which they inflicted. These ideas were part of his Spartan philosophy, and I think that to this day he still applies to dentists the maxim of "no pain, no good". Certainly he always succeeded in selecting a dentist who did hurt, and, when we were living in Broughty Ferry, we were sent to a fierce old man who was too shortsighted to be able to avoid hurting. On one occasion he gave a jab at one of my molars with an instrument like a bodkin. The jab missed its mark and went through my cheek. "Does that hurt, boy?" he asked. It was his usual refrain. This time a well-planted punch in his stomach informed him that the answer was in the affirmative. This incident wrought a change in our lives, for I developed an abscess in my cheek, and from then on my mother chose our doctors and dentists.

Apart from my operation I have nothing but the pleasant-est recollections of my stay with my grandmother and would gladly have prolonged it indefinitely. We did no work, unless compiling letters to our parents can be counted as work. Most of my letters were written to my mother, and I still possess them, for she kept these early manifestations of genius, and they came back to me after her death. They show no signs of precocious talent. The handwriting is smudgy and unformed and the composition monotonous with the word "aweful" recurring in every sentence. They are mostly bald chronicles of what we had done and seen during the day, and the only letter which throws any light on my better nature is one which contains an account of a dead dog which we found in the canal near Craiglockhart. It had a stone tied round its neck and had obviously lain at the bottom for some days until, swollen with decomposition, it had risen to the surface. To-day, I should not hesitate to say that it had been thrown into the canal by some callous brute. But as a child I had kinder thoughts, and in three long, unpunctuated sentences I developed for my mother's benefit the theory of a poor family who loved their dog, and, unable to feed it, had finally decided to drown it. And in order that the children might not know, the father and mother had stolen out in the middle of the night and, after a tearful farewell, had consigned it to its watery grave!

Unfortunately, pleasure, like everything else in life, never stands still, and one morning towards the middle of September my grandmother informed us that we were to leave in a few days for our new home in Broughty Ferry. We were now made much of, and as a grand finale of farewell my uncle Tom gave us a treat. This consisted of a giant tea followed by a trip to the Braid Hills golf course where we acted as caddies to my uncle and Roland Gulland, another Old Merchistonian. We did not get back to my grandmother's house until nearly ten o'clock at night.

The old lady was sitting in the hall. She was surrounded by her faithful servants. Her bottle of smelling salts was in her hands, and the stopper was out. She had been, as Maggie, the tablemaid, at once whispered to us, in communication with the police. These were signs of an agitation which should have touched our inmost heart, for it showed that she was fond of us and took her duties as our custodian seriously. Moreover, the agitation was fully justified, because my uncle had forgotten to inform her that he was taking us to the Braid Hills. But I observed none of these signs. Innocent, yet strangely conscious of some unrealised offence, I watched her eyes, waiting with apprehension for the wrath to come. And come it did, its volume increasing as her righteous indignation drowned her first feelings of relief at our safety. But on this occasion her grand remonstrance was reserved exclusively for my uncle. It was delivered in her best manner, her low solemn voice rolling out one quotation after another from the Bible. It ended with gloomy forebodings about Tom's future and a final phrase, which later I myself was to hear all too often: "Unstable as water, thou shalt not excel."

Two days later, with a new sovereign in our pockets and a new Macgregor dress kilt in our trunks, we left for Broughty Ferry.

CHAPTER TWO

THE APPROACH TO our new home on the north bank of the beautiful Firth of Tay is an imposing one, but of that first journey from Edinburgh to Broughty Ferry I remember nothing except the emotional rapture of crossing the Forth and Tay bridges.

Of these two famous bridges the Tay Bridge made the stronger appeal to my imagination, not merely because on account of its low parapet it always gave me a tremulous sensation of riding on the sea whenever I crossed it in the train; not merely because it was then the longest bridge in the world, nor yet again because its many-legged spans could be seen from my bedroom window at Seafield, but because of the great disaster of 1879. On the night of December 28th a furious gale raged over the east coast of Scotland. It reached its height in the early evening when the train from Edinburgh to Dundee was due. That ill-fated train passed the south end of the bridge at fourteen minutes past seven. It never reached Dundee. The frail, spidery bridge, built only eighteen months before, buckled under the combined pressure of gale and train, and, with the collapse of a large section of the centre portion, engine, van and five carriages were plunged into the storm-tossed estuary of the Tay. Counting railway servants and passengers, the total complement of the train was eighty persons. All perished.

Although this great disaster took place nearly sixteen years before we went to Broughty Ferry, it was the major event in the life of every grown-up person in the whole district. Some of our friends had taken part in the work of rescue or had stood in the excited crowd on the Dundee Esplanade on that terrible night when even to crawl along the bridge involved the risk of being lifted by the wind and hurled into the mountainous waves below. And every Christmas in our drawing-room at Seafield, the tale would

be told and re-told: the long drawn-out drama of the re-
covery of the bodies, the tragedy of the newly-married
couple on their honeymoon, the man who escaped death by
leaving his carriage at Leuchars in order to talk to a friend
and thereby missing the train, and the curious fate of the
engine, finally recovered after two failures and still running
in active service until we left Brought Ferry. Whenever
there was a gale, and every winter there was nearly always
at least one storm, my mother would shudder with super-
stitious forebodings, and the next morning, as soon as it was
light, I would rush to the window to see if the new bridge
was still standing.

If the bridges are my only recollection of that journey to
Broughty Ferry, my first day at Seafield House remains
clear-cut in my memory. To small boys the exploration of
a new home is always a source of unfailing delight, and we
had scarcely kissed our parents and answered their questions
before we were off on an exciting voyage of discovery.
Although smaller than Spier's, Seafield was far more like a
private house—which, indeed, it had been until my father
clapped a school building on its east side. Situated on a hill,
it commanded a fine view of the estuary, and from the
windows of the nursery, an apartment which we frequented
but to which we no longer belonged, I could see the Fifeshire coast, and with my telescope could even make out the
lettering of the Waterloo Monument between Tayport and
Newport on the other side of the Firth.

Our first visit was to our domain upstairs: the day-nursery
and our bedroom which in term-time was converted into a
guest room. They satisfied our requirements. They were
higher and more spacious than our rooms at Spier's. With
more awe than enthusiasm we inspected the new school-
buildings—a big roomy hall convertible into two large
classrooms by a curtain, and later, by a sliding wooden
partition—and the new changing-rooms with their foot-
bath and long rows of basins.

But it was the queer corners and the outside policies which interested us most. Below the house, stretching for unknown distances, was a network of cellars, dark and gloomy and full of unknown terrors. I don't think that even as a big boy I ever explored them thoroughly or alone, and even with my brother there were moments of tremor when the candle blew out and we would stand still, afraid to go forward or even backwards, until we could strike a match and relight the wick. Outside, the house faced the sea and had a noble front with two stone staircases leading to gardened terraces running down to what formerly had been a park below. The park, of course, had been converted by my father into a tennis court and playing fields, and at once my eye, sweeping over the new vista, fixed on this tennis court as a suitable arena for the renewal of our cricket and football duels. The top of the terraces, too, was soon discovered as an ideal spot from which to drive golf balls, for the raised border of the grass, where it joined the avenue, made a natural tee. It was for long our ambition to hit a ball into the road which, shut off by a low wall, skirted the end of the playing field. This ambition was not achieved until some years later when I was in my "teens". To-day, any ten handicap player could carry the distance with a number five iron.

But it was the back and west sides of the grounds which we at once selected as our outdoor kingdom. At the back were stables with new masters' rooms above, four greenhouses—each with a deep well or water-tank, a big hen-run, and a potting-shed where we kept our tools and made unsailable boats and, later, unfishable fishing rods. Here were the riddles which, propped up by a stick with a long string attached to it and with a plentiful supply of breadcrumbs below, served as traps for live jackdaws, sparrows, and even, I fear, for robins, for they were the boldest and most easily caught. Both stables and henhouse yielded rats, which we caught in live traps and drowned afterwards in the greenhouse tanks. When this cruelty—and it takes an incredibly long time for a rat to drown—was stopped by parental authority, we used to take the rats down to the playing field, let them loose, and finish them off with golf clubs or, better still, with ash single-sticks. As the rat was supposed to have a chance, this was considered "sporting" and was officially sanctioned.

As boys, my brother Rufus and I were not entirely without humane feelings and, when these were stirred, we could be roused to high indignation. Not long after our arrival in Broughty Ferry, Carlo, my father's retriever, was so stricken with old age and rheumatism that he had to be destroyed. His destruction was entrusted to Coventry, the gardener, and this blue-nosed, blue-cheeked old villain must have bought the wrong kind of poison or else Carlo must have possessed the immunity of Rasputin, who on a somewhat similar occasion suffered no ill-effects from the strychnine cakes which were given to him. At any rate Carlo refused to die, and, having taken his poison, lay watching us and, although unable to move, wagged his tail vigorously. Then, almost before we knew what was happening, Coventry stepped forward, seized Carlo's head and slit his throat with a sheath knife.

This incident so worked on our emotions that for several days we spent our time in devising various plots for wreaking vengeance on the incompetent old gardener. The schemes included "tarring and feathering", of which we had recently heard, but, not knowing what it meant, we contented ourselves with running after him and calling him "murderer" from a safe distance. These epithets drew terrible blasphemies from the old man, who always reminded me of Billy Bones in *Treasure Island*. "Little booggers," he used to mutter savagely, "wait till I catch you." And from him, I fear, we learnt our first swear words.

To the west of the house were lands of pleasanter and less bloodthirsty memories: a roomy plantation with chestnut trees, copper beeches, and rhododendrons from whose shade

an occasional "pot" with an air-gun could be made at a
sitting rabbit, two large kitchen-gardens separated by a wall
and sloping down a hill to the end of our grounds, where
there was an old peach house and a burn, in reality a muddy
ditch and long since filled in, which ran through another
plantation alongside the boundary wall. Here we were completely out of sight of the house, and here on a Sunday,
always a grim day, boats could be sailed without fear of
detection.

In this new world which we had entered there were many
new friends to be made in the servants' hall, for although a
few faithful servants, like Susie, had come with us from
Beith, there were many newcomers. Chief of these were
Murray the cook, and Munro the page boy. Very soon
Murray, a thin, scraggy Aberdonian, became one of the
family. She had some drawbacks. She was extravagant and
unpunctual. She was, too, a laudanum addict, although we
did not discover it for many years, and, like Baudelaire,
could take incredible quantities of the drug with apparent
immunity. How she managed to procure the stuff we never
knew, but it came every week by post in two bottles. Its
only effect seemed to be to increase her capacity for work.
With the passage of time, she grew more wizened. Her hair
became thin and grey. But her industry never flagged, and
her greatest fault in a large household was a willingness to do
everyone else's work in addition to her own. She was devoted to my mother, serving her with unfailing loyalty and
remaining with us, in spite of occasional protests by my
father, for nearly thirty years. To us children she was incredibly good. She could be relied on to provide a hot meal
at any hour of the day or night, to dry one's clothes when
one had fallen into the burn, and to cover up one's iniquities
with a series of plausible excuses or, if necessary, well-told
lies. In school-time, too, she was a dependable ally. Our
dormitory window was just above the kitchen window.
By a pre-arranged signal we would let down a Condor

skate key on a string and make it tap on the window below. The string would then be taken in and a basket of cakes and other delicacies attached to it by Murray. In this manner she provided us with the ingredients for a delicious midnight supper—an offence, which, if detected by my father, would have meant her instant dismissal. Fortunately, school-masters are less suspicious than most boys imagine them to be.

Like most Scottish spinsters, Murray was a great reader. Her literature was the type of penny novelette in which the lady's maid, after valiantly but narrowly resisting the amorous solicitations of the peer's son, marries a steady business man slightly above her station. Of these novelettes Murray received a fresh supply every week. In the early stages of puberty I read them with avidity.

Munro, the page boy, also had an addiction, but his was association football—a drug which in Scotland at least is as deleterious as laudanum. Then a sturdy lad of fourteen, he had only one ambition: to become a professional footballer. At the back of the kitchen there was a gravel court, which, shut in on all sides by walls and a paling, made an excellent miniature "soccer" ground, and here my brother and I took part in strenuous contests which served to keep the page boy in training and to initiate us into the mysteries of a game which, as a "rugger" purist, my father despised. To Munro's early training I owe the fact that, although brought up in a "rugger" school, I was able later to play in a French "soccer" Cup Final, and, as a member of the winning team, to gain in 1912 the gold medal of the Moscow League Championship.

When Munro left us, after two years, to join a junior professional team in Edinburgh, we were inconsolable. For some time I followed his career with interest, corresponding with him and learning with pride of his progress from junior football to the ranks of "The Hearts" or "The Hibs". Then, like so many other people during my career as a wanderer, he passed completely out of my life.

I still retain my interest in a game which Scotland has made peculiarly her own. Indeed, I sometimes wonder whether Scotland, which used to supply the New World with its best emigrants, has not already reached that stage of decline where its greatest export will be professional footballers. Not only has she supplied for years the leading clubs of England with her best players, but she has taught the game to the whole world. I have met Scottish football trainers in every part of the globe, and in my post-war years at Prague, the two coaches of Slavia and Sparta—the great Czech clubs now fully equal to the best that England or Scotland can produce—were former players of those two warring rivals, the Glasgow Rangers and the Celtic.

Another friend, although not human nor, indeed, very friendly to us, was "Bob" the pony. On him we learned or were supposed to learn to ride. Then young and frisky, he reversed the usual rôle of horse and rider, for from the word "go" he always took complete command. At first we used to be taken by a groom round a circular course, the last stretch of which began with the crossroads at Claypots Castle. Afterwards, when the groom was withdrawn and I was sent out alone, "Bob" used to amble round the circle peacefully. But if I tried to make him go in another direction, he jibbed. Then, if this was not effective, he gave a passable imitation of rodeo bucking and soon deposited his burden on the road, leaving me to walk home by myself. Ponies are very like schoolboys. Both these perverse creatures know instinctively from the very first moment whether they can take liberties with their master. In the end I let "Bob" have his own way, and with this surrender my enthusiasm for riding waned. It was the same with my brother Rufus, and the only one who ever mastered "Bob" or, indeed, any of our ponies was my brother Rob, who was horse-mad from the day he could walk. This was perhaps not surprising, for our Seafield ponies were proletarians and cricket professionals before they were riding ponies. In addition to being driven in the dog-cart, they had to pull the heavy cricket roller and also the huge grass-mower, and doubtless they resented the presence of small boys on their backs as an unjustifiable interference with the eight-hour day and an unwarranted affront to the dignity of labour.

One enemy I encountered during these first days at Seafield. This was the telephone; an instrument which I have had to use more than most people, especially in my journalistic life. At Beith we had no telephone, but at Seafield we found already installed an old-fashioned contraption with a bell-handle which one could turn for hours without response from the exchange, and it was here that I made my first acquaintance with an instrument which I have always hated more than any other invention of modern science. I have never learnt to use it effectively, and my first attempt was serio-comic. My mother was ill, and my father who was administering first-aid sent me to telephone to the doctor. I gave what I was told was the right number, and presently a male voice answered. "Are you Dr. Mackness?" I asked. The voice seemed to answer "yes", so I rolled off the message like a parrot: "I'm speaking for my father, Mr. Bruce Lockhart. He wants you to come to Seafield House at once." Twenty minutes later the school butcher arrived. When he was told that he was not wanted, he seemed annoyed, and I was blamed by both the butcher and my father for my carelessness. It was not my fault, for I gave the right number, and in any case the butcher's name was not in the least like the doctor's. But in those early days of telephoning in Broughty Ferry almost every kind of mistake was possible.

To-day, the telephone has reached such a stage of efficiency that it is now used even for important diplomatic conversations. Mistrusting the instrument as I do, I disapprove of this practice, and I have incontrovertible evidence of its dangers.

Not long ago the first long-distance telephone was

established between London and the capital of an important South American Republic. To inaugurate this epoch-making advance of modern science, a special conversation was arranged between Mr. Anthony Eden, the British Secretary of State for Foreign Affairs, and the Foreign Minister of the important South American Republic. Unfortunately, for he is a young modernist, Mr. Eden had to go to Geneva, but, before leaving, he arranged for Sir Robert Vansittart, the permanent Head of the Foreign Office, to represent him. Again, unfortunately, for he is equal to all emergencies, Sir Robert was called away just as he was about to begin his conversation. Rapidly, he handed the receiver to one of his senior colleagues, a staunch Conservative who has grown old in the service of his country and who, like myself, is a confirmed enemy and therefore an incompetent user of the telephone. In the presence of the private secretary, the following conversation took place:

"This is the Foreign Office, London, speaking. I am representing the Secretary of State." The voice was loud—too loud perhaps for the delicate microphone, but so resonant that it could be heard down the corridors of the Foreign Office. It was followed by a gurgle of Latinity from the far-off capital which, in turn, was countered by a stentorian "Speak up, Speak up, I can't hear you." This produced more gurgitations and more Latin, followed by further roars of "Speak up" from the British side. The exchange of verbal machine-gun fire lasted for several minutes until the British official, becoming agitated, began to punctuate his invocations for clarity with a series of resounding damns. At last, abandoning an unequal contest, he put the receiver down with a final damn of disgust.

Seventeen days later, an efficient British diplomatic service, which now piously collects Press cuttings and the other new impedimenta of modern diplomacy, sent back from the South American capital to the Foreign Office the reports from the local newspapers describing the inauguration of the long-distance telephone. The account in the leading government organ ran as follows:

"To-day, the first long-distance telephone service was inaugurated between London and ——. The audibility was perfect. Every word could be heard as distinctly as if the discussion were taking place in a room, and Senor ——, our Foreign Minister, was able for ten minutes to carry on an important and useful conversation with the British Foreign Secretary, Sir Robert Van Damn."

Between our arrival at Seafield House and the opening of the school term, there was an interval of only ten days. We spent most of it in acquainting ourselves with the lay-out of the little town which for the next nine years was to be our kingdom. In this pre-motor car era Broughty Ferry was the residential suburb of the rich jute merchants of Dundee. It was only four miles from that city, and the merchants, sober, silent men with a strong streak of Presbyterianism in their character and a rigid regard for the Sabbath and other forms of Scottish respectability, used to go into business daily by train, walking to and from the station for the benefit of their figures. They were careful spenders, but had fine houses built of stone and situated in the best residential area on the spur of the hills overlooking the sea. A stone mansion was solid, and solidity, both financial and moral, was the summit of their ambitions. Building was therefore the only temptation which led to extravagance, and before our arrival there had been a great architectural competition between two wealthy jute families, the Grimonds and the Gilroys. In our time the Gilroys were very much on top, for the Grimonds' palace was in the town, had little land round it, and was, I think, unoccupied, while the Gilroys had a magnificent fortress, which bore the historic-sounding name of Castle Roy, on the crest of the highest hill.

These were, of course, modern mansions. But Broughty Ferry boasted two real castles: Claypots, which was less than half a mile from our house, and Broughty Castle which had a commanding situation on a sea-rock at the narrowest point of the Firth of Tay. Claypots, now a ruin, was said to have been built by the famous Cardinal Beaton as a residence for one of his discarded mistresses. But I suspect that this legend is a Presbyterian libel, for Beaton was dead many years before the first stone of Claypots was laid. In my time it was in a disgraceful state, being used by the local farmer on whose ground it stood as a rubbish depository, by jack-daws and starlings as a nesting ground, and by tramps as a night-shelter and lavatory. When I revisited it not long ago, it had been completely cleaned, and neat tickets on the doors and an accurately compiled historical guide bore witness to the excellent restoration done since the war by His Majesty's Office of Works.

Broughty Castle has a more clearly defined place in history. Built during the fifteenth century, it was captured and occupied by the English after Hertford's victory at Pinkie in 1547. Three years later it was retaken for the Scots by French troops. This exploit, one of the rare Scottish rewards of the Franco-Scottish alliance, gave little satisfaction to boyish patriots like ourselves, and we were rather ashamed of it.

Broughty Castle was restored in the nineteenth century and has now few aesthetic attractions. In our time, it had a small and insignificant garrison and it played no part in our lives. During the topsy-turvy period of the Great War, when employees became generals and colonels and big jute bosses served humbly as second lieutenants, it came into its own again. It became the spearpoint of the Broughty defences, and here Colonel Adamson, the local commanding officer, had his headquarters. A war-time officer, taking to soldiering as a sea-trout takes to its spawning bed, he was a blunt and plain-spoken disciplinarian, who, if he feared God, kept his fear to himself and showed none in the execution of his duty. As Broughty was on the coast, one of his main tasks was to see that no lights in the town were showing. Going his rounds one evening, he found a lamp blazing on the seafront. He turned to his orderly. "Put out that lamp at once. Use all the for-rces that nature can provide." Eventually a shower of large pebbles restored Broughty to the safety of darkness.

The next morning a deputation of local authorities waited on the Colonel at the Castle. There had been an outrage the previous evening. A valuable street lamp had been wantonly smashed. There were grave suspicions that a soldier was responsible. Would the Colonel take the necessary measures to enforce discipline?

Coldly the Colonel informed them that the soldier who smashed the lamp was himself or, at least, was acting on his orders. He vouchsafed no other explanation, but the storm gathering on his brow should have warned the local dignitaries of the dangers of further questioning. Pompous and full of self-importance, they failed to read the signs. Doubtless, said their spokesman, the Colonel had his own reasons for his action. But who was to pay for the valuable lamp? The storm broke in a loud sustained blast. "Your lamp was blazing right across the Firth. You'll pay for it yourselves." Then, breaking into the broad Dundee vernacular, the Colonel thundered: "Now, remember this. A'm the greatest b——r o' hell in this place and if a've any more of your truculence a'll keep your damned town in darkness until the end of the war." Till the end of the war the Colonel himself was known throughout the length and breadth of Angus as the "G.B.O.H."

It would be foolish to pretend that during these early days of my Broughty Ferry life my thoughts were occupied by the historical associations and topographical features of the locality. Looking back to-day, I realise that the central figure in my life was my brother Rufus. Red-haired, snubnosed, and freckled, he was far more than a brother. Until I went abroad, he was my closest friend. Rarely, I think, does one find two brothers whose likes and dislikes coincide as ours did. We did everything together. Indeed, it never occurred to us that our pleasures could be divided. And if my brother subordinated his wishes to mine, this self-sacrifice never marred the harmonious smoothness of an ideal companionship. Our amusements were cheap and healthy and our interest was concentrated whole-mindedly on such simple and natural attractions as the sea-front with its bathing boxes, the two wooden piers where, later, with a long line of flies fished with a heavy sinker, we caught hundreds of "podlies" (small pollack), and the Broughty-Tayport ferry boat with whose captain and crew we soon established a lasting friendship. But perhaps the most important event in our youthful lives was the discovery of "Blair's", a small "sweetie" shop about a hundred yards below the side gate of the playing field. Here a bottle of Kola was to be had for a halfpenny, and for a penny we could buy a large "poke" of Bull's eyes—black and white peppermint balls which with economic care could be made to last for an hour, and whose only disadvantage was that, unless one had a gumboil, they could not be sucked in school without the certainty of detection. And here, with unfailing regularity, we spent our pocket-money—twopence a week supplemented by occasional small tips, for large tips were confiscated and banked in a large wooden money-box as soon as received.

Much of our time, at first, was spent in preparing for school, and there was much trying on of football shorts and jerseys, blazers and school-caps—dark green with a crest and the Virgilian motto "Audentes Fortuna Juvat".

"Colours" play too large a part in the life of the average British schoolboy. They certainly make far too large a hole in the pocket of the average British parent. But I doubt if even walking down the steps from the chapel and shaking hands with the captain of the fifteen in front of the whole school—the Fettes mode of bestowing football honours—can ever equal the rapture and pride of manhood which come with the donning of one's first jersey.

The school outfitter had his shop in Dundee, and in this manner I made my first visit to a city which, although the third largest in Scotland and after Glasgow the most important commercially, has never captured the imagination of the outside world in the same manner as its rival, Aberdeen.

My first impressions of Dundee are naturally rather vague, if only because I was to visit it so often during the next nine years of my life. But they were not pleasant, and even to-day I never hear its name mentioned without feeling a vague smell of whale oil and marmalade in my nostrils. Indeed, in spite of its glorious situation with the Sidlaws forming an almost Highland background, it is a place which lacks all charm. The docks, with their graceful clippers and whalers—sailing ships which in my time were still engaged in the Arctic or the Indian trade but which now alas! have vanished—were a world in which youthful fancy could make romantic flights. But otherwise the city was sombre and forbidding. The smoke which belched from its factory chimneys spread an atmosphere of foggy gloom over its streets, and the large proletariat, composed mainly of Irish mill-girls, was harddrinking, hard-swearing, drab, and unattractive. Even then it struck me as a city of spires and "lums", and my return to it a year ago, after I had seen half the world, only confirmed and strengthened this early impression. One main street, Constitution Road, is known locally as "Mount Zion" because it contains so many churches, and Dundonians are as proud of Cox's "lum" as Australians are of Melbourne Cathedral.

For the benefit of my English and American readers I had perhaps better explain that "lum" is good Scots for a chimney. The word is perpetuated in the Scottish saying "lang may your lum reek" (long may your chimney smoke), which, incidentally, is Mr. Ramsay MacDonald's favourite Christmas greeting to his Scottish friends.

With the passing of September, our long holiday ended, and one afternoon, tremulous with excitement and full of vague fears, we watched from an upper window groups of small boys driving up in cabs loaded with luggage, to the front door. Seafield House opened as a school for the first time on October 1st, 1895. My fears of the unknown were justified. Spier's had been a play-school in which my brother and I had been privileged and protected players. Seafield House, if not the real thing, was the beginning of it, and at any rate a school in which a boy had to find his own level. The arrival of those cabs meant that I had passed from the sheltered backwater of the nursery into the outer edge of the whirlpool of life.

CHAPTER THREE

IT IS A mistake for a schoolmaster to send his sons to his own school. He is in much the same position as that of a footballer who, called on to referee a match in which his own club is engaged, either favours his own side or, in his desire to be strictly impartial, is unfairly severe to it. Although I was beaten often enough, my father undoubtedly favoured me, and in consequence the other masters and the boys took special pains to correct the balance. Seafield was therefore my first experience of the rough edges of life.

My father's new venture opened with twenty-nine boys, fourteen of whom were boarders. Half a dozen or so were sons of professional men—doctors, chartered accountants, lawyers, but the parents of the vast majority were Dundee jute manufacturers. Thus most of the boys came from well-to-do homes, but few, if any, of them were spoilt by luxury. Nor was there any modern softness in the education provided at Seafield. Our life was Spartan. The east wind was a kill-or-cure tonic, and, as we wore the kilt, our knees and a part of our thighs were exposed to the full rigour of the cold. As a school dress the kilt is an admirable garment, but it has one disadvantage. Knees not washed properly after football are exposed to the full gaze of punctilious masters, and my first imposition was to copy out twenty times in large copperplate handwriting John Wesley's text "Cleanliness is next to Godliness", supplemented by the assistant master's corollary: "Therefore I must wash my knees thoroughly after football." This imposition was repeated with irritating frequency, until at last I mastered the hardest lesson of a small boy's life, for there was no hot water in the changing-rooms, and the skin of knees, scrubbed with cold water and a dirty nailbrush, always cracks.

The oldest boy in the school was just over twelve; the youngest was my brother Rufus, who was then only six years and six months and thus could claim the rare distinction of having been the youngest boy at two successive schools. With him I had shared a bedroom almost from the day of his birth. School life made a break in this domestic companionship, for we were now detailed to separate dormitories. Here, even in the hardest frosts, there was no heating, my father throughout his life supporting cold with an immunity which has made him callous to the shivering of others. In winter we dressed with chattering teeth; and a succession of chilblains, the inevitable result of warming ill-dried hands before the school-room fire, had a permanent effect on my handwriting.

Nearly every boy in the school had a nickname. Mine was "Letter-Box". School nicknames are singularly, and often brutally, appropriate and are generally indicative of popularity or the lack of it. From my nickname, which I secretly disliked, readers may draw their own conclusions of the attractiveness or otherwise of a small boy with a wide, half-open mouth and a head too large for his body. At first I had not a very easy time, although there was no bullying except for a little mild blanket-tossing which some fiend had learnt from *Tom Brown's Schooldays* or *Eric*, then the two most popular school stories in the library. But once a week we trooped off to the town gymnasium for physical drill and gymnastics. This gymnasium was in the centre of the town, near the station, and our way to and from it led by a narrow and rarely frequented lane. Here, one day, we came upon an organised fight between two big boys from the local board school just opposite Seafield. It was, I realise to-day, a fierce and brutal fight. One boy, his eyes already blackened and blood streaming from his nose and mouth, had been heavily punished, but the ring of spectators round the two antagonists made surrender impossible.

I am afraid that the only effect of this spectacle on the boys of Seafield was one of emulation. It produced an epidemic of fighting, harmless enough but sufficiently widespread to provoke official intervention and a severe ban on these duels.

Following on this ban, a fight was the cause of the most terrifying experience of my life at Seafield. I was caught scrapping with another boy by one of the assistant masters, a powerful athlete who played "rugger" for the local club. Although my opponent was older than I was, the master fixed on me as the culprit. He punished me by taking me into the changing-room and making me stand with my back to him while he practised drop kicks with a "rugger" ball at my head. One shot, which caught me on the back of the neck, sent me sprawling on the stone floor, and for half an hour afterwards I shook with convulsive sobs which came admittedly more from fear than from actual injury. This master left us after the first year and subsequently became a Church of England parson.

This unpleasant experience, although it checked my ardour at school, did not put a stop to my youthful propensity for fighting. Led by another school companion, who was as brave and as reckless as a Zulu warrior, we used to engage in bloody combats with a gang of small "keelies" who, resenting with true Scottish democratic instincts the privilege of our more expensive education, sneered at our school caps and called us names in which the word "gentry", liberally preceded by uncomplimentary adjectives, occurred with provocative regularity. We would retort with a challenge to a fight and name some secluded lane as a suitable meeting-ground. These encounters generally took place in the dusk of Saturday afternoons and, although we always fought fair and generally won, we often carried home such marks of victory as face-cuts from stones and shin-bruises from kicks. I cannot say that I ever liked this form of amusement in which I took part more from fear of being thought a coward than through any lust for fighting.

Work at Seafield was not neglected. The place of my football-kicking assailant was taken by W. D. Miller, who was by far the best assistant master that my father ever selected. He was the very best type of Englishman, cultured, widely travelled, and full of that tolerant understanding which is the unique virtue of the English character. By his example and gentle insistence some of the roughness was rubbed off our Scottish manners, and his method of suggesting rather than instructing led us to a new and more serious outlook on life. Moreover, he was a truly great teacher, strict but inspiring, and, thanks to him as well as to my father, I learnt more at Seafield than I ever did anywhere else with the one exception of my student years in Germany.

In those days Scottish boys certainly worked harder than English boys and, I think, developed more rapidly. At Seafield the standard of work was high, and we had several brilliant boys. I held my own among them, collecting several prizes, most of which were for history, but I by no means excelled. Nor was my father the only parent who took an interest in his son's education. Many of the day-boys who did their preparation at home were coached by fathers who believed in work as they believed in the Bible, and who, realising that the greatest battle in life—the conflict between self-discipline and self-indulgence—has to be lost or won in early youth, saw to it personally that there was no relaxation of effort in their sons' home studies.

This parental influence created a healthy rivalry between boarders and day-boys which was as strenuous in the form-room as it was on the field of play. Admittedly, Dundee has produced few famous scholars and artists. Indeed, the only Dundee poet that I can remember is William McGonagall, who died about the time I was born and whose verse lives by its badness. And McGonagall, as his ode to Glasgow shows, was not very grateful to his native city.

"The ships which lie at the Broomielaw are most beautiful to see;
They are bigger and better than any in Dundee.
O beautiful city of Glasgow I must conclude my lay
By calling thee the greatest city of the present day."

But, if in those days the poetic soul of Dundee was dead, the intellectual standard of its commercial leaders was high. There was then—and for all I know may still be—a Homer Club in Broughty Ferry of which my father was a member and which met regularly to read the *Odyssey* and the *Iliad* in the original, and over cocoa and biscuits to discuss the more abstruse passages. I cannot recall all the members, but three of them were well known to me. These were Mr. Troup, a local Presbyterian minister, Dr. Peterson, afterwards Sir William Peterson, Principal of McGill University, and Mr. James Cunningham, a learned jute manufacturer, who was more interested in the classics than in Indian fibres. Three of their various sons have achieved high distinction in the service of their country. Admiral Troup is now head of the Admiralty Intelligence Division, Mr. Maurice Peterson is the present British Minister in Sofia, and Sir George Cunningham is to-day Governor of the North-West Province of India.

This atmosphere of the classics was translated to our form-room, and at the age of eight I was already wrestling for the main part of my school hours with Latin verbs and the impenetrable mysteries of gender rules. Translation, which has always appealed to me more than grammar, was more exciting; Caesar's *Invasion of Britain* and *Eutropius* were even enjoyable. I have already referred to my father's belief in the value of learning poetry by heart. At Seafield we learnt reams of Scottish poetry, and incipient nationalism, which scarcely needed this encouragement, was stimulated by the chanting of the most patriotic passages of Scott. Youthful memory trained in this manner is marvellously retentive, and even to-day I have only to be given a start in order to be able to roll off line after line of "Breathes there the man with soul so dead" or of the famous encounter between Fitzjames and Roderick Dhu in *The Lady of the Lake*. Scott's poetry may be dead to Scottish youth to-day, but in our time it was very much alive. Seafield could claim even a boy poet whose masterpiece was a parody of *The Lay of the Last Minstrel* in which the hero was a musical tramp on a bicycle, then, bar the railway train, the quickest means of locomotion in the world. The poem began something like this:

> "The way was long; the wind was cold;
> The bicycle was stiff and old.
> The lamp, its rusty outside joy,
> Was carried by an organ boy."

I am bound to admit that as materially minded Dundonians we regarded the poet as mad, but with the cold courage of intellectual contempt he never allowed "ragging" to limit his productive capacity. Under his inspiration we produced even a literary magazine called *The Flamingo*. It contained a full-length historical romance, borrowed crudely from Stanley Weyman, a school story, a tale of travel, and, of course, several pages of verse by the school poet. *The Flamingo*, like most productions of this nature, was short-lived, and, much as I should like to think of myself in those days as an incipient author, I never contributed to it. The school poet went into business. So much for the unfulfilled promise of early youth.

In those days my father was very fond of music. Even now in his retirement he still hammers out accompaniments on the piano with fingers which never learnt to play, and to his slow and hesitating chords he sings Scottish songs in a resonant bass voice which in summer carries through the open windows almost to the neighbouring golf course. At Seafield, therefore, singing, which fortunately counted as work, occupied two hours in our weekly timetable. Our mentor, frequently assisted by my father, was Miss Young, an effective and strict mistress, who had taken up teaching after her father had lost his money in a Glasgow bank failure. Under her tuition we learnt such Scottish favourites as *Scots Wha Hae*, *The Hundred Pipers* and *The Bonnie Banks of Loch Lomond*.

Alas for the disillusionment which a thirst for curious knowledge brings in its train! For forty years *Loch Lomond* was an integral part of my life. It has meant to me something more than Scotland. The shores of the loch, where Rob Roy had one of his strongholds, had been trampled by the feet of my Macgregor ancestors, and in my lonely home in Malaya the plaintive melody of the song, rustily rendered by a second-hand phonograph, induced in my soul that state of delicious wistful melancholy which is the prerogative of all Celtic exiles. Since I have discovered that the song was not inspired by Loch Lomond, its charm has been dispelled. As the line "and I'll be in Scotland afore ye" clearly shows, the place where my true love and I were never to meet again was the bonnie, bonnie banks not of Loch Lomond, but of Loch Morie.

In view of Scotland's genius for capitalising the attractions of her scenic splendours, I assume that, as Loch Morie was then a distant and inaccessible Highland loch, some Glasgow forerunner of Cook or Lunn, realising the tourist possibilities of Loch Lomond, must have persuaded the composer for a trifling consideration to alter the title of his song.

Apart from singing, instrumental music was also included in my school curriculum. Even at Beith I had begun to learn the piano and soon after coming to Broughty Ferry I was made to abandon that instrument and to transfer my efforts to the violin. For this change I bear my parents a lasting grudge, for the violin, which demands years of constant practice even to make it tolerable, is no instrument for an amateur who has to earn his own living. Although I continued my studies until I was twenty-one, I never reached even the stage of playing a solo at a charity concert. Had I devoted anything like the same amount of time and effort to the piano, I should be able to-day to provide real pleasure to myself and even mild distraction to my friends. I took my violin with me to Malaya, played it intermittently in the heart of the jungle, and left it there when I came home.

Nevertheless, as a boy violinist I was proud that I was not as other boys, who hammered out scales and Weber's *Huntsman's Chorus* on the school piano. My exclusive talent, too, gave me a place in the family orchestra which performed in the drawing-room on Saturday evenings. My mother was an excellent pianist, but our greatest asset was John Fleming who played the 'cello really well for an amateur. His wife sang, and occasionally I was allowed to play the violin obbligato to her rendering of Denza's *Call Me Back*—a performance of mine which gave mixed pleasure and amusement to everyone except the singer.

John Fleming was a relation of Robert Fleming, the Dundee financier, who went to London and who died only a few years ago. Robert has a permanent place in financial history as the creator of the modern trust company. He was the grandfather of Peter Fleming, the brilliant young author of *Brazilian Adventure* and other books of his own exciting travel experiences in the wilds of China.

The musical talent of my mother and the robustious singing enthusiasm of my father have been inherited in varying degrees by my brothers and sister. My brother Rufus relieves the cares of headmastership by playing the piano and the 'cello. Both my youngest brother Rupert, who was born at Seafield, and my sister Freda have been on the stage, and my youngest brother now earns his living as a professional singer.

Religion, too, was firmly implanted in our youthful minds. In school we learnt Scripture from the *Old Testament History* of Canon Glazebrook, a former headmaster of Clifton College, and morning prayers with a chapter of the Proverbs read by my father were a cold and daily prelude to breakfast. Sunday was the grimmest day in the week. My father, although a great churchgoer, was never a partisan churchman, and doubtless his experiences at Beith had taken the edge off his early Presbyterian enthusiasm. At any rate, at Broughty Ferry we went to the local Episcopalian church. No inclemency of the weather ever freed us from morning service, and, as my father liked singing hymns, we sometimes attended evening service as well.

These incursions into what is virtually the same as the Church of England were the only non-Scottish part of a Scottish Sabbath which was kept with the Presbyterian strictness of those days. Games of any kind were forbidden, and, in spite of my father's devotion to cricket, one of the worst thrashings that Rufus and I ever received was for practising bowling on Sunday with a tennis ball against the garden wall. A walk was tolerated as part of my father's open-air religion, but for the rest of the day we had to conduct ourselves in much the same manner as a prisoner of the second division, the only difference being that we were given a better dinner. Our own story books being strictly banned, we had to read a good book, and in this way I made my first acquaintance with Bunyan's *Pilgrim's Progress*—a work which since then I have never been able to read to the end.

History, fortunately, was counted among the serious books suitable for Sunday reading, and in my father's library I discovered a treasure which for several years was to provide me with more enjoyment than any story book. This was a copy of Mackenzie's *History of Scotland*, which was given to my father by his grandfather in 1869. As history it has a strong Presbyterian bias and is, I suppose, long since out of print, but there was one chapter entitled "The Hammer of the Witches" which could always be relied on to transport me from the gloom of a Seafield Sunday into a world of make-believe very different from the whimsical never-never-land of Barrie. It told the story of the persecution of the witches by that egregious wiseacre, James the Sixth of Scotland, whose treatise on Demonology must take first place among the many foolish literary productions of monarchs. There were fearsome descriptions of the "pilniewink", a kind of finger-screw, the "cashielaws", an iron case in which the legs of alleged warlocks and witches were enclosed and then roasted, and other instruments of torture to which the victims of James's perverted superstition were submitted. There was a grisly woodcut of the Devil, complete with tail, horns, and eyes of burning coal, preaching with claw-hands outstretched—marvellously like the picture of John Knox addressing Mary—to a man seated below and surrounded by four women dressed in the ample robes of the Stuart period. The woodcut was taken from a contemporary print illustrating the story of an unfortunate woman, inappropriately named Samson, who on the rack had made a bogus confession describing how she and other witches had attended a meeting held by Satan in North Berwick Kirk. Samson's confession did not save her. After her torture she and those whom she had denounced were strangled and burnt together. This picture haunted the dreams of my boyhood as no other nocturnal apparition, although in winter the figure of Pew, the blind beggar-pirate in *Treasure Island*, tapping his way along the frosty road, ran it a close second.

Mackenzie, the author of this history and the grandfather of a Broughty Ferry boy friend, was nothing if not a Scottish patriot. In the moralising comments with which he concluded every chapter he sought to minimise James's cruelty by ascribing it to political opportunism. James, he said, had his eye on the English throne and had been taught by his advisers to do everything to make himself popular with the English. Persecution of witches began in England. Its chief instigators were the English bishops.

Although James's list of victims, which included several men and women of high station, was appalling, it may be said in extenuation of his mania that he was not the originator of this form of persecution even in his native Scotland. In 1537 his grandfather, James the Fifth, put to death on a charge of witchcraft a personage more distinguished by her lineage and progeny than any of his grandson's victims.

This was Lady Glamis, the widow of the sixth Lord Glamis. She was born a Douglas and was already suspect in the King's eyes because of her brothers whose aggressive power had aroused James's antipathy. After the death of her husband, a relative of his fell in love with her. She spurned his advances, and in revenge the rejected suitor informed James that Lady Glamis and her young son, Lord Glamis, were plotting to destroy the King's life by witchcraft. The King, neglecting no opportunity of enforcing his authority over an unruly nobility, had the lady and her son arraigned. They were tried and sentenced to death.

On the same day Lady Glamis was burnt upon the Castle Hill of Edinburgh "with great commiseration of the people in regard of her noble blood, being in the prime of her years, of a singular beauty, and suffering all, though a woman, with man-like courage". The death sentence on her son was deferred, and after James's death he was set free. Fortunately he succeeded in securing the release of his estates and title which had been forfeited at the time of his sentence. Otherwise the history of the British Empire might have been different. The burning of Lady Glamis took place in the summer of 1537, and the quater-centenary of her death coincided almost to the day with the coronation of her direct descendant, the former Lady Elizabeth Bowes-Lyon, as Queen of Britain. Thus the ancient family of the Lyons, whose ancestral home of Glamis is only fifteen miles from Broughty Ferry and which, later, I visited more than once, has the unique distinction of having provided from its female members one lady who was burnt by a king and another who is now married to a king.

To these royal persecutions of alleged Scottish witches I owe my relief from the drabness of a Scottish Sabbath which inspired in me few feelings of religious sentiment and none at all of devoutness. In his old age my father has relaxed his own rigorous observance of the fourth commandment. He no longer goes to church with the same unfailing regularity. He has accepted Sunday golf, and he has been known to play even cards on a Sunday, a form of amusement which he never tolerated during his fifty years as a schoolmaster. In this as in most other things he has moved marvellously with the times.

In my inmost heart I deplore this departure from an austerity, which, although beyond my compass, I admired even as a boy. I deplore it mutely in the same way as I am moved to melancholic regret by the sapping of a giant oak which for centuries has withstood unbowed the ravages of the fiercest storms. It is not merely that my father has bowed his head to Time. In his personal acceptance of different standards I see a symbol of the national decline. Something solid, something that I feel instinctively was of inestimable value to our Scottish heritage, has departed from the Scotland of my youth.

CHAPTER FOUR

THE SONS OF schoolmasters have one great advantage over other boys. They live perforce in large houses with playing-grounds almost on the doorstep. Given even a minimum of natural talent, they should therefore excel at games. The famous Foster brothers were sons of a schoolmaster and were brought up in the rackets court of Malvern. Henry Brougham, one of the best all-round athletes among my contemporaries, whose sister Mona my brother Rufus married, was the son of a Wellington house master, and I could quote many other examples.

In our case the enthusiasm of my father was supplemented by the games-playing skill of my mother who at Broughty Ferry was the local croquet and badminton champion. Even when she was fifty she could make my brother Rufus, a first-class ball-games player, go all out in a badminton single. In these circumstances we acquired inevitably a certain proficiency, and, counting an uncle who played for Ireland, we have three generations of "rugger" internationals in the circle of our near relatives. My sister-in-law Mona, however, has the best family record, for she has had a brother, a husband, and a son, all of whom have won international caps for rugby football.

At Seafield I had my first experience of organised school games. During the two winter terms rugby football was played daily in all weathers, and several times a term we matched our skill against other schools. Although there were only thirty boys in the school during my first two years, I was neither big nor good enough to gain a place in the football fifteen. I played my first match at the age of ten in the Christmas term of 1897. Our opponents were the first fifteen of Merchiston Preparatory School, and the match took place on one of the junior pitches of the famous Merchiston ground in Edinburgh. The Merchiston side included two subsequent

internationals, and in our own team we had a future Oxford
and Scotland captain in George Cunningham and two subsequent Trial internationals in J. E. McIntyre and E. W.
Tawse. After a fierce encounter on a muddy field we were
beaten by a single try. We then put on our coats and sweaters
and walked across the ground to watch the final stages of a
Schools Championship match between Merchiston and
Loretto. Tired but strangely elated, I returned home with
several bruises on my shins and a chest swollen by a further
infection of football mania. Although I played for Seafield
until the end of the Easter term of 1900, I never enjoyed myself so much as in this first match against heavy physical odds
at Merchiston.

Nevertheless, during those early years of my football life
personal interest in my own performances was dwarfed by an
experience which in its emotional appeal far transcended all
other raptures. This was my first international match. My
father was then a member of the Scottish Rugby Union
which selected the Scottish side, and in March, 1897, he took
me with him to Edinburgh to see England play Scotland.
Inverleith, let alone Murrayfield, was not yet in being. Raeburn Place, where previous internationals had been staged,
had become too small to house the growing army of spectators, and for the first and only time in the history of Edinburgh at any rate, for the Scottish Rugby Union has a formidable reputation for the purity of its amateurism, the
match was played at Powderhall, a ground given over to
professional sports.

Not national pride alone makes me affirm that the atmosphere which envelops an international match is more electric in Edinburgh than in any other capital of the four home
countries. Twickenham, with the King in the Royal Box and
with its tiers of stands frowning down on the green sward
below, is an imposing spectacle, but the presence of large
numbers of women who know nothing of the rules of the
game disturbs the concentration of the enthusiast. Twicken-

ham has become too like a social function. There is a glorious Celtic exuberance about the atmosphere of Dublin, especially when the emerald green jerseys of Ireland are sweeping their way to victory in one last desperate rush. I pay a just tribute to the emotional stimulation of Cardiff where the superb singing of *Land of Our Fathers* attains a religious fervour. No crowd, too, is more generous in its appreciation of the finer points of the game than a Welsh crowd.

But to the spectacular glories of Twickenham, the fierce exuberance of Dublin, and the emotional fervour of Cardiff, Edinburgh adds a grim earnestness which has its roots in the most cherished traditions of the Scottish race. The crowd is a vast concourse of experts, and it is little wonder that for years the Scottish Rugby Union refused to number its players, for, except the unfortunate exiles on leave from abroad, every member of the throng, from the smallest schoolboy to the oldest greybeard, knew them by sight and by Christian name, even if he had never met them, and had studied their football careers from the donning of their first jersey to their final appearance on the field of fields. I have attended bull-fights in Spain and baseball matches in the United States. At "soccer" matches in Prague and in Vienna I have watched national hate and political differences of opinion fan the frenzy of the crowd into a riot. At Lord's I have seen dignified statesmen weep with emotion when at a critical moment a Harrow fieldsman has dropped a catch in the cricket match against Eton, and in the same arena I have heard Mr. "Gerry" Weigall raise a raucous voice of warning to a Cambridge batsman who has played back when in the Weigall opinion he should have played forward.

But the emotions engendered by these various spectacles are spasmodic. The frenzy of the Central European crowds lacks the restraint and refinement essential to any sporting contest. There are tedious moments in cricket and bull-fighting and even in baseball. All these games lack the sustained unity of palpitation, which, especially when Scotland is playing England, makes every Scottish heart in the huge crowd beat as one during eighty minutes of concentrated struggle. In this emotional tumult there is something of the spirit of Bannockburn. It is the annual reassertion of Scottish independence and of a national pride which, although the Scot conceals it successfully in foreign countries, is more boastful and more aggressive than even the casual arrogance of the English. And the crowd is animated by one fierce, exultant desire: to see Scotland triumph over the old enemy.

Something of this spirit I had absorbed naturally when, wrapped in my warm Inverness cape, I took my place in one of the best seats in the centre of the stand. All around me were members of the Scottish Union and old "rugger" internationals whose names had long been known to me and whose deeds of valour, recounted on many occasions by my father, had assumed legendary proportions in my eyes. There was Bill Maclagan, hero of twenty-five Scottish caps, "Judy" Macmillan, greatest of Scottish forwards and an old pupil of my father's, Harcourt Davidson, a giant of a footballing minister of the kirk, and, most attractive of all because he was also a world-famous cricketer, Gregor Macgregor.

Dominating this circle of giants was a small sallow man with bushy eyebrows and a generous moustache. He was an old school friend of my father, and, as long as I could remember, I had heard him referred to almost daily as "Jock McCraw". His real name was J. Aikman Smith. Like Burgess, the Merchiston coach, he was no footballer, never attaining higher distinction in the game than that of reserve for the fourth fifteen of the Royal High School. But he was a born leader of men, ruthless in the face of opposition but generous and warm-hearted in spite of a pugnacious exterior, and for forty years he dominated Scottish rugby football. He died, too, a footballer's death, collapsing with heart failure in the train as he was accompanying the Scottish team on its journey to Wales.

To all of these heroes I was introduced. Pride swelled my

heart as I shook hands gravely with them and was greeted with such admonitions as "see that you become as good a footballer as your father". On that day I was proud of my father, who wore the little blue velvet badge surmounted with silver braid and bearing the magic lettering Scotland v England, 1897, which in those days was always given for every international to members of the Union. At Seafield I made quite a collection of these badges. With my other football trophies they were confiscated by the Bolsheviks, when they arrested me in 1918, and never returned.

My knees knocking together with anticipatory excitement, I sat down to while away as best I could the ten minutes which still remained before the game was due to start. There was interest enough to captivate the attention of a small schoolboy: the swaying of the crowd, the pipe band of Dr. Guthrie's Industrial School, the huge Scottish thistle which obstinately refused to stay in my diminutive buttonhole. Then abruptly the field was cleared and the pipers scurried across the green turf to take up their position at one end of the stand. From the other side of the field a great cheer announced that the head of the first English player was visible, and presently the English team, spotless in white shorts and white jersey with a red rose on the heart, ran on to the field. There was a long minute of silence broken only by the hard zip of leather meeting hands as the Englishmen warmed themselves with a little preliminary passing. Then the band struck up *The Barren Rocks of Aden*—a tune which later was to become all too familiar as a scabrous Fettes anthem sung at "Pops" to coarse words—and to the skirl of bagpipes and a long sustained roar of "Scotland", the Scottish team made its way through the narrow lane which led from the dressing-room to the ground. I saw a glorious vision of royal blue, and, almost before I could distinguish the rock-like chests and burly calves of the forwards from the more sinuous figures of the backs, the game had started.

A detailed description of the match would be superfluous.

Indeed, I have since seen far too many internationals to remember all its incidents. But the last quarter of an hour will live in my mind as long as memory lasts. The struggle, hard and pitiless but without the trickery which ruins much modern football, had been remarkably even, fortune swaying, now this way now that, with irritating fluctuations which kept the crowd in a constant fever of excitement. But the balance had turned in England's favour, and with only fifteen minutes to go the English team was leading by a try.

With the shadow of defeat hanging over it, the crowd roused itself to a frenzy, and in a shrill treble I added my discordant note to the swelling chorus of "Feet, Scotland, Feet". And nobly the Scottish forwards responded to the call. In a succession of fierce rushes they swept their way towards the English line. It was almost suicide to go down before this terrible phalanx in which the spears were the flying feet of H. O. Smith and young "Saxon" McEwan, then the forerunners of the famous "Darkie" Sivright in fierce, not to say coarse, play. But the Englishmen never flinched, and, as Scot after Scot tried to throw himself across the line, the English defence hurled him back. To a roar of cheers the redoubtable Mark Morrison was over, but was called back by the referee. And the cheering changed instantly into a groan of disappointment. Time trembled in the balance, and the spectators, looking anxiously at their watches, trembled with it. Then, with only two minutes to go, the Scottish forwards made one last desperate rush down the centre of the field. Close to the line it was temporarily stopped. But the English defence, battered by the succession of fierce onslaughts, buckled, and from a loose scrum a Scottish forward seized the ball and hurled himself over the line behind the goal posts. The crowd became delirious. My father, holding his stick with both hands and hammering with it on the wooden floor or on his neighbour's toes, was crying and laughing at the same time. Everyone in the stand stood up, and for a moment the field below was blotted out from my view by a wall of bowler hats and overcoats. I did not care. At that moment of exultation nothing mattered. That glorious try on the verge of time meant certain victory for Scotland. The kick in front of goal was the easiest in the game.

It was entrusted to Tom Scott, a Hawick working man and a reliable goal-kicker, who had converted scores of tries from every angle. As he began to prepare for his kick, there were cries of "Sit Down", and, instinctively mindful of the nerve-strain on the Scottish kicker, the spectators settled into their seats. The cheering died, giving way to a silence like the hush of prayer. And in that moment of suspense many fervent prayers were whispered to the god of Scotland. Tremulously I held my breath while Tom Scott made his heel-mark in the ground and carefully wiped the mud from the toe of his boot. Then, giving the signal to the prostrate half-back to put the ball down, he took two steps forward and kicked. The ball rose feebly, hung for a moment in the air, and passed outside the right-hand goal post. The mighty Tom Scott had failed with a kick which even a schoolboy of ten could have successfully converted five times out of six. Scotland had been robbed of a victory which two minutes before had seemed all too sure, and in mortified silence the great crowd began to file away.

In my own disappointment there was something of the bitterness of defeat. That Scotland had finished on equal terms was no consolation. Only the year before, Scotland, after four successive victories, had thought it unnecessary to go to the expense and bother of taking the Calcutta Cup, which goes to the winners of this annual match, to Manchester. There Scotland had been defeated. The terrible humiliation of having to confess that they had "forgotten" the Cup made victory at Powderhall doubly necessary. The victory had been wrested from us when it was in our grasp. The shame had not been wiped out. In this bitter moment, like that great sportsman, Sammy Woods, I had no use for "draws" except for bathing.

I should have liked to linger by the battle-field, perhaps realising subconsciously that novelty is the mainspring of every emotional experience and that no future international, however decisive Scotland's victory might be, would ever be quite the same as that first Calcutta Cup match at Powderhall. But my father was already in a bustle. Before taking me back to Broughty Ferry he had to attend a committee meeting at which the deeds of the players would be submitted to the cold scrutiny of individual criticism. Greatly privileged, I took my place between him and Mr. Aikman Smith in a supplementary official bus which contained several of the Scottish players. They were too tired and perhaps too disappointed to speak, and in sympathetic silence I gazed at their muddy boots and huge raw-boned knees. When we pulled up at the old Royal Hotel in Princes Street, the great "Jock McCraw" himself helped me out of the bus. Then, putting his hand in his pocket and giving me two half-crowns, he turned to my father. "Man Lockhart," he said, "if yon bungler had not foozled that kick, I'd have made it a golden sovereign." To others this parsimony inspired by bitterness may seem hard and even typically Scottish. But even then I understood it and accepted it naturally. In my eyes the fifteen shillings which I had missed represented the just difference between glory and the anti-climax of that terrible moment when the pride of Scotland had been suddenly exalted and so suddenly let down.

Holding as I do that a "rugger" international is the most soul-stirring spectacle of all athletic contests, excelling in its concentrated excitement polo, baseball, or any other game, I find it strange that rugby football should have enriched the English language with so few words and should occupy such a minor place in English literature. Cricket has furnished scores of expressions which, from "keeping one's end up" to Mr. Baldwin's moral standard of "not cricket", have passed into the language. "Rugger" shares with association football only one general phrase: "to have the ball at one's foot".

Cricket, too, has supplied the theme of numerous books, but, apart from Sir John Squire's noble poem and one or two restrained efforts by Sir Hugh Walpole, "rugger" has been neglected. Even school-story writers have preferred other games, although I must make an exception in the case of Mr. R. S. Warren Bell whose *J. O. Jones* is a splendid tale of a bad school rescued by a rugger-playing headmaster.

In my Seafield days Warren Bell was one of my two favourite school-story writers, sharing pride of place with a young author who had just begun to write about this time and whose *The Gold Bat* did for cricket in my eyes what Warren Bell's *J. O. Jones* did for rugby football. The young author, then or a little later, used to write for *The Captain*, and it was in the pages of that now defunct boys' monthly magazine that I first saw his name. It has since become famous in every corner of the English-speaking world. The young school-story writer was Mr. P. G. Wodehouse.

Although cricket is a game to which the Scots have never taken kindly, it was, strangely enough, just as popular at Seafield as was rugby football. This unnatural preference was inspired partly by the enthusiastic zeal of my father and partly by the fact that the assistant masters were always Englishmen. I can remember no assistant master who was more than a very moderate "rugger" player. In L. G. W. Wilkinson, A. C. Miller and H. S. Pink we had three masters who as cricketers were on the verge of first-class.

Thanks to my training as an infant at Beith I gained, at the age of eight, a place in the eleven of a school most of whose members had never before handled a bat. In that first year we played, or rather travelled to play, only one match, but in one sense it was the most exciting of all the numerous matches in which I took part during my five years at Seafield. It was against the juniors of Glenalmond, the famous Scottish public school which owes much of its success to the initial support of Mr. Gladstone and to its superb and inspiring situation in the heart of the Perthshire Highlands.

We started at seven in the morning and before we reached home we had been more than eight hours on the road—an Odyssey which is a sufficient comment on the transport difficulties of those pre-motor car days in Scotland. The match was never played, rain coming down in torrents before a ball was bowled. But on the way home two of our team refreshed themselves with a drink from a bucket at a wayside well and developed typhoid fever, and in consequence of this alarming outbreak all our other matches were cancelled.

My first cricket trophy was a bat presented to me by David Addison Smith, one of Scotland's greatest cricketers, for making top score in my first match. Our opponents, the redoubtable Merchiston Preparatory, made 126. We were dismissed ignominiously for 26, of which my score of 11 won the bat. As a small boy, however, I showed more promise as a slow bowler than as a batsman, and at the age of not quite eleven I made my first appearance in public print as the result of a bowling performance which would make even Rhodes's best average seem expensive. Playing against St. Salvator's, a St. Andrews' private school whose boys were obviously better at golf than at cricket, I took in their two innings thirteen wickets for six runs, clean bowling twelve of my victims and dismissing four in successive balls. This performance was duly chronicled in the Dundee newspapers under such captions as "Small Boy's Astounding Feat".

This prodigy of bowling was never repeated, but as a member of the eleven I had a joyous time and to the detriment of my work travelled as far afield as Edinburgh, Glenalmond and St. Andrews to play against other schools. At Seafield I had my first experience of those blood-matches which were later to develop their full venom in the form of inter-House matches at one's public school. These were the annual encounters between Day-boys and Boarders. At Seafield they were played in a far keener spirit of rivalry than any school match, and they generally produced close finishes, the star batsmen often failing in the hour of crisis and the rabbits rising to heights of unexpected prowess.

But far more exciting than our own games at Seafield was the cricket at Forthill, the ground of the Forfarshire county team. The ground was only ten minutes' walk from Seafield, and, as my father loved watching cricket, we went there frequently. Indeed, I think that the matches were a greater stimulus to our cricketing zeal than either the enthusiasm of my father or the technical coaching of our English masters.

Forfarshire cricket in those days was run by W. R. Sharp, one of four brothers, each of whom left a fortune of several hundred thousand pounds. "W. R.", a rotund and jovial sportsman, excelled at all games. As a golfer he had played in the amateur championship. At rugby football he was once selected to play full-back for Scotland, but in those days even international games were kept in proper proportion, and with a casualness which now seems difficult to understand he declined the honour because it entailed a long journey to Wales. His cricket he had learnt in England as a schoolboy at Clifton College. He was kind to boys, and whenever he made a good score there was always tea for us in the pavilion which was his gift to the county.

The great event of the season was the match against Perthshire, and in his keenness to defeat the enemy "W. R." used to collect a side by methods which did not always appeal to the other members of the club. In this annual encounter both sides were limited to the service of one English professional. Great care was taken to secure the very best available, and, indeed, some of England's greatest professionals, notably Haigh, Ringrose, Smailes and Andrews, have made their debut for Forfarshire or Perthshire. "W. R.", however, went outside the spirit of this restriction by enlisting as amateurs such talented cricketing football professionals as Hillman, the Dundee goalkeeper and J. Sharp, then the Dundee full-back.

The annual match at Forthill was always played on the

Perth holiday, and thousands of Perthshire supporters made the journey to Broughty Ferry. The atmosphere was therefore that of a Yorkshire v Lancashire match supplemented by extraneous excitements which are absent from Bramall Lane or Old Trafford. The Perthshire supporters brought ample supplies of whisky, and there were few present who had not a bottle in their pockets. Like the football supporters of the Rangers and the Celtic in Glasgow, the rival factions took up their stand on opposite sides of the ground, and woe betide the unfortunate Forfarshire cricketer who happened to be fielding close to the Perthshire partisans. He was subjected to a running fire of venomous back-chat, which covered his ancestry, his physical appearance, and the cut of his trousers with a completeness which is to be found neither in Debrett nor even in the *Dictionary of National Biography*. If he were an Old Harrovian like Charlie Gilroy, he was regarded as a "bloody to-ff" and was told so with a frequency which was as insistent as it was irritating. And, if he happened to make a catch to dismiss a Perthshire batsman, a shower of bottles, bananas and ham sandwiches ensured that he missed the next.

Infected by this partisan exuberance, we watched every ball of these encounters with eyes glued to the pitch, and I remember one tie not only for the glorious thrill when, with the scores equal, Whitehead, the Forfarshire fast bowler, knocked the last Perthshire batsman's off-stump out of the ground, but also for a more painful emotion when, as I was leaving the ground with a last whoop of jubilation, a disgruntled Perthshire "tough" lunged viciously at me and gave me a stinging crack on the seat of my pants with a heavy blackthorn stick.

Occasionally we followed the fortunes of Forfarshire when they played away from Forthill, and in this way I paid my first visit to Glamis Castle in order to watch a match between a Forfarshire eleven and a Glamis team captained by Lord Glamis, now the Earl of Strathmore and father of our present Queen.

In regard to cricket my father is single-minded, and on this occasion I was not allowed to detach my interest in the game by even a cursory glance at the Castle. Indeed, many years were to elapse before I was to enter its portals—to see the great baronial hall with its mixture of ancient treasures and rather cold modern comforts; the old rooms with King Duncan's bedroom which our present King uses as a dressing-room; the fine Lazlo portrait of the Queen in the Countess of Strathmore's boudoir; the bedroom, now decorated with the Scott tartan, in which Bonnie Prince Charlie and Sir Walter Scott slept; the eerie old kitchen with almost no windows and no outside light, and the huge chimney stretching from the basement to the top of the castle—to behold from the platform of the square tower the finest view in all Scotland with the Sidlaws to the south and the Grampians stretching in a succession of mountainous waves to the northern horizon; to inspect in the billiard-room the cast of the great 6 lbs. trout caught in the Dean burn, which runs through the grounds, and to cherish secret hopes that one day I, too, may be privileged to throw my fly on these delectable waters.

I never played cricket at Glamis, but before we left Broughty Ferry my brother Rufus took part, I think, in several matches. On one occasion, when the visiting eleven were batting and were doing badly against the deliveries of the Glamis fast bowler, a little girl of five gave great amusement to the batsmen who were awaiting their turn. Every time a wicket fell she clapped her hands and jumped around with partisan glee. "Who is the man bowling?" asked one of the visiting team. "That's James," said the little girl gravely. "I'm going to marry him when I grow older." James was one of the Glamis footmen. The little girl is now Queen Elizabeth.

To-day, there is no cricket at Glamis. The Earl is now eighty-two, and his family is scattered. He is still fond of games, and, when he is at Glamis during the late autumn, still goes to Forfar on fine days to watch the local professional team play association football. But the family are now increasingly rarely in residence, and in view of the Earl's age their absence is scarcely surprising, for with all its charms, its superb situation and its glorious park, Glamis, like most castles, cannot be a comfortable dwelling-place. Every room, however, bears evidence of that simple home life which surrounded Queen Elizabeth's Scottish girlhood. There is one great bed with curtained hangings on which the name of every member of the family with the date of birth has been embroidered by the Countess of Strathmore herself. The Queen's age is easy to remember. It goes with the date of the year, for she was born in 1900.

CHAPTER FIVE

IF ORGANISED WORK and organised games occupied most of our time and overshadowed the background of our school days, there was always a friendly light on the horizon which pointed the way to a life of independence. This was the weekly whole-holiday on Saturdays.

The boarders at Seafield were weekly boarders. It is not a system which I should recommend to parents, for the weekly visit home unsettles both the minds and the stomachs of small boys. But to my brother and myself whose home was school and whose fare on Saturdays was simpler than during the rest of the week, this holiday was a day of joyous adventure which was more than sufficient recompense for the gloom of the Sunday to come.

We were free from breakfast-time, and, as soon as the last weekly boarders had left, we rushed upstairs and changed into our oldest clothes. Old clothes meant escape from regimentation, and when we put them on we felt like the happy tramp in the fairy story whose shirt the king tried to borrow in order to acquire happiness himself and who had to go away sorrowing because the tramp was shirtless. Our own appearance must have been tramp-like, but my father and mother did not seem to mind and either by intention or by indifference refrained from imposing unnatural restraints.

And here let me venture to address a word of advice to the mothers of Scotland. Take no heed if your children show no interest in clothes and prefer to eat their food with unclean hands. Do not buy a new pair of braces when you find your son's trousers hanging precariously by a piece of string and two buttons. A generous amount of deliberate letting of children shift for themselves is perhaps the chief essential of a sound education, and the time will come all too soon when your sons will evince an unhealthy interest in striped socks, gaudy shirts, manicures, and the other peacock vanities of modern civilisation, and you yourselves will be wringing your hands over tailors' bills for which your own extravagance or your own high standard of luxury will be responsible. For the faculty of imitation is at its strongest in boyhood, and in a higher degree than charity it begins at home. To-day, when I see the young men in remote Highland villages plastering their hair with Anzora cream, wasting their money on gramophones and dancing, and seeking any job which will lead them speedily to the dole, rather than work in the fields, I often wonder if our elementary education is infected by a dangerous taint of imitative snobbishness or if these things are signs of the pre-ordained decadence which luxury brings inevitably to every race.

At any rate, I am grateful to my parents for the measure of neglect that they gave us. My Saturday pleasures at Seafield were healthy and innocuous and they ranged from catapults and chestnut contests to air-guns and golf. As the Forfarshire coast of the Firth of Tay forms a series of natural links, golf was an early enthusiasm. Barnhill, little more than an approaching and putting course, but then dignified by the name of the ladies' course, was the first scene of my early attempts to master a game whose chief charm consists in the fact that even the greatest expert can never be certain of producing the same degree of skill in two successive rounds. From Barnhill I advanced by a natural combination of progress and ambition to Carnoustie, and, once having reached this delectable links, I remained true to it.

On these Saturday golf expeditions I sometimes played against other Seafield boys, but my chief and favourite opponent was my brother Rufus. We travelled by train and took our lunch with us. Our matches were strenuously and rigorously fought out, and for me at any rate were an excellent test of self-control. For, although a year-and-a-half younger, Rufus could hold his own with me. Even in those days he had an admirable games temperament, and, when down, would set about in dour silence to redress the leeway.

At times I found this perseverance irksome, and in our early encounters more than one match ended in a fencing duel in which irons took the place of single-sticks. Fortunately, these quarrels never lasted more than a few minutes, and very soon I learnt to master my temper and to accept my occasional defeats from a younger brother with proper equanimity. I do not think that since then golf has ever provoked me to anything more than a mild self-irritation.

Nor was golf the sole attraction of Carnoustie. When we had lost all our balls in the icy coldness of the unfriendly Barry burn, we would seek shelter from the wind in a high bunker and, munching our egg sandwiches, look at the wild birds and the salmon nets off the Barry sands. I have always liked wide horizons, and on fine days I could see the Bell Rock lighthouse which was well known to me as the scene of the tragedy of Sir Ralph the Rover, the pirate, who, having removed the warning bell placed there by the good Abbot of Aberbrothock, had run his own ship on the rock and had perished there with all his crew. Southey's poem was a favourite of my father's, and I had learnt it by heart at an early age. Of still greater interest to me was the fact that the lighthouse, which inspired not only our admiration but a youthful desire to spend a night in the tower, had been built by Robert Louis Stevenson's grandfather.

When the weather was too cold, we repaired, if we had any money, to one of those cottages which even in those days supplied modest refreshments to poor golfers. Our first experience of this kind led to a financial tragedy exceeding in bitterness the far greater financial disasters of my subsequent career. Driven off the course by a shower of hail, we found a dirty-looking cottage with the magic word "Teas" displayed outside. We went in, and presently a blowsy, hard-bitten woman dumped down a teapot and a plate of scones and butter and raspberry jam before us. Our combined exchequer amounted only to sixpence, and, as soon as the woman left the toom, Rufus whispered to me: "this spread will cost more than our sixpence, we must be careful." We held a council of action and decided that we should buy one bottle of kola and eat one scone each. Kola we knew was cheap, and a scone could not cost more than a penny. We finished our meagre meal and, still famished, tapped on the plate with a knife for our bill. We put down our six pennies, but the woman snorted.

"The charge for teas is sixpence a head and cheap at the price. And there is an extra twopence for the bottle of kola," she said.

We pointed out timidly that we had not touched the tea and had eaten only two scones.

Her eyes blazed. She had heard this tale before from dirty "keelies" who had come in to fill their bellies and to cheat an honest woman out of her money.

In vain we protested our innocence, declaring that our father lived in a big house and would send the money by the next post.

Perhaps we looked like "keelies". At any rate, she did not believe us, and her anger now swelled into a torrent of abuse. Thoroughly frightened, I made a sign to Rufus, and, after retreating backwards out of the room, ran for safety to the friendly shelter of Simpson's, the golfing shop of the well-known Carnoustie club-makers.

To-day, Carnoustie has blazoned its name on the map of the world. Through the medium of its sons who have left it in order to become golf professionals in the New World, it has become a household word in the United States. As the home-town of Stewart Maiden, the golfing mentor of Bobby Jones, it has acquired something of the atmosphere of Mecca, and to meet the requirements of the army of tourists the number of cottages supplying teas has increased a thousandfold. The town has altered in size and in character and was a sad disappointment to David Low, the brilliant cartoonist, whose father was born in Carnoustie and lived there until he emigrated to New Zealand.

David, a former colleague of mine, took his father back to Carnoustie a few years ago. When I saw him on his return, I asked what he thought of the place. David, whose faith in Europe and in the rights of small nationalities has suffered many rude shocks during the last few years, shook his head sadly. "The only Scottish tang about the place was my father," he said.

In my Seafield days Carnoustie was little more than a village, and golf a game confined almost exclusively to Scotland. In England, it is true, there were a few courses, but in London, Mr. Balfour, the first British statesman to play golf, was regarded as a comic eccentric, and Liberal cartoonists caricatured him as a golfer with the same malicious intent with which French cartoonists drove M. Briand out of office after his famous golf match with Mr. Lloyd George at Cannes. How limited was the popularity of the game may be gauged from the fact that in both the British and the American first editions of *Catriona*, published in 1893, Stevenson thought it necessary to insert a note to his chapter entitled "The Tee'd Ball" to explain that this was a ball placed upon a little mound by golfers for the convenience of striking.

But in Scotland itself the game was played with a sombre and serious dignity. Pullovers were unknown, and a golfer who ventured to play in shirt-sleeves would have been hounded from the course. Greatly daring young men sported knickerbockers, and golf captains and other aged dignitaries of the game wore a tightly buttoned red coat. But at Carnoustie, and at the more exclusive Barry, respectable Dundee jute manufacturers like the Sharps and the Boases played in trousers.

We boys played in kilts, a dress which has certain disadvantages on a wind-swept course. I remember one occasion when as a small boy I was playing at Barry with a young nephew of John Sharp, the eldest of the four brothers. A gale of wind was blowing, and at one point where two tees were almost adjacent we saw John Sharp. My companion hailed him. "Hallo, Uncle John," he said in a shrill treble. "What are you going round in?" John Sharp, a genial, kind-hearted man with a large corporation and an attractive burr in his speech, looked for a minute at the two boys, their kilts swirling in the air and exposing a generous proportion of bare thigh, and shook his head. "I'm going r-round in my tr-rousers," he said gravely. Discomfited by the guffaws of laughter which came from his opponent and their two caddies, I smote my ball into a bunker.

Although the standard of golf among Seafield boys was high, neither my brother nor I ever achieved any marked degree of skill in the game. At the age of fourteen I took part in my first competition on the medal course at Carnoustie. I handed in a card with the figure 116. It was not quite the worst score, but several boys broke 90, and the winning boy returned a card of 83. In those days of guttie balls and inferior implements this was a remarkable score for a youngster, and four of my Seafield contemporaries were subsequently good enough to play in the amateur championship.

In summer, golf was subordinated to watching cricket, my father, like many Scots of his generation, holding that golf was essentially a spring and autumn game. In winter, if there was frost, we skated on a pond in the shadow of Claypots Castle. To my boyish imagination it seemed a vast lake, and I pictured it as the last line of defence of an impregnable fortress. Revisiting it after an interval of over thirty years, I was sadly disillusioned. It was little more than a glorified puddle.

Summer and winter alike we went on wet days to the saltwater swimming baths in Dundee. To me the baths, situated in the dock area, were attractive less for their own merits than for the opportunity they provided of inspecting the whalers, India merchantmen, and an occasional destroyer which were berthed alongside, and the smell of tarred ropes was a pleasant stimulus to the travel blood in my veins.

In the Dundee baths was enacted a dramatic scene in our family life. On one occasion my brother Rufus, then unable to swim, got out of his depth. He was just able to touch the floor of the bath with his feet and kept bobbing up and down in an effort to breathe. Everyone thought he was playing, and he would have drowned in a crowded bath had not an attendant realised the true situation and, jumping in with all his clothes on, lifted my brother out. I was born on a Friday, whose child, according to the rhyme, is loving and giving, and I remember my mental agitation lest my father, magnanimous in big things but parsimonious in small, should fail to reward the attendant suitably. He gave him, I think, five shillings—a premium which some schoolboys may consider excessive for the life of a future headmaster.

These normal pastimes were supplemented by more boyish amusements of our own devising. At an early age we acquired a Daisy air-gun. Constant use gradually weakened its spring until even a sparrow was impervious to the best-aimed slug and merely shook its feathers vulgarly when hit. It was then that we devised a new game which owed its origin to Rufus's passion for stories about Red Indians. Creeping out after dusk, with the air-gun held straight down from the armpit, we would walk innocently along the quiet roads of the best residential part of Broughty Ferry. Then, waiting anxiously until the street was clear, we would enter the drive of a large house, lie down under a fir tree, and from a distance of thirty yards fire a slug at a lighted window. One slug was nearly always sufficient to cause an immediate reaction. The window would be thrown open, and a slightly anxious voice would cry out: "Who's there?" A second shot would produce a panic. Bells would be rung, and presently servants armed with lanterns would come out to examine the grounds before the house. Safely hidden beneath the dense branches of the fir tree, we would lie very still, scarcely daring to breathe, while our nerves tingled with the fear of detection.

We were never found out, but this game came eventually to its inevitable end. From private houses we went to farms. Somehow we had discovered that a slug truly aimed at the hindquarters of a cow produced a glorious exhibition of bucking and a most comic elevation of the cow's tail. This practice had to be carried out by day. The risk of detection was therefore greater, but gradually we grew careless. What a sparrow could withstand, a barn fowl would endure with comparative immunity; and from cows we turned our gun on hens. One day, when our supply of slugs had run out, my brother inserted a dart in the gun and, firing at short range at a hen, stretched it lifeless on the ground. While we stood regretting this tragedy, the farmer, who had evidently been watching us, came up from behind and, taking us by the scruff of our necks, marched us off to my father. The gun was confiscated.

If I was allowed to go my own way, I was not entirely excluded from the social life of my parents. My father and mother dined out frequently and in return gave dinner-parties and an occasional dance in the Big School. These functions always took place on Saturdays, and then I had to put on my dress kilt and black jacket with silver buttons and come in for dessert, shake hands with the guests, and remain for the first dances. With an instinctive loathing I hated these formalities and the inspection of nails which preceded them, and, as soon as I could, I stole away with Rufus to the kitchen to regale myself with the good things which these Saturday evenings provided. One of these kitchen raids nearly cost me my life, for, having eaten a large number of meringues too quickly, I contracted a violent headache, and, to ease it, I ran upstairs to the bathroom and plunged my head into a basin of cold water. Somehow or other my head stuck under the taps and I could not get it out. Fortunately, the bathroom was over the dining-room, and my mother, hearing my frantic tramping on the floor, rushed upstairs just in time to save me from an ignominious drowning.

Sometimes my father would take us on a trip which lasted the whole day, and it was on one of our Saturday holidays that I made my first journey to St. Andrews. Rufus and I were then very small boys, and at Leuchars, where we had to change trains, my father, after depositing us in the St. Andrews train, stepped out on the platform to talk to a friend. While he was still engrossed in his conversation, the train started without him, and, sobbing in each other's arms, my brother and I were carried on alone.

Fortunately, the journey which lasted about a quarter of an hour was long enough to enable my father to telephone to the St. Andrews stationmaster, and when we arrived at the terminus we were met by a kind official who took us into his room and, by showing us the mysteries of the telegraph and the ticket puncher, helped us to pass away the time until my father arrived by the next train. But the mental distress of those first moments when the train steamed out of Leuchars was very real, and to-day it dominates all my memories of my first trip to St. Andrews.

A little later we paid a more pleasant visit to the grey city by the sea. On this occasion we had been invited by the Cunninghams, who had moved to St. Andrews from Broughty Ferry, and at their house I met Andrew Lang. He was the first author that I ever saw, and, quite apart from his striking appearance, I was duly impressed, for as the author of the Yellow Fairy Book and, greater still, of the Red True Story Book he was already someone more than a friend in my estimation.

To my disappointment the conversation at lunch was mostly about golf, for Lang took an aesthetic interest in the game, and James Cunningham, the father of my friends George and Freddie, was a fine golfer as well as a classical scholar. Indeed, a portrait of him in golfing attitude appeared as a model for beginners in almost the first book on golf ever written.

On this occasion I played my first round on the classic Old

Course, paid my first visit to Rusack's and was taken up to the proprietor's room on the top floor, the view from which has been described by so great a traveller as the Duke of Windsor as the finest in the world. In the afternoon we made a Baedeker tour of the sights: the Old Castle, the University buildings, the Cathedral, St. Regulus Tower, the Blackfriars Chapel, and the cemetery where the great Tom Morris now lies buried. In the streets, I saw for the first time the resplendent red gowns of the students and learnt to call a Freshman "bejant", a corruption of the French "bec jaune", which is the equivalent of our "greenhorn". And from the lips of a parrot-like guide, who swung his lantern down into the grim Bottle Dungeon of the castle and who had to start his tale all over again every time that he was interrupted, I heard, on the actual spot, the grisly story of murder, rape, and martyrdom which have given to the city a unique place in the annals of Scottish history. Historical details absorbed in this manner make a lasting impression on imaginative boys, and, as the guide rolled off the list of names, I saw a sleek and well-fed Cardinal Beaton gloating over the burning of Wishart, the Reformer, only to be murdered himself a few months later and to have his corpse exposed on the battlements. As I looked down on the turbulent sea below, I visualised the taking of the castle by the French fleet and John Knox being carried off as a prisoner to the French galleys.

Doubtless the pictures which I formed were wholly incorrect in detail, but at any rate they remain very clear in my mind and have not altered to this day. They are, indeed, my lasting memories of a city whose very name endears it to every Scot. Royal and Ancient St. Andrews, home of the classics and of golf, you, too, must rank among the dream-islands which always float in my imagination as a refuge from the mainland of reality.

On rare occasions we went to spend a Saturday to Monday visit at the home of a weekly boarder. One of these visits touched a new chord in my heart—sympathy with the under-dog. We went to stay with a boy whose father, Captain Scott, was commander of the *Mars*, an old "wooden-wall" of the British Navy, which was anchored off Newport, close to the Tay Bridge. It was used then as a reformatory school for Scottish boy-criminals. Doubtless, the atmosphere of the ship was far healthier than that of a prison. The boys, dressed and disciplined like sailors, were given a useful practical training and were taught to play games in the right spirit. Many of them subsequently chose the sea as a career, and one or two even rose to executive rank.

But in their hard faces I could see signs of revolt, and if there was fear in my heart there was also a great pity. And in the cutter which rowed us ashore, I wanted to give all my money to a boy-rower whose thumb had been hacked off by a knife in a fight and whom I pictured as a counterpart of Ransome, the cabin boy in *Kidnapped*.

These first feelings of humanitarianism received a further stimulus when, after accompanying Willie Miller, our assistant master, on a day's shooting up the Tay, we used to pass through Dundee on a Saturday night on our way home. In changing stations, we had to walk along Dock Street in which every second door opened into a public-house. "Drunks" of both sexes encumbered the pavement. Brawls were frequent, and on one occasion we had to make a wide detour to avoid a bottle fight. Beneath the yellow light of the street lamp I saw a man fall, his head smashed open by a broken bottle. His opponents were kicking him. I should have liked to rush in to stop this brutality, but my knees knocked with fear. And, indeed, to a small boy the crash of broken glass, the pools of blood lying on the pavement, and the vision of the pale, sodden faces of the men and women, more like animals than human beings, were terrifying enough.

In those days many of the public houses belonged to the father of a man who subsequently became my journalistic colleague and friend in London. When the father died, he left a considerable fortune to his son, but the latter, mindful of his youthful days in Dundee, refused to touch a penny of it. The son is now editor of a great national newspaper.

Similar feelings of fear and pity animated my mind when we went to stay with a boy whose father was a rich jute manufacturer. In this case the house was close to the jute mill, and even then I could not help contrasting the luxury of the owner's house with the pinched poverty outside. Dundee employers, on the whole, were capable, honest, God-fearing men who worked as long hours as their workmen and who had a high conception of their civic duties. But they were products of the harsh industrial revolution, and, Free Traders by tradition, they never hesitated to import the cheapest labour and to house it as inexpensively as possible. With the employers of Glasgow and other industrial centres, they or their fathers must be held responsible not only for the vast importation of Irish immigrants, but also for the stunted growth of the present-day industrial proletariat of Scotland.

The somewhat hypocritical ease with which they managed to reconcile hard business with their religious feelings filled me with an early distaste, not for Liberalism itself, but for the Liberal Party; for, in my Seafield days, Dundee was and always had been a Radical stronghold. The Radicalism was represented not only by the working classes. The pioneers of the jute industry were self-made men who had then little use for peers, landowners, and other pillars of the Conservative Party. They, too, held as strong views as their workmen on Free Trade and the franchise, and the youthful Gladstone, delayed in Dundee on his way south from his father's estate in Kincardineshire, shortly before the passing of the Reform Bill, received a lasting impression of the city's Radicalism from the passage of a procession with banners, one of which bore the inscription: "DOWN WITH THE HOUSE OF LORDS. TO HELL WITH THE BLOODY TYRANTS."

The Radical tradition remained after the burgh was granted two seats and the population had been sharply divided into "haves" and "have-nots". Until Miss Horsbrugh was elected in 1931, Dundee had returned only one Conservative member in its long political history. Returned is perhaps a misnomer, for this first Conservative, a local provost, was elected originally as a Liberal. Shortly before the end of that Parliament he was seen helping Disraeli on with his overcoat in the lobbies of the House of Commons. His obsequiousness to the great Conservative leader was noticed by watchful Liberals, and at the next election he was accused of nursing secret Conservative leanings. Outdoing St. Peter, he denied the charge on every platform on which he spoke and was duly re-elected as a Liberal. Soon after the opening of the Parliamentary session he crossed the floor of the House and took his place behind Disraeli.

Personally, I think that many Dundonians were Liberals mainly by conservatism. At any rate, it is a curious fact that the farther north they live, the more conservative in their opinions the Scots become. And that is why, to-day, the last strongholds of Liberalism are in the far north.

I must pay a tribute to the Dundee business man's knowledge of the world. The Englishman, who rules the greatest empire the world has ever known, is amazingly ignorant of geography. No such nescience characterised the Dundonian of the Victorian age. The jute manufacturer knew his map of India and of China rather better than many cartographers, and in an era when America was an ignored and almost unknown continent I learnt more of the American Civil War from Dundee jute kings than I ever learnt at school or university. Their knowledge was not entirely disinterested. In the early days of the jute industry, when Dundee led the world, huge fortunes were made by supplying nose-bags and sacking to the armies of the North and South.

The whaling industry made everyone interested in the Arctic, and as there was a brisk flax trade with Russia I heard much about that country without having any idea that it would subsequently claim the best years of my life or, indeed, any inclination or ambition to visit it. It was in Dundee that I first saw a Russian uniform. It belonged to Harry Rennie, a friend of my mother and a Dundee flax merchant who then occupied the post of honorary Consul of the Tsar.

Although they preferred hard facts to sentiment, these Dundonians of the end of last century were kindly, hospitable men whose family life was a model of decent Scottish respectability. There was no night life in Dundee. If they strayed from virtue, they erred far from home, accepting the Mohammedan dictum that a sin in the sight of men is more offensive than a sin known to Allah alone. Impassive in triumph and in crisis, they had, too, a sense of humour sometimes expressed unconsciously as, for example, when Mr. Edward Robertson, who sat as a member for Dundee and who was afterwards elevated to the peerage, chose as his title Lord Lochee of Gowrie. This title, perhaps the most euphonious that has ever graced a lord, was taken from the grimmest suburb of Dundee and one of the most beautiful carses in Scotland. But their greatest virtue was the shrewdness of their judgment, and rarely did their innate commonsense lead them into errors of recklessness. It was a Dundee flax merchant who during the Great War gave to the War Office the tersest and best advice that it ever received on the Russian revolution. Called in as an expert on Archangel, he was asked by the big-wigs to give his opinion regarding the value of Allied troops in that semi-Arctic port as a rallying-ground for the "loyal" or anti-Bolshevik forces. "If it's your intervention you mean," said the Scot, who, although a bitter anti-Bolshevik, could sum up a situation without bias, "it's no more use than farting against a gale of thunder." Unfortunately, this blast of commonsense did not deter the red-tabs from an enterprise which served merely to galvanise the Bolsheviks and to damage British prestige in the eyes not only of all Russians but also of the whole world.

The Great War cost Dundee many lives, and no city has a better war record. It also shook Dundonians out of a prosperous complacency which had lasted for more than seventy years and forced them to fall into step with modern progress. Dundee to-day is a changed city. In the face of Indian competition the prosperity of the jute industry is a thing of the past. But Dock Street is now a well-built, respectable thoroughfare, and in Miss Horsbrugh the town has a Conservative member who is a stouter fighter for improved social conditions than were the old Liberals of the past. In 1937 she secured the Royal Assent for her "Red Biddy" Bill and thus achieved the distinction of being the first woman for six years to put her name on the Statute Book. Her Bill imposes restrictions on the sale of "Red Biddy", the popular name for a villainous concoction composed by adding methylated spirits to cheap wine, which, when the increased post-war duties made whisky and gin too expensive, enjoyed a wide sale among the working-class population of the large Scottish industrial cities. On "Red Biddy" a man or woman could get drunk for twopence. Now that the new Act has come into force Dundee, and even Glasgow, may become sober cities.

Of my own politics during my Broughty Ferry boyhood I have only vague memories. During the only election which I remember clearly, I wore the colours of Captain Ramsay, a member of the Dalhousie family, who was the Conservative candidate, and engaged in wordy and sometimes physical combat with the "keelies" who, to a man, supported Mr. Sinclair, afterwards Lord Pentland, the successful Liberal champion.

During the Boer War, which began while I was still a schoolboy at Seafield, I was certainly a patriot and, therefore, presumably a Conservative. I bought cheap and gaudy buttons with coloured portraits of Buller, Gatacre, "Fighting Mac", Wauchope, and the other British leaders during the first year of failure. I learnt, too, by heart the popular war-songs of the day, like "Dolly Gray" and "Goodbye, Little Girl, Goodbye", and can hum their tunes and repeat their words to-day when the retention of the most popular croon-song of the moment defeats my memory. Owing to our family connections I had already a fair geographical knowledge of South Africa, and on a large map I followed with flag pins the varying fortunes of the British generals.

But of the magnitude of the early failures I was sublimely unconscious, nor did I realise, as I was to realise later in my Continental life, that the rest of the world was delighted to see the supercilious British beaten to their knees and forced to admit for the first time for a hundred years that, so far from being "not as other men", they were in essence the same mixture of strength and weakness as the rest of humanity.

Of the origins and moral or immoral justification of the war I had no knowledge. To us schoolboys the Boers were "slim" scoundrels who hit below the belt, and I remember a school anagram which was given to us to solve. One of the lights ran somewhat as follows:

> "Old man who forced on war and bolted when
> He heard the advance of guns and tramp of men."

Small boys are not good at solving anagrams, but I doubt if there was a boy in the school who failed to write in "Kruger" for this light.

It would be absurd to attach the label of Conservatism to my youthful patriotism. My instinctive nationalism was the result of environment, which, according to its trappings, produces Conservatives, Liberals, Socialists and Communists by the same natural process. The truth is that boys not yet in their "teens" do not reason. They follow their natural bent, into which, thank God, politics do not enter.

BOOK III
HIGHLAND HOLIDAY

A HUNTER's fare is all I would be craving,
A shepherd's plaiding and a beggar's pay,
If I might earn them where the heather, waving,
Gave grandeur to the day.

Neil Munro

CHAPTER ONE

ACQUISITIVENESS IS PROBABLY the only characteristic which is common to both the Scots and the English, and in the minds of the upper and middle classes of both nations the idea of heritage is linked with the idea of property. This is, I think, a false idea of the true value of possessions. For possessiveness is a state of mind rather than a right, and in a man's life there is only one possession which is not subject to the laws of change. The possession which I prize most cannot be measured in money or in terms of the material goods which a man inherits from his father. It is not tangible; yet it is visible and always present even in its physical absence. It is to be found in that environment of mountain and stream, of green meadow and slow-flowing river, of wood and plain, and perhaps even of town and factory chimney, which forms the indelible background of a man's youth, influences for better or worse his character, and colours his whole outlook on life. It is expressed in the words, my country—the country being not England or Germany or Scotland or even Kent or Inverness-shire, but that range of landscape which is limited by the ocular vision and which represents more strictly than any mansion or cottage what a man calls home. And to this wide interpretation of home we return again and again with the certain knowledge of comfort and consolation when we are tired of the burden of our active life or have been stripped of all our material possessions.

As a schoolmaster my father led a peripatetic life, and to me, neither to-day nor when I was a boy, have Anstruther, Beith, Broughty Ferry and Sandhurst ever conveyed an atmosphere of home. At Seafield our Saturday whole-holidays provided a pleasant escape from the discipline of school life. The Christmas and Easter holidays extended the range and duration of that escape. But the supreme joy of my existence was the annual migration to Strathspey for the long summer holiday of August and September. Throughout her life my mother lived for this moment, and as very small boys my brothers and I inherited and shared this nostalgic longing. During the winter months we talked of little else and planned fishing and other expeditions which, if magnified by anticipatory imagination, rarely failed to fulfil expectations.

By the middle of July we were already in a fever of excitement. Old clothes were sorted out and laid in neat piles. Fishing rods were burnished and revarnished. An insistent inroad was made on the money-box, and a whole delicious Saturday morning was spent at Gow's in Dundee in the purchase of fishing tackle. At last the great day would arrive, and with an army of servants, cart-loads of luggage, and Teufel, the most pugnacious of Irish terriers, we would set out for the station.

As far as Perth we would be fidgety and impatient. But from there began a journey into fairyland. We always had an engaged carriage, and with complete disregard for the wishes and comfort of our parents my brother Rufus and I tossed a coin for choice of the two corner seats facing the engine. If my father demurred, my mother, placid and marvellously sweet-tempered, quickly diverted his attention. When one lives for only seven weeks in the year, everyone dear to one must be happy in order to ensure one's own happiness.

Our choice, in fact, was not dictated by fear of train-sickness, but by the knowledge that the corner seats facing the engine commanded the best view. For from now on began an enchanting pastime. As fields of oats and turnips gave place to birch-clad hills and ranges of low brown mountains, we sat with eyes glued to the windows. It was the beginning of the Highlands, and, pencil in hand, we noted down the lochs, the rivers, the burns, the historical landmarks, the first heather, and the various head of game. These last constituted the elements of an exciting competition. Such inferior animals as rabbits, pigeon and moorhen, counted only one;

partridges, hares and pheasants counted two, and a whoop of triumph greeted the spotting of a covey of grouse, for, brought up to regard as heresy the Sassenach idea that a partridge or pheasant is in any way comparable to a grouse, we rated that noble bird at four marks.

The choice of seats was always a problem. The west side revealed not only the larger quantity of game but also the first view of Killiecrankie, of the rivers Tummel and Garry, and of Loch Ericht. But the east side had one supreme consolation, and for that reason I always chose it when the turn of the coin favoured me. From Struan began the long ascent to Dalnaspidal. With many puffs and snorts the engine crawled its way up Glen Garry through scenery that every moment grew wilder and grander, past the Athole Sow and the Boar of Badenoch, on which occasionally a red deer could be seen looking down on the train from a high rock, until at the Druimuachdar Pass it reached the top of the watershed.

And here the holder of the east side corner redoubled his vigilance. For a few hundred yards there was a kind of waterless no man's land. Then a small stretch of reedy marsh came into view and from it issued the tiny beginnings of a hill burn. It contained the merest trickle of water, a trickle which in a dry summer scarcely damped its peaty bed. But it showed what to us was the beginning of the Highlands, and it was greeted with a solemnity which betokened far deeper feelings than those of triumph. Just before Newtonmore we had our first view of the Spey. At Aviemore, where we always stopped while our carriage was attached to another train, the Cairngorms unfolded themselves in their full grandeur, and at Grantown ended a journey which has become an integral part of that dream-life which, like every man, I live in my quiet hours of reflection.

It is difficult for any man to say with accuracy what have been the great moments in his life. In my own, foreign travel and a background of hills always seem to have been associated with happiness, and there is one meeting under the shadow of the Alps which is among the few holy things that I shall carry with me into the grave. Every train journey, too, has for me the promise of adventure, and like Neil Munro I feel that half the joy in life is in starting and the other half in getting on the way. But the emotion engendered by the journey to Strathspey is the one emotion which no repetition can ever dull and which remains as strong in me as it was in the beginning. To-day, I still count the landmarks and the game by myself, for it is many years since Rufus and I have made that journey together. And, even if I leave London by the night sleeper, I never fail to wake at Struan and to wait in the early dawn for the first view of that tiny trickle just beyond the top of the pass.

A year or two ago I took part in a series of broadcasts organised by the B.B.C. under the title of "The Spice of Life". My theme was the escape from the cramping thraldom of big cities. With simple truth I said that for me home begins where the water flows north. That one phrase brought me more letters and made me more friends than any book that I shall ever write.

The part of Strathspey which was to be my summer home for so many years, and which I still revisit with increasing frequency, is an oval of which a cross line drawn from Lochindorb to Tomintoul marks the greatest width. Lengthwise, the Spey from Kingussie to Ballindalloch divides it almost equally. This oval protrudes into a corner where the three counties of Inverness, Moray and Banff abut, and it is as fair a land as any that graces Britain. Through the valley, warmed by the sun even when the hills are clouded, the river runs like a silver thread. After the rain the fields glisten in a shimmering kaleidoscope of different greens, and to the south-east stretches the long range of the Cairngorms, at some moments distant and enchanting, at others gloomy, threatening, and alarmingly near, yet always mysterious and majestic.

It is a land whose history has been written in blood; and

the ruined castles on the islands of its lochs, and on the rocky crags overlooking the river, tell the story of fire and sword more graphically than any war memorial. To the island stronghold of Lochindorb came Edward I, the Hammer of the Scots, to suppress the revolt raised by John Comyn, or Cumming, whose descendants to-day still wrest a difficult existence from the Strathspey soil. When the train stops at Kingussie, the English tourist may see, if he cares for such things, the ruins of Ruthven Barracks, built after the "Fifteen" by the English in order to keep the Highlands in submission. Here, after Culloden, the Highlanders assembled to make their last stand for Prince Charlie, and between those dates of 1304 and 1745 peace reigned but seldom in the valley of the Spey.

Interest in this period is largely absorbed by the grim record of the Celtic-Catholic effort, weakened by internal clan feuds, to resist Saxon-Presbyterian encroachment. The bitterness created by this struggle has not entirely disappeared and the possibility of its revival cannot be wholly excluded. It has made of Scottish history the patchwork of bias and prejudice that it has become in the writings of nearly all Scottish historians.

I have already described how my great-grandfather walked across the hills from Tomintoul to Balmenach to create what was virtually a new farm and to start the distillery which was to raise my mother's family from the lowly position of simple crofters to one of considerable affluence. Cromdale was the focal point of our annual summer incursion, and of all houses to which we were invited, or which we leased, Balmenach, the home of my Macgregor relations, remains clearest and dearest in my memory.

The old house, built in grey stone over a hundred years ago, faced south, and on the east an avenue of trees protected it from the cold winds which blew from the Cromdale Hills. Various additions to meet the needs of a large family had made it into a long, rambling affair ideal for hide-and-seek. Behind the house were the large farm buildings with a dairy and an enormous pig-sty where the best worms for fishing were to be found. Flanking the whole of the west side and almost touching the house was the huge distillery with its tall chimney, its long rows of warehouses, its vast, rather terrifying vats, and its roomy malt barns. Behind the distillery were the neat, trim houses of the government excise men who controlled the output of whisky and the payment of the duty. In front of the house was a plot of grass which sloped down to a garden enclosed by an old stone wall. On the carriage drive which flanked it was a huge stone which even as a grown man I could not lift. It was said to have been thrown over the wall by my grand-uncle Gregor, who like all the Macgregors of his generation was a giant.

The house stood in an open valley at the foot of the Cromdale Hills. Between house and hills were the fields which, in former days at any rate, provided the barley for the distillery, and stretching far up the mountain side until they were almost indistinguishable from the grey-white boulders were the countless sheep which formed the financial sinews of the Macgregor farm. The hill water, essential to good whisky, came from the Cromdale burn which, swelled by three other hill burns, flowed past the back of the house. In those days it teemed with trout, and to small boys a further incentive to fishing was the ever-present vision of my uncle's spliced salmon-rods, which, supported by two huge nails, lay ready for use on the verandah wall of the house.

The village of Cromdale was a mile away to the north, and its little station was connected with the distillery by a private railway. Far older than the tourist town of Grantown on the other side of the Spey, Cromdale, which means the "crooked plain", had been a free burgh in the time of James VI. Its former glories have long since vanished, and to-day it is a tiny hamlet with a school and a post office as its main buildings. Just over half a mile beyond the village is the old church where my Macgregor ancestors lie buried. Shaded by huge beeches it stands by the banks of the Spey, and by the church wall runs the Minister's Pool from which I took my first salmon.

To small boys Balmenach was a complete world in itself. And what more could a small boy want? Was there not a real engine to ride on, with Long John, the warm-hearted engine-driver, allowing me to hold the levers and to pretend that I was really driving, while Rufus and my cousin Ian sat on the buffers? Were there not stables with horses and two prize Shetland ponies, a farm with cattle, powerful rams, and fierce goats that had to be held by the horns to prevent butting, and, last but not least, a burn which in a "spate" would yield trout, not by the brace, but in dozens?

The distillery was a whole world in itself. It was exhilarating, if slightly terrifying, to be lifted up and held, while one looked down into the huge vats with the yeast burbling in a thick porridge below. With my mind full of possible disaster, I would gravely ask my uncle Jim what would happen if one fell in. "Come out as whisky," was the invariable reply. I think I took the answer quite seriously. Exciting, too, were the long grain-chutes down which one could slide and the little room in which were kept the whisky samples.

Inevitably, even as small boys, we learnt much about the making of whisky. It was a surprise to discover that it was colourless and had been so drunk by the Scots for centuries until the distillers set out to capture the English market. In those days the English, regarding whisky as a kind of inferior gin consumed by Scottish savages, spurned it. Then by various artificial processes the Scot added the sherry colouring. Blending was also introduced to please the English palate, and in this manner whisky conquered England. More tragic from the Scottish point of view were the economics of the trade. The first duty imposed was only three shillings and fourpence a gallon, and the excise officers took the distiller's word for the amount of his production. Gradually the need of finding fresh sources of revenue and the demands of the temperance reformers brought about successive increases of the duty, and to-day it stands at the high figure of seventy-two shillings a gallon.

Although my Macgregor relations of two generations back had breakfasted off whisky, I never touched it until I was twenty-one. As boys, however, we were allowed to taste the "worts". This is the liquid extract of malt before it is fermented into whisky. It was pleasantly sweet and very good for growing boys. Perhaps the greatest attraction of the distillery was the huge malt barn, which, when the mysteries of whisky-making palled, could be turned into the best arena imaginable for indoor cricket or, better still, for indoor tip-and-run. Here, on wet days, while we waited for the "spate", we had riotous games into which my aunt and uncle and as many of the staff as could be stolen from their work entered with full zest.

But the hillside was our real playground. Here history could be studied at first-hand almost on the doorstep. The Battle of Cromdale, where in 1690 the Highlanders made their last stand for the ill-fated James VII against the forces of William of Orange, was fought on a hill close to Balmenach, and I remember my awe and excitement when one Easter some men who had been cutting peat brought to my uncle two old claymores, rusty but still serviceable, which had been thrown away by the Jacobites in their flight.

I do not know what side, if any, the Macgregors took in this battle. The Grants, the dominant local clan, sided definitely with the forces of King William under Sir Thomas Livingstone. Their chieftain put Castle Grant at Sir Thomas's disposal and from its tower revealed to him the Highlanders' position. The Jacobites were beaten but were saved from annihilation by the friendly intervention of a morning mist, and I like to think that, as Children of the Mist, the Macgregors were then on what I still regard romantically as the right side.

The story of this battle made a profound impression on my youthful mind. Without the aid of a map, and assuredly with complete inaccuracy, I pictured in my mind the disposition of the forces, the course of the struggle, and even imaginary individual incidents. When we went to the mouth of the Dalchapple burn, the starting point for our favourite fishing stretch on the Spey, I saw its limpid waters in a "spate" of blood. And, coming down from the hillside in the gloaming, I sometimes frightened myself all too successfully by conjuring up the apparition of the bloodstained piper who, according to local legend, was supposed to haunt the battlefield.

At Congash, halfway between Cromdale and Grantown, was a farm which formerly belonged to Captain Grant, an uncle of my great-grandmother. Here were traces of a Druid circle and of the ruins of an ancient chapel with a graveyard whose curious stones I erroneously connected with human sacrifices.

More interesting than these incursions into the remote past was the history of the Macgregors, if only because I felt myself a part of it. At all times ancestor-hunting is an unprofitable pursuit, for it rightly arouses the derision of others and frequently reveals unpleasant truths which destroy the whole fabric of romance. Nevertheless, it flattered my pride to learn that the Macgregors were regarded as the most Celtic of all Scottish clans, that they were descended from a Scottish king, and that the clan motto "E'en do and spare not" was taken from the words of another Scottish king whose life was saved by a Macgregor. On that legendary occasion the king was in danger from the repeated charges of an infuriated boar, until his Macgregor attendant tore up a young tree by the roots and with this improvised weapon held the animal at bay.

In so far as the words "E'en do and spare not" have any application to my own Macgregor relations, their truth is expressed in the reckless family generosity which has never spared the money that most of its members have shown some ability in making.

There was, too, a pleasant intoxication from the knowledge that the clan had suffered unjust persecution, and had been deprived not only of its lands but of the use of its name. The final proscription of the Macgregors was the direct consequence of their success as fighters. In 1602 a band of Macgregors marched from their own lands near Loch Lomond against the Colquhouns in order to avenge the murder of two of their clansmen. The battle took place in Glen Fruin and, although the Colquhouns had the advantage of numbers, resulted in a crushing victory for the Macgregors. Their triumph was short-lived. James VI was then King of Scotland and at the time was in residence at Stirling. Sixty Colquhoun widows, each bearing the bloodstained shirt of her slain husband, appeared before him to demand vengeance, and the sight of these grim proofs of bloodshed was too much for a monarch who, even at a review, could not bear to look upon a naked sword.

The king acted swiftly and without inquiry. He issued an order for the extermination of the "viperous" Macgregors, who were henceforth forbidden to use their name and to carry weapons. From this date until 1795 the Macgregors were outlaws.

Of these outlaws the best-known is Rob Roy. Although my mother's people were descended from a sept of the Rob Roy family, Rob himself was not one of my boyhood heroes. I detested his politics, and his conduct at Sheriffmuir, where he sat on the fence and thus prevented a complete Jacobite success, filled me with disgust. He was, indeed, little better than a cattle thief, and his fame rests largely on the fact that he was the first racketeer and the father of modern insurance. The racket took the form of the combined operation of stealing cattle and offering protection to the landowners against cattle-lifting. The insurance genius consisted in his ability to extract premiums from the landed proprietors whose cattle were stolen by Rob's own followers. In spite of this rather unsavoury record, his Christian name Rob, as I have already indicated, has been liberally applied to members both of my own family and of the families of my Macgregor relations.

The Macgregors, I feel, had many faults. They had, however, the redeeming merit of picturesqueness, and for that reason they occupy a larger place in Scottish literature than any other Highland clan. It is true that the Lowlanders who have made that literature have not flattered the Macgregors. In his delineation of James More, one of Rob Roy's sons, Stevenson has drawn a portrait of the poorest human fish in literature, and neither in *The Legend of Montrose* nor in *Rob Roy* does Scott make any attempt to gloss over the savage cruelties of a clan which, forced to live as outlaws, wreaked a bitter vengeance on society. Stevenson, however, has given us in *Catriona* a model Macgregor heroine; and I do not forget his efforts to trace his own descent from the Macgregors and his disappointment when his researches proved fruitless. And Scott, who as a borderer had more of the clan spirit, is to be forgiven for the sake of that inspiring line: "Macgregor, despite them, shall flourish for ever."

At Balmenach I had ample opportunity to study the clan spirit in so far as it remains in the Highlands to-day. In a large family like the Macgregors it expressed itself in a readiness on the part of all its members to criticise each other without restraint and in an immediate closing of the ranks whenever any criticism was made from outside. Its greatest virtue, and perhaps its chief vice, was the inherited tradition that in times of financial trouble even the most worthless member of the family must be helped out of his difficulties. From this traditional generosity I myself subsequently benefited on more than one occasion.

This peculiar interpretation of family solidarity in no way diminished the family tendency to engage in feuds. I was too young to remember more than vaguely the days when my grandmother held undisputed rule over Balmenach, and my memories of the place are associated with the never-failing hospitality of her eldest son, my uncle Jim, who by his kindness to us boys, his skill in fishing and shooting, and his knowledge of Highland lore, gained an early and lasting hold on my affections. But, not very long before, a feud had only just ended which in its bitterness had divided the whole family for more than a decade. When my Macgregor grandfather was brought home from New Zealand in order to restore the fallen fortunes of the distillery, he found his mother surrounded by a large family of sons and daughters. It was easy to see that extravagance, idleness and mismanagement were the cause of the distillery's decline. True to the Macgregor tradition, however, my grandfather was about to put his money into the common pool when his father-in-law, a shrewd man of business, advised caution. If my grandfather was to invest his fortune in the business, the distillery must be his. The deal was carried through on these lines, and my grandfather's mother and her other children were transferred to Burnside, another Macgregor house about three-quarters of a mile farther up the burn.

My great-grandmother was a Cumming and prouder than any Grant, for she regarded the Grants as interlopers who had deprived the Cummings of their rightful lands. She had never approved her son's marriage to my grandmother. That she should now be moved from the home which her husband had built in order to make way for her daughter-in-law fanned a natural dislike into a bitter enmity. For years she never set foot in Balmenach, and the ban which she imposed on herself was extended to her children.

By the children, of course, the feud was not taken seriously. Indeed, it added to the adventure of life, and between the boy cousins of Burnside and the girl cousins of Balmenach there was more than one clandestine romance carried on by means of letters placed under stones half-way between the two houses and collected and delivered by conniving servants.

But between the principals the feud must have been bitter enough, for, as usually happens in family quarrels, it was conducted by the women, and both my great-grandmother and my grandmother were cast in granite mould. In her youth my great-grandmother had been a classic beauty. In her old age she smoked a pipe, and never rose before midday. Her sense of dignity is best illustrated by a story of the local doctor's visit. In those days there was only one doctor between Kingussie and Forres, and his services were rarely requisitioned. But when she was about sixty-two my great-grandmother fell ill, and the doctor was summoned. He examined her carefully and then shook his head.

"Your bones are too old to mend," he said bluntly.

The old lady was so angry that she rose from her bed and hounded the doctor out of the house. She lived for twenty years longer.

I never saw her, for she died a few months after I was born. But in a tiny cottage at Balmenach there lived an old, wrinkled woman whom we knew as "Grannie Simpson". She was very old and spent most of her time in a curtained box-bed, emerging only to hobble like a witch to the door to feed her hens. She had the gift of prophecy, and, although a little nervous, we boys liked the queer sensation of having our fortunes told. When we visited her cottage, she always took some time to fit us into the proper place in her memory. "Come here, my bonnie boy," she would croak, and very gingerly I would advance to the bed. For a moment she would peer at me with head bent forward.

"Ye'll be Miss Florence's boy? Master Bertie, is it no?"

I would shyly say Yes, and she would nod her head in gratification at her own omniscience.

"Aye, old Grannie never forgets," she would repeat several times.

Then came a series of low mutterings, and finally the words of prophecy.

"I see ye in far-off lands. There's black and white men at

yer feet. Aye, and there's much money passing through yer hands. But drat it, I canna see that ony o' it sticks." I have spent many a pound note on less accurate prophecies.

As a figure suspended between two worlds, Grannie Simpson roused in me that sense of the supernatural which is never far absent in the vicinity of mountains. She smoked an old, black clay pipe. I was frightened of her and never visited her alone. And to-day it is her picture that comes back to me when I think of my great-grandmother.

It needed no gift of second sight to predict that I should visit foreign lands. There were no members of my mother's family who did not have the travel-bug in their blood and most of them had spread themselves over the face of the earth. If heredity means anything I was likely to follow their example.

By the time Balmenach became a conscious factor in my life, the feud had ended. My grandmother had left the house, and her eldest son, Jim, himself summoned back like his father from New Zealand, reigned in her stead. Of her other eight children only my youngest uncle and my youngest aunt were not of age. My other aunts had married. My uncle Alister, later a pioneer of the plantation rubber industry, was planting coffee in Malaya. Rob had died in the Argentine, and Tom, the hardest-working and the most successful in later life, was learning banking in Edinburgh. Of my mother's numerous cousins some were in New Zealand, others in the Argentine, and one owned a couple of South Sea islands.

About this time the full control of the distillery passed out of the family's hands. In 1896 the sales of whisky amounted to 200,000 gallons, and in 1897 the distillery was floated as a limited company with a capital of £120,000 divided into 6,000 Ordinary shares at £10 each and 6,000 Preference shares at the same price. The family, it is true, kept the vast majority of the Ordinary shares, and my uncle Jim was appointed resident and managing director. It was, therefore, still very much a Macgregor concern.

But the formation of the company and the departure of my grandmother marked the end of an epoch. Balmenach had nourished, supported, and sent out into the world three generations. They had passed on; and the new generation, which was growing up, would never take their place. As the eldest grandson of my Macgregor grandparents I had just touched the fringe of that epoch. It was a period of opportunities boldly taken and sometimes recklessly thrown away. These characteristics were to be in some measure the keynote of my own life.

CHAPTER TWO

THERE WAS ONE principle which governed my parents' choice
of a home for the summer. My mother insisted on being near
her own mother. It was a consideration with which my brothers and I were well pleased. My grandmother was un-
swerving in her fidelity to Strathspey. She possessed the
Kaiser's facility for attaching God to her own environment,
and a shell-pink sunset or a gathering storm rarely failed to
evoke from her lips a sonorous and majestic rendering,
given in the approved but ungrammatical metrical version,
of the first two lines of the hundred-and-twenty-first Psalm:

> "I to the hills will lift mine eyes,
> From whence doth come mine aid."

For her the hills of Israel were the hills of Cromdale, and
rightly, for those brown sentinels of the soul have a grandeur that is not to be found in Palestine. She possessed her full
share of the clan spirit and liked to have her children and her
grandchildren round her. My brother Rufus and I were
brought up on very simple fare. Even at school at Seafield,
where the other boys drank tea and had meat for breakfast as
well as in the middle of the day, we were confined to milk
and were allowed meat only once a day. During the holidays
meat was often replaced by potatoes and milk, and not until
I was sixteen was I allowed to come down to dinner in the
evening. But at my grandmother's house there was more
licence. In her presence even my mother, fearless and sometimes rebellious, was chary of asserting herself. And when
the old lady, stroking the rings on her well-shaped hands,
would say innocently: "Florrie, why shouldn't the boys have
trifle?" the boys had trifle. We, too, liked to be near our
grandmother.

Her own choice of a Strathspey residence for the summer
was dictated by considerations more material than those of

my mother. It was governed largely by the state of the whisky market. When sales were good, she took a large house with a small shoot. When times were bad, she contented herself with a smaller house and no shoot.

In the first summer holiday in Strathspey which I remember clearly, times cannot have been too good, for she had leased only a large farmhouse which was close both to Grantown and to Balmenach. As my parents could then ill afford a house of their own, we all stayed with my grandmother.

That holiday is imprinted on my mind and on my facial appearance by two disasters and one crowning and permanent happiness. With hereditary instinct we made the farm our playground, rode the cart-horses, helped to round up the cattle, and of course became firm friends with the farmhands, one of whom claimed, and doubtless rightly, relationship with the Macgregors. For some time all went well, and I should probably have retained for the rest of my life that unconscious fearlessness which is given only to children who have early contact with animals. But there was a bull, a sturdy, well-shaped poll-Angus who had taken several prizes at the Grantown cattle show. Perhaps in those innocent days I was scarcely conscious of the difference between cows and bulls. Perhaps the bull himself disliked the green of my Seafield blazer. At any rate, one evening as I was romping gaily round the field and shooing the cows homewards, Mr. poll-Angus seemed to resent this interference with his harem. He began to paw the ground viciously and to lower his head in a most menacing fashion. I advanced boldly. Then I saw a red blaze in his eyes which destroyed my fearlessness for ever. I bolted for the fence. The bull followed, and by a big rent in his shorts and a flesh wound in his posterior from the barbed wire, Lockhart won his best race.

Perhaps I provide an unnatural attraction to bulls. When I was a child in arms, my mother saved herself and me on a somewhat similar occasion by throwing me over a hedge. Be this as it may, I have ever since retained a profound respect for bulls, and even for cows, and prefer on all occasions in their presence to take the long way round.

The second tragedy made a more enduring mark on my exterior but left my inmost feelings unaffected. In front of the house was a small park which my father, with his usual enthusiasm, converted into a cricket field. A cricket match for grown-ups was arranged, and, although I was just nine, I was pressed into service to complete one side. While I was fielding in the long field, where I was supposed to be out of danger, Forbes, my grandmother's burly coachman, hit a full-blooded swipe which went so high that it never seemed to come down. It went straight to me, and with an unholy desire to show off I stationed myself under the falling ball. Perhaps I grew tired of waiting, for my hands failed to connect with the ball which landed with a thud on the bridge of my nose. It was the first break of an organ which, broken subsequently both at football and boxing, has defied the efforts of London's most expensive surgeons, not only to put it straight, but even to make it function properly.

But the supreme bliss of that holiday—a bliss which in retrospect still stirs me to lyrical rapture—was the serving of my apprenticeship as a real fisher. Most anglers write at least one book on fishing, even if it is only an unliterary record of their own captures. If I have not yet followed their example, it is not from lack of temptation. During my life I have played most games and practised most outdoor sports with a zest keener than that of the average man. But fishing is the only pursuit to which I have remained unyieldingly constant, and the solitude and the intimate contact with nature which it affords have given me a peace of mind and a happiness of soul for which I am eternally grateful.

Since the beginning of historical time certain fish have been regarded as noble and even sacred. The wise men of Syria worshipped a fish goddess, and in a temple in the heart of Java I have found holy carp whose capture would have been followed by instant death for the sacrilegious poacher. At least one country, the Ukraine, has a fish for the chief emblem on its national flag. Before Culloden, Bonnie Prince Charlie fished in the Beauly and during his weeks of hiding lived, like Thor, on salmon. And to-day there is scholarly support for the theory that Jason's quest of the Golden Fleece was a fishing expedition for tunny.

Something of this reverence for fish and fishing has come down to us moderns, and in August, 1923, when Mr. Baldwin wrote to Mr. Neville Chamberlain offering him the Chancellorship of the Exchequer, Mr. Chamberlain, who was then fishing the Aberdeenshire Dee, wrote back rejecting this honour. But in his letter of refusal this outwardly unemotional Englishman allowed himself one lyrical outburst. "What a day!" he wrote. "Two salmon in the morning, and the offer of the Exchequer in the afternoon!" He put the salmon first, and so would any true angler.

German Nazis, who profess to despise our statesmen for taking their hobbies more seriously than their politics, will deride Mr. Chamberlain for the order of his preferences. There are not only Nazis but also Englishmen who worship poorer gods, and Mr. Chamberlain is in good company. Everyone knows the selfish angler, the man who is out to kill the most fish and the largest fish and who is offensive when he succeeds and insufferable when he fails. He is at his worst in hotels, where he rises early in the morning in order to fish another guest's beat on his way down to his own. Fortunately, such egregious egotists are rare among anglers, who constitute as clean-living and as clean-thinking a fellowship as exists in any sport.

Quite apart from angling parsons like Charles Kingsley, some of the best Christians in the world have been anglers; and mention of Mr. Chamberlain will make most people think of Lord Grey, not only the finest statesman-angler that Britain has produced, but a man who knew how to extract from angling the hundred-and-one other pleasures which it affords apart from the mere taking of trout and salmon. The Foreign Office, over which Lord Grey presided, has inherited some of his skill and zeal, and two of my former chiefs in Sir George Clerk and Sir Francis Lindley are keen anglers who, like myself, have fished in many countries and under many different flags. And to a rare skill Sir Francis Lindley adds the merit of being able to write about his art with the same charm and much of the same philosophic outlook as Lord Grey. More than most people great bankers seem to find in fishing a pleasant relief from the trammels of figures, and I am sure that the right place and moment to approach Mr. Anthony Rothschild for an extension of one's unsecured overdraft would be the banks of the Ness just after he had landed a twenty-pounder. And if there be a Communist who on reading these lines is tempted to sneer at fishing as the sport of bloody capitalists, I would bid him remember Lenin. For, in addition to being an ardent cyclist and the father of modern "hiking", that great man was a passionate lover of outdoor life and a sportsman who, if he preferred shooting, did not disdain the angle.

In the years of his triumph he was too busy with such mundane affairs as world-revolution to be able to tear himself away from Moscow. I saw him many times in moments which were as exciting and as dangerous to me in my humble capacity as they were to him. I see him now, his legs wide apart, his hands holding the lapels of his jacket, facing the angry mob in the Moscow Big Theatre with a smile of amused indifference and quelling it, not so much by the persuasiveness of his oratory as by the sheer force of the personality of a man who, confident in himself, was supremely conscious of his own superiority. But the portrait of him that lives in my imagination is one which I never saw in the living flesh. It is of a young man keeping himself bodily fit and mentally sane in exile by touching his toes fifty times every morning and tramping the tundra with a gun in search of snipe and duck or watching his line by the banks of some

Siberian lake. Very bitterly do I regret that I never mentioned fishing to him during those critical months in 1918 when I discussed with him allied intervention and the other delicate problems of an enigmatic situation in which I never knew whether Britain and Russia were allies or enemies. Had I done so, history might have been altered. Fishing, I feel, would have been the only personal approach to that most impersonal of men.

Let no hunting fanatic curl his upper lip in contempt of a sport which he crudely imagines is suited to the exercise of contemplation rather than of the muscles. There is a tributary of the Spey called the Avon, and please pronounce it "A'an". It flows by my ancestral Tomintoul and is the fastest river in Scotland. It is as clear as crystal, but its bed is a cavern of huge granite boulders and its banks are lined by tree-clad precipices. And in a "spate" its waters come down with a speed and force which bring destruction in their torrential course. You may be wading in two feet of water under a blue sky, when suddenly, if it has been raining in the Cairngorms, you will hear a roar behind you. And if you are wise you will rush to the bank as fast as the slippery boulders will allow you. Otherwise you will be swept from your feet never to rise again. If it is your good fortune to hook a salmon on light tackle, he will take you down half a mile of this Niagara, while, with a speed which you scarcely realise that you are capable of, you try to follow him, clambering over rocks and risking life and limb as you plunge rod and reel into the water and strive to crawl under a tree whose branches lie close down to the surface of the stream. And whether you succeed in landing him or, as more often happens, he breaks you because even your fish-fed courage boggles at a precipice which would defy a goat, you will throw yourself on the bank and pant for breath. Every bone in your body will be aching. You may be badly bruised. You may have even broken a finger-joint or a knee-cap. But you will have known an exhilaration that you have never experienced before, and, if you are over thirty, you will certainly wish that you were ten years younger. The Avon is no river for old, or even any but the fittest middle-aged men, nor, except for the rich who fish the more expensive beats from a boat, is its mother river, the Spey. In my own lifetime three of my acquaintances have been drowned salmon-fishing in the Spey in the one short stretch between Inverallan and Pollawick, and there have been others. The Avon, too, has taken its toll of victims, and its seeming innocence is well expressed in the local rhyme:

> "The River A'an, it flows so clear,
> T'would beguile a man o' a hundred year."

Such skill as I possess as an angler I owe to my uncle Jim, who taught my brother Rufus and me, both by precept and by example, to throw a fly and who introduced us to the best pools of the Spey. He would have made a great surgeon, for he had wonderful hands and also very definite opinions about the right and the wrong ways of doing things. Not only did he teach us how to tie knots and how to look after our tackle, but, with a patience rare in grown men in their attitude towards boys, he devoted his time to imparting to us something of his own skill and knowledge. During our boyhood my aunt and he were unfailingly kind to Rufus and me, always inviting us to Balmenach for the Easter holidays and putting themselves to much trouble not only to cater for our amusements but also to enter into them wholeheartedly and unselfishly. If it is any gratification to them in their old age, I can assure them that kindness to boys is a heritage which they treasure far more than the hospitality and assistance they receive in later life.

But our first fishing mentor was my youngest uncle, Ian. In that summer of 1896 he had just left school, and, himself a keen angler, he took us with him on his fishing expeditions. There were no motor cars in those days, and Rufus and I had not yet risen to the dignity and luxury of a bicycle. Nor were there any burns near my grandmother's house. Ian, however, solved our transport difficulties by adapting his own bicycle to the use of three passengers. A waterproof cape tightly rolled round the handlebars made a comfortable if precarious seat for Rufus. The step on the back wheel provided a safe but exhausting stand for myself. Mounted in this fashion, which to-day is forbidden by law, we would set off early in the morning on the five-mile stretch to Balmenach. Then, leaving the bicycle there, we would begin our long tramp up the Cromdale burn.

There are four stages in a fisherman's life. The first is characterised by the desire to catch a fish by any means which the ingenuity of man can devise. The second is the slaughterous stage of numbers, when a man is satisfied only by counting his captures in dozens. In the third stage this numerical boastfulness is replaced by the vainglory of size. In the fourth and best stage a man is content not to fish too much, to allow his concentration to be divided pleasantly by those open-air pleasures of the mind and eye to which angling is the best gateway, and, when he does fish, to come as near to nature as he can and to pit his skill against trout or salmon with the delicate weapons of the true artist.

My uncle Ian was then far advanced into the second stage. My brother and I were just entering it, but our means of satisfying our lust for numbers were severely limited. For in our straggling procession up the hill the stern rule of "seniores priores" prevailed. Ian, who had fished the burn from his childhood, went first, I came next and Rufus brought up the rear. Such fish as escaped Ian's deftly dropped worm suffered a second temptation from mine, and my brother's pickings were meagre and truly hard to obtain. At the end of the day, when we laid out our catch of seven or eight dozen on the grass, Ian had generally accounted for eighty per cent. of it, leaving a mere twenty per cent. to be divided in much the same proportion between Rufus and myself.

Nevertheless, there were compensations even for the under-dog. In those days the dam which supplied Balmenach with water was carried to the house in a swift-running lead covered by rough flag-stones in which the ravages of rain and snow had made open gaps. Rufus, even then possessed of an investigating mind, soon discovered, by inserting his worm between the gaps, not only that huge trout lurked below but that they took readily. He revealed, or was made to reveal, this secret to me, and from the day of that discovery we always waited behind, not merely with the deliberate intention of giving Ian a good start but also with the realisable ambition of being able to confront him afterwards with a trout or two far larger than any that he had captured in the burn itself. And this was our first approach to the third stage in an angler's life.

Then there was the walk itself. In those days we trudged what now seem to me incredible distances for small boys, tramping far up the lonely hillside until even the tall chimney of the distillery looked no higher than a wax taper. We were soon above the tree-line, for the hills of Cromdale, over 2,000 feet high, are something more than mere hills, and the English would rightly glorify them as mountains. The burn grew ever smaller and smaller until at times its course would almost disappear under the encroaching cover of heather and wiry grass. Then, every few yards or so, would come a small waterfall which splashed noisily into a wide basin. And in this basin were lusty and ever more unsuspecting trout. There was the combined sweet smell of heather, peat and moss to sustain us, and the purest air in the world gave a second wind to our lungs and a tireless energy to young legs.

Our way led us into the heart of Highland bird life. Coveys of grouse, resenting this intrusion into their privacy, would start almost at our feet and with a noisy "Go-back—go-back", skim gracefully over the heather. In every little bog we flushed a snipe which, with many twists and turns, darted backwards down the burn. Overhead, curlews pursued their cumbersome flight, raising their mournful note to the heavens in protest against this unwarranted disturbance. Every now and then a heron, standing like a stone sentinel at some pool, would dispute our fishing rights, and more than once a hare, crouching with ears back in the hope of escaping detection, would be seized by the back of the neck and added to the bag.

Generally it rained all day, for our expeditions were timed to the weather and the possibilities of a "spate". We would be soaked to the skin. Red patches of cold would show themselves through the slippery grime of our worm-stained hands. But we did not care. At the end of the day we were sure of a glorious tea and a warm fire at Balmenach. And if on the way home Ian had to stop his bicycle several times in order to enable me to get down from my perch on the step and relieve the pins and needles in my right foot, there was always the compensation of that breathless moment when the three boys on one bicycle rode down the dangerous Cambrae hill. At the bottom it turned sharply to the left, and, if the turn was not successfully negotiated, only a low stone parapet separated us from the Spey, where the whirling waters of the famous Garro Pool surge their way past a miniature precipice of tree-clad rock. We reached home tired but triumphant. I knew no Browning then, but assuredly on days like these all was well in our Strathspey world.

Since that summer of 1896 I have fished all over the world in settings as romantic and as adventurous as any man could desire. In Central Europe and the Balkans I have cast my fly in waters flowing past ruined medieval castles. During the fiercest moments of the Russian revolution I have caught pike in the Moscow river, with illiterate Red Guards, armed to the teeth with loaded rifle, revolver and hand grenade, struggling to read my pass signed by Trotsky. At Wilton, most beautiful of all old English homes, I have stalked the chalk-stream trout from the lawn on which Shakespeare once staged his own plays. In my own country I have enjoyed equally both poor man's and rich man's fishing. Thanks to a rich uncle I have taken salmon from the most expensive beats of our Scottish rivers, including the famous Grimersta in the Hebrides, where a man can be alone the live-long day and where the dying sun has a glory which no tropical sunset can equal. They have been days and nights of delight, but I doubt if they have ever given me the same carefree rapture as when, as a boy, I followed the Cromdale burn almost to its source.

To-day, like the other hill streams of the Highlands, the Strathspey burns have lost their fecundity. Motor cars have made them too accessible to the ever-growing army of anglers, and the cutting of hill drains, the pollution from modern roads and factories, and the indifference of land owners and other authorities to the preservation of trout, are rapidly destroying a great natural asset.

It is true that there are still burns which yield as large baskets of trout as ever they did, but they lie far beyond the range of car or bicycle, and are to be reached only by hardy young men prepared to face the wind and the rain, to walk sixteen miles, and, if need be, to sleep on the hillside.

I know one such burn halfway between Tomintoul and the Cairngorms. But to me it is only a dream which without seven-league boots will never be realised. Yet it is to it and not to the great salmon rivers like the Dee, the Tweed and the Spey that my fancy flies when the fogs of London and the futility of my city round turn my thoughts towards a cleaner, better life. There is no angler in the world who has ever lived as good a day on river or loch as the one he dreams by his winter fireside.

CHAPTER THREE

AFTER THAT SUMMER of 1896 near Grantown, my grandmother took the low-ground shooting of Rothiemurchus,
and for three out of the next four years our summer headquarters were Inverdruie, a little clachan or hamlet about a
mile and a quarter from Aviemore. The Doune, the ancestral home of the Grants of Rothiemurchus, which would
otherwise have gone with the shooting, was let to Lord
Manvers, and my grandmother lived at Inverdruie House,
which, although too small for all her guests, commanded a
superb view of the Cairngorms.

In this summer of 1897 we had a house, or rather, cottage,
of our own, which was only ten minutes walk from Inverdruie. It is the custom of the farmers of Strathspey to build
a stone house which they let during the summer months to
holiday visitors, and the rent they receive is frequently their
most reliable source of income. During my mother's lifetime we must have leased a score of these houses. They were
uniform in design and in internal decoration. There was a
drab dining-room with a heavy mahogany table and horse-
hair chairs. If the house was in the Grantown district, there
was certain to be a large print of the old Countess of Seafield
and one, slightly smaller, of her bearded factor. At Aviemore
the Laird of Rothiemurchus, who was poor and modest, did
not distribute his likeness with the same largesse, and here,
with a wider loyalty, the farmer-tenant substituted the
portrait of Queen Victoria for that of Caroline, Countess
of Seafield. The change made little difference, for the two
old ladies were remarkably alike in appearance. The drawing-
room was a rickety affair in which the only solid pieces were
the two stiff armchairs draped with antimacassars. Fragile gilt
chairs, cheap vases with artificial flowers, and streaky water-
colours, left as a legacy by ungifted amateurs, completed the
room which was no place for sturdy boys whose hair was

anointed neither by oil nor even by water and was, indeed, rarely touched by a brush. Antimacassar was a mouthful which was never explained to us, and little did I think then that Macassar itself would one day provide the setting for one of my happiest pilgrimages. A winding wooden staircase led to the bedrooms on the first floor. Above were the attics, with ceilings so low that even a boy of ten could bump his head unless he stooped. And here Rufus and I slept.

Aviemore was then the smallest of unspoilt paradises, and our cottage the tiniest that we ever occupied. I do not think that it was even dignified by a name. We called it "Blair's", after Blair, its genial red-faced owner who preferred telling tall stories to credulous boys to working the sawmill which gave him his daily bread. To Rufus and me the cottage was a fairy castle. Close by flowed the Druie, a clear, swift-running stream which figured on the map as a river, and in the spring was one, and within a boy's stone-throw of the back door was a shallow muddy dam, where, in the dusk of evening, eels would show themselves and, after much circumspection, slowly swallow the worm which we dangled before their jaws. They were nasty, slimy things whose capture was extravagant, because it involved the loss of the hook which they always seemed to take right down into their belly.

Still, they were not entirely unprofitable, for they could be used in order to frighten our Scottish servants, who regarded eels as the descendants of the serpent in the Garden of Eden and would willingly have starved rather than eat one. Very silently we would steal into the kitchen and drop our eel down the back of Murray, the cook. The effect was electrical, for she would run round the kitchen screaming for someone to pull it out. This cruel trick had a different ending when I tried it on Mackenzie, our tablemaid. Her reaction was swift, and I bolted out of the door. The boy who had already played in cricket and football matches for his private school was no match for the sturdy Highland girl. She caught me within twenty yards, and with a hand as hard as my father's tawse cuffed my ears until I howled for mercy.

But most of our time was spent by the banks of the Druie. That summer we started fly-fishing, and in a shallow rapid, which straightened out my clumsy cast, I caught my first fish on the fly. I strongly suspect that this fish was a salmon parr, for the river was full of them, but it was taken home, solemnly eaten, and entered in the book of deeds as a trout.

Fly-fishing was merely an added discovery in the technique of angling. It did not mean that I had become a purist or had abandoned worm or, indeed, less legal methods of capture. Between the dam and the river was a deep backwater in which night-lines could be set, and in this way Rufus and I captured our biggest fish, including a young pike.

Farther up the river was a large pool, deep but swiftly flowing at the top and gradually widening into a flat, calm shallow with a gravel bottom. Here I bathed every day with my father and my uncles. Although Rufus and I had been given many swimming lessons at the Dundee Baths, we had never learnt to swim, being, indeed, little water-funks. My uncles soon remedied this defect. They took us to the top of the pool and in spite of our struggles hurled us into the deep end. The current was swift enough to carry us to safety without any more serious result than the swallowing of an unpleasant amount of water, and in this manner we soon learnt to swim. Whatever Dr. Freud may think of this method, it was efficacious and, as far as I know, imposed no inhibitions on my character.

A year or two later, we used to have our morning dip in the deep hole of the Spey under the Aviemore Bridge. It was rather an eerie performance, for the water was dark and sinister-looking, and I was not altogether unhappy when these morning plunges were unexpectedly stopped by outside intervention. Being little more than children, Rufus and I bathed without drawers. On a hill on the other side of the river was a house inhabited by two maiden ladies. In view of the distance and of our tender age, they would have needed a telescope to see anything to shock their Presbyterian prudery. But apparently they did see, for they made a complaint to the local policeman. As nudism had no place in the Scotland of those days, we returned to the safer seclusion of the Druie.

It was a pleasant and little-frequented river. At Coylum Bridge it divided into two burns, both of which had their sources in the very heart of the Cairngorms. Being in the deer forest, they were rarely fished, and here my brother and I filled our baskets with small trout, captured, I fear, on the worm, for the banks were too wooded for such inexpert fly-fishers as we then were. Here I would tramp for what seemed miles, wandering far ahead of Rufus, and not returning until the sun sank behind the tree-tops and the shadows filled me with fear. In a silence that seemed supernatural, even the crack of a twig made an alarming noise, and, with my mind full of kelpies and eldritch phantoms, I would run back to Rufus, hurrying to escape the sound of my own feet.

Not even the Malayan jungle ever inspired me with the same fear of the unknown. We never saw a living soul the whole day, and, indeed, the only inhabitant of that lonely forest was an old woman who lived in a cottage by herself. She never came out, and in the eyes of my brother and myself acquired the qualities of a witch. She died while we were at Aviemore, but her death was not discovered until several days after it had taken place. She was found by the postman, who had called to deliver a rare letter from some grandson in far-off parts, and I remember even now my horror at hearing the postman tell our servants how the old woman's face and arms had been eaten by rats. At that time, rats loomed large in the beastly things of my world, for Blair's and, indeed, all the houses by the Druie were infested by a peculiarly ferocious and bold type of rat which invaded the kitchen, the dining-room, and even the nursery, where one took a bite out of the cheek of my young brother Norman who was then a baby. And here I must subscribe to the theory of the permanence of childhood influences, for ever since I have hated rats with a fierce loathing and would rather sleep with a cobra than hear a rat in the wainscoting.

Picnics, which were my grandmother's favourite recreation, shared an equal place with fishing in my affections. In my opinion, Aviemore lacks the rugged grandeur of the Cromdale district, but, although to-day it sticks in my mind as a resort for elderly spinsters, I shall never deny that its proximity to the Cairngorms and the splendour of its birch woods and pine forests give to it a soft and special beauty which is not to be matched in any other part of the Highlands. It was here that I first came under the spell of the scenic influences of mountain, river and loch. Susceptible to the changes of colour, I was always ready to climb, preferably by myself, the nearest hill to see the sun go down and to watch the shell-pink sky change slowly into an afterglow of mother-of-pearl. And certainly no boy among my acquaintances was more interested in local history or more avid in his desire to reach into the romantic past.

My range of discovery was restricted by the limitations of my grandmother's wagonette, but, seated on the box beside the coachman, I travelled a world which seemed wide enough, and in this manner I visited Loch Pityoulish, Loch Moirlich, Loch Garten, Loch Balladern at the foot of Craigellachie, the rallying place of the Clan Grant, Loch Vaa, and Loch Alvie, where my grandmother always had tea with the local minister while Rufus and I explored the banks of the loch and looked in vain for the snout of a basking pike.

Readers of Colonel Thornton's *A Sporting Tour* will recognise Loch Alvie as the Loch "Alva" where, in 1786, that intrepid Yorkshireman had his famous encounter with the giant pike. After a struggle of an hour and a quarter, the pike was finally landed and its capture greeted with a "whoop which re-echoed through the *whole* range of the Grampians". This pike measured five feet four inches from eye to fork—a size which, if the measurements were correct, would give it a weight of nearly fifty pounds. A colonel's truthfulness is not to be doubted, but Colonel Thornton's accuracy may be gauged by his lyrical description of the Cairngorms, in which he asks his readers to imagine him standing on a crag with a mountain of "at least 18,000 feet above him and a steep precipice of 13,000 feet below!"

There are still pike in Loch Alvie, and with the good minister's permission I have fished for them more than once. I hooked only one—a fish which, if not reaching the dimensions of Colonel Thornton's monster, looked large enough, when he showed on the surface, to be compared afterwards with the trunk of a tree. Of course, he got away, and the reader, mindful of the Loch Ness monster, will rightly conclude that the imagination of Gaelic anglers is sometimes quite as vivid as that of a Thames fisherman.

A favourite place for picnics was Loch an Eilean, a small Highland loch which has the added picture-postcard attraction of an island with a castle on it. It was within the confines of my grandmother's shoot, and was reached by a private road which steered a rough and unmetalled course through woods of birch and pine. Rickety plank bridges afforded an uncertain passage over two burns, and then, as one turned the corner of the Ord Ban, a knobbly hill inhabited by black game and capercailzie, one came suddenly upon the silver stretch of water lying like a mirror with the wide range of the Cairngorms, now marvellously near, as its frame.

My grandmother had a boat on the loch. Although Loch an Eilean is also mentioned in Colonel Thornton's classic as a haunt of large pike, we used the boat, not for fishing, but for rowing out to the castle and inspecting the ruins. The castle had been one of the strongholds of the notorious Wolf of Badenoch, a son of King Robert II of Scotland, who, at the end of the fourteenth century made himself the terror of Strathspey and Morayshire. He must have spent his time building castles, for there are many castles in these parts, and all, or nearly all, are reported to have been haunts of the Wolf. To-day, the moss of legend has so covered his exploits that the truth is no longer to be dug out. That he was a man of Titan stature and sadistic temper is generally admitted, and his ill-treatment of his rich wife, the Countess of Ross, is as much a matter of history as is his wanton destruction of Elgin Cathedral, the one architectural jewel of the Highlands. His motives may have been no worse than those of many medieval barons, but there can have been few who excelled him in cruelty, reckless pride and unnatural savagery. In all probability he belonged to the type of brigand whose hand is turned against all men. In his case the fist was used most unsparingly against the Catholic bishops whose treasures he coveted.

Like many other men who have misused their youth, the Wolf repented in old age and lavished on the Church the wealth that he had amassed by plunder.

Even legend has little to say about the Wolf's tenancy of the island castle on Loch an Eilean. Yet the stronghold has a small place of its own in legitimate history, for here, at the time of the Battle of Cromdale, Grizzel Mor, the wife of the Laird of Rothiemurchus, who, like all the Grants, supported William of Orange, successfully defended the stronghold against an attack by the Highlander adherents of James VII.

The loch, moreover, had a special claim on my interest, for one side of it was skirted by an old track made by Rob Roy in order to facilitate his cattle driving. This track must have been trodden often by the sept of Macgregors whom he settled there and who were the forbears of my mother's family. Rob himself, whose loyalties were governed by his pocket, came at least once to Rothiemurchus.

On that occasion he came to help a Grant laird who was having trouble with some Mackintoshes. To the surprise of the laird, Rob arrived alone and was at once taken to task for not bringing the promised aid. Rob whistled for his piper, and commanded him to play "Macgregor's Gathering" before the laird's house. Soon, in twos and threes, fully armed Macgregors sprang out of the forest. In the face of this force, the Mackintoshes withdrew. This episode is celebrated in a reel tune called "The Burning of the Black Mill".

A more immediate attraction to young boys than these historical associations was the pair of ospreys which, in the "nineties", came regularly to the castle and built their nest of stout twigs and sticks on the highest corner of the wall. Although we should dearly have liked to inspect the nest, we were forbidden on pain of a thrashing to do so. The prohibition was wise, for, some years later, one of the shooting tenants put our secret desire into practice and inspected the nest with the unfortunate result that the ospreys abandoned it and never returned. They were graceful birds, and we often saw them bringing back fish to their young, as we rowed our boat in front of the castle to hear the echo which, when one speaks even quite softly in front of the castle door, returns one's voice with a clarity that is almost sinister.

A silent testimony to the dangers of the loch, which is very deep in parts and full of springs, is the granite tombstone erected in memory of Major-General Walter Brook Rice who was drowned while skating there some fifty years ago.

To-day, thanks to the increasing number of tourists, Loch an Eilean has acquired a national reputation as the Loch Katrine of the north. In solemn truth it is far more beautiful than that much over-praised stretch of water. But it was even more enchanting forty years ago. During my grandmother's tenancy of the shooting, a disastrous hill fire broke out on the far side of the loch. It lasted for several days, and, blackened by the smoke and with eyebrows singed, Rufus and I helped in the exhausting work of trying to stem the onset of the fire. Its ravages have long since disappeared, but they have robbed the loch of some of its sylvan symmetry.

My grandmother had also a boat on Loch Gamhna, a mountain tarn full of small dark trout and famous for its profusion of waterlilies. Here Rufus and I had one of those minor adventures which happen only to small boys and which, because they are unforeseen, remain long in the memory. We had just beached our boat at Loch Gamhna when a carriage drove up with an old man and his wife inside it. The carriage stopped, and the old lady pointed with her parasol. Self-consciously, for we were dressed like tramps, we thought that she was calling her husband's attention to our rags. There was a minute's conversation, and then the coachman came over and asked us if we could gather some waterlilies. Back into the boat we went and collected two armfuls of lilies, which we carried to the carriage.

"What lovely lilies—and what beautiful red hair you have," said the old lady, turning to Rufus. With trembling hands the old gentleman fumbled in his purse and took out five shillings. For a moment Rufus hesitated, while Highland pride wrestled with his conscience. But I gave him a quiet dig in the back, and he took the money. It went into our common pool. The old gentleman and his wife were Lord and Lady Manvers.

As a boy, I liked old men. It is true that in my reckoning of age every one who was over thirty-five counted as old, but I preferred the "over thirty-fives" to the young men. They were less impatient, and more willing to answer the questions of small boys, and they could tell wonderful stories of strange lands without giving one the feeling that one's leg was being pulled.

At Inverdruie there were several "over thirty-fives" who, because they expanded to a small boy, live in my memory as friends. First, there was old Louis, the gardener, who dug worms for us, showed us how to set night-lines, and gave us the choicest strawberries from the garden. He was a staunch ally in time of trouble, and when my grandmother, who knew small boys, inquired why there were no strawberries in the garden, Louis would perjure his Presbyterian soul and discourse learnedly on the evil propensities of blackbirds which, in spite of all his precautions, picked holes in his nets. Because of his name we assumed, probably quite erroneously, that he was of French extraction and listed him in our minds as a descendant of a French nobleman who had come over to help Prince Charlie.

Then there was John Peter Grant, the laird. He was a grave, bearded man who bore his poverty with all the dignity of a long pedigree. His estates had been encumbered by the extravagances of his ancestors, and his own life had been clouded by an early sorrow, for his first wife had left him. He lived very frugally, rarely laughed, but had a pleasant smile and had always a kind word for Rufus and me when we met him. Long after we left Aviemore, we had only to ask him, to be given a day's fishing on his loch or in the Spey. He liked talking politics with my father, and it was during a conversation between them that I heard my father profane the Deity for the first and almost only time. It was in September 1899, a few days after my twelfth birthday. We had just come out of the little church at Rothiemurchus, and my father had stayed behind to talk to the laird.

"I've just heard privately from London", said the laird, "that Dreyfus has been condemned again."

"Good God!" said my father, strangely agitated, "the incarnate devils."

I was much impressed. Even then I wondered why my father, who would walk through the drunkenness of Dock Street in Dundee without appearing to give it a thought, could work himself up into a fever of excitement about the fate of a foreigner.

Later, when I myself became engaged in foreign affairs, I was to realise that this peculiarity was not confined to my father but was, indeed, a form of national mania which has embarrassed the foreign policy of successive British Governments and will probably continue to do so until the character of the British people changes.

In the little church at Rothiemurchus, where the lairds are buried and where the collection bag is, or used then to be, handed round on a long pole rather like a fishing net, I met Dr. James Martineau, the famous Unitarian divine, and a regular summer visitor to the district, and also Dr. Macgregor, the famous Edinburgh minister of St. Cuthbert's.

Dr. Macgregor was not even a distant relative, but he was my grandmother's favourite preacher. He was then spending the summer at a house close to Inverdruie and, of course, was invited to preach at the local church. A little slip of a man who, we were told, had to stand on a hassock in order to be seen in the pulpit, he was a truly eloquent and magnetic preacher, and there was no desire to fidget and no possibility of sleep during his sermons. He was a puzzle to my boyish mind. He had then recently married for the second time, but in his sermon he told his congregation more than once that he held daily communion with his dear, dead wife. As his second wife was sitting in the pew immediately below him, I found it hard to understand how he performed an act which in those days I interpreted physically.

But the old man who attracted me most at Inverdruie was my grand-uncle Will. He was my grandmother's elder brother and was then really old, with good features and a white beard which gave him the appearance of a pre-war professor. He had lived well and, when he was gouty, had to be approached with circumspection. But he was a man of such wide reading and varied knowledge that even my father was impressed, and he had certainly led a remarkable life. He was an admirable raconteur, with a fine precision in his choice of words, and from his lips I heard wonderful tales of ships and war-prahus, of aborigines and cannibals, of gold diggers and bushrangers, in the new world of Oceania where he had made and lost more than one fortune.

Quite apart from the examples of the Macgregors, it was from her two brothers, Will and Tom, that my grandmother acquired her own remarkable ability to make and spend money. My grand-uncle Tom I never saw, but until the end of my grandmother's life I was to hear his name very often. He was the greatest money-maker of all my various relations and had the genius and the ultimate fate of the born gambler. He made two fortunes in gold mining in Australia, and had at one time a house in Park Lane. His first fortune he lost, while he was at home in London, through the dishonesty of a friend. The second he gambled away on a single card. His confidence in his lucky star was unbounded, but the star refused to shine again. He then went downhill rapidly, married as his second wife a Sydney barmaid and lived with her until he died in Australia, leaving behind him a considerable family whom none of us has ever seen.

Recently, however, I received evidence of their continued existence from an Australian coronation visitor who told me how he had walked into a Sydney greengrocer's with a copy of my book *British Agent* under his arm. The woman serving him pointed to the book and said, "I've read it too. The author is a relation of mine." Doubtless she was one of my grand-uncle's children.

This grand-uncle was a sore disappointment to my grandmother, who had to keep him, and, serving as a text for my own waywardness, he was frequently held up to me as an example of the dangers of profligacy.

Another old boy, although not then at all old, who kept us in roars of laughter, was my uncle Stewart Bruce. He married my mother's sister, belonged to an old Ulster family, and lived in Ireland. A powerfully built man with the arms and chest of a Sandow, he excelled at any form of game and outdoor pastime. He had played Rugby football for Ireland, had broken his school record for the long jump, had putted the weight incredible distances, and was even then just about the best shot in Ireland.

He had been at school at King William's College, Isle of Man, which has a place in school history as the scene of Dean Farrar's *Eric or Little by Little*. It was my uncle Stewart who first shook my faith in the reliability of that school classic. Anything less like the boys in *Eric* than my uncle would be difficult to imagine. His tongue would have tripped over words like "introspection" and "morbidity", and, if he ever mentioned his soul, it was to bless it or to damn it.

It was as an incorrigible ragster and practical joker that he appealed to us. On one occasion, one of the guests, who had probably suffered severely, cunningly loosened the seams of Uncle Stewart's evening trousers in the hope that he would put them on without noticing and that when he sat down to dinner, the garments, which Mr. Jack Hulbert has defined as "plural when you wear them, and singular when you don't", would split asunder.

Uncle Stewart appeared at dinner in his dress trousers. There was, however, no crack. It had come before—in the dressing-room, and Uncle Stewart had put on another pair. He took a masterly revenge. The next day he spent in chopping up reams of horse-hair, and the results of his choppings he sprinkled on the inside of the dress trousers of the man who had tried to play the trick on him. On this occasion there was no premature detection. Nor did the unfortunate man suspect anything, but sat through dinner writhing in increasing irritation and wondering if he had the itch.

It was a revenge and a triumph which inspired Rufus and me to imitate our uncle's prowess. But our own successes were rare, and soon we discovered, sometimes painfully, that the practical jokes of small boys are not considered so amusing as those of grown-ups.

I was thirteen when I spent my last summer at Aviemore. It was a holiday marked by two outstanding events in my small life. I learnt to shoot. I did not go out with the guns but was relegated to the dell and the bracken-covered hill beside Loch Pityoulish, where, under the tuition of Cox, an English sergeant turned keeper, from whose lips I heard my first words of Cockney, I shot scores of rabbits, with a few hares, pigeon, snipe, and an odd grouse or two, to make up a mixed bag. On one occasion, while walking through a silver birch wood, I came full on a roe-deer not more than ten yards before me. For a moment it stood and looked at me as if rooted by surprise. "Shoot 'im," whispered Cox, "you can't miss 'im." But there was a feminine appeal in those clear, staring eyes which made me hold my finger, and, as I limply lowered my gun, he disappeared with a graceful bound behind the birches.

Since then I have had numerous opportunities of shooting deer, both in Scotland and in Central Europe, but I have never fired a shot at one, preferring to-day to do my stalking with a camera. It is a curious example of illogicality in a man who has no compunction about shooting pheasants or knocking a fish on the head after it has made a glorious fight for its life. This form of illogicality is confined to the English-speaking peoples, who are alone among the races of the world in the equal intensity with which they pursue the fox and revile the lout who maltreats a dog or a horse.

Having shot over many famous moors and coverts, including Konopišt, the Bohemian home of that fanatical slayer of game, the Archduke Franz Ferdinand, I should be guilty of pose were I to say that I do not care for shooting. I do, and, moreover, I still shoot when the opportunity offers itself. I admit that, as far as the actual shooting is concerned, driven partridges, driven grouse, and pheasant covert-shooting provide in that order the finest test of skill. But personally I prefer going out by myself with a gun and a dog to all those organised drives and battues which, for their success, demand a Prussian regimentation of one's time and position, and at Whittingehame I have taken more pleasure in inspecting the late Lord Balfour's library, curiously limited to works on philosophy, music, and dietetics, than in the pheasant shooting.

As a pastime I rate shooting well below fishing. It gives me almost as much pleasure to see someone else play a salmon as to catch one myself, whereas most people cannot watch even the best guns for more than half an hour without being bored. And this, I think, represents the difference between a technical skill which achieves perfection when, as is not uncommon, your crack shot rarely if ever misses, and a delicate art which not even the best angler in the world can ever master in a lifetime.

The other eventful episode of this holiday was my first appearance as a performer at one of those concerts which, during the months of August and September, the visitors to Strathspey inflict on the inhabitants for the benefit of local charities.

In those Victorian days the programme was heavily charged with drawing-room ballads and piano solos. The solos were usually played by young girls who, in pink dresses and with pink bows on their pigtails, repeated the pieces which they had learnt laboriously at school in the previous term. The ballads were sung by the married women and by middle-aged spinsters who, when they were not frowning in mute wrath at the accompanist for playing too loudly, bade one "Come into the Garden" with an eagerness which unmasked the tragedy of their wasted lives.

Occasionally local talent was represented by a blacksmith or a gamekeeper who, in a remarkably pure, natural voice, sang some old Scottish favourite like "Highland Mary" or "Gae Bring tae Me a Pint o' Wine" and then stumbled off the platform, loudly cheered by the youths in the back seats. Finally, when the torture was ended, the laird, or some visiting plutocrat who had been pressed into taking the chair, congratulated the singers and announced that the success of the concert had succeeded the success of all previous concerts, and that the fund for the provision of coal to the inmates of the local workhouse had been swelled by a magnificent contribution of seven pounds nine shillings and ten pence halfpenny!

These concerts brought radiant joy to my father, who found in them an opportunity both for exercise and for giving to the world a voice which at other times was heard at its best in the bathroom. Generally he favoured sentimental soldier songs like "The King's Own" or rollicking cavalier ballads of the "God for King Charles" order. On rarer occasions, for my mother put a check on these higher flights, he would attempt the more sugary arias of Wagner, and I remember him once singing "Still wie die Nacht" in a voice which disturbed whatever previous stillness the night possessed.

A few years later the combined musical talents of my brothers did something to raise the standard of these concerts to a brighter level, and one summer our performance of potted musical comedy was in great demand all over Strathspey. My contribution to these extravaganzas took the form of supplying the topical verses, and one tilt against the Grantown Town Council, which was then engaged in a long dispute over the respective merits of petrol gas and electricity for lighting purposes, went with a bang which even shamed the Council into decisive action.

But at Aviemore I made my debut unsupported and alone. I sang a comic song and added my name to the unknown thousands of amateurs who have murdered "When Father Laid the Carpet on the Stairs". I am glad that my brothers were not big enough to realise the enormity of my offence. A year later, when Fettes had made me into a self-conscious schoolboy, wild horses would not have dragged me on to the platform. At Aviemore, however, my song, the only comic one on the programme, was received with far greater applause than a much later performance when, complete with kilt and tam o' shanter, I attempted to repeat Harry Lauder's rendering of "I'm fou' the nou' " in Grantown. Highlanders, perhaps not unnaturally, do not, or did not then, appreciate Harry Lauder. They liked still less the attempts of people who should know better than try to imitate him, and in his criticism of the concert, Tulloch, the editor of *The Strath-spey Herald* and a staunch supporter of the family, was severely critical of my buffoonery.

CHAPTER FOUR

IT IS MY profound conviction that a man's character is influenced far more by the environment which surrounds his boyhood than by the sins or virtues of his ancestors. Only those who are born and bred in great cities can adapt themselves successfully to the unnatural conditions of city life. A man who has the scent of the heather in his nostrils from childhood is damned from the start in a metropolis like London and seeks in alcohol and in night clubs the only available escape from an intolerable situation. In course of time his friends laugh at his love of the country and with superficial judgment register him in their minds as a man who cannot live without the artificial attractions of great cities.

This conviction came to me early in life and was enforced by personal experience. In our four years at Aviemore there was a gap which was caused by a temporary illness of my grandmother. In 1898 she did not feel strong enough to run both a house and a shoot and went instead to Grantown. Almost at the last moment my parents took a house in the centre of the same summer resort.

Grantown, made popular by Queen Victoria's visit in 1860, is not a city. But it is certainly not the country, and, except for my father who had his golf and his tennis at his doorstep, our summer experiment there was not a success. There was no fishing within reasonable distance, except in the Spey, and at Grantown that noble river yielded little else but small parr to the lures of inexpert boys. Tennis I then regarded as a game for girls.

It is true that life was not without its excitements. The golf links were the centre of Grantown life, and, having little else to do, I golfed assiduously with my brother Rufus, confining our efforts to the short course by day and venturing, like shy sea trout, into the wide stretches of the big course in the evening. In 1898 it was still a nine-holes course, and I remember it less for its golf than for the excellent ginger beer supplied by Mrs. McLean, the club-house attendant. Since then I have played on it often, both as a boy and as a grown man, and to-day it lives in my memory for its picturesque surroundings and for my first meeting with Bobby Cruikshank. When I first saw him, Bobby, the son of a Grantown tailor, was a caddie on the local course. But even then he showed signs of the prowess which was to raise him to the highest pinnacle of professional golf. Some years later one of the shooting tenants at Castle Grant or Revack gave him a chance in life and sent him to Edinburgh University. But Bobby's genius was in his wrists and fingers and, after serving in the Great War, he took his courage in both hands and went off to the United States to try his luck as a professional golfer. Like Walter Hagen, he is a great angler as well as a great golfer, and he is one of the small band of poor Grantown boys who have found fame, and, I hope, fortune, in the New World.

Another memorable diversion was the Grantown Cattle Show, for it attracted a travelling circus, and here for a whole week Rufus and I lived on the merry-go-round and in the boat swings. An even greater attraction was the shooting booth, where, thanks to our previous practice with air guns, we were able to show off before the local farmer-boys by knocking down celluloid balls and clay pipes and collecting large numbers of cheap vases and little monkeys made of wire and wool, as trophies of our skill.

The Show itself was a one-day affair, and, apart from the appearance of my uncle's Shetland ponies in a driving con-test, we found the official programme slow and wearisome. But as a study of Highland humanity the Show was a revelation to youthful minds. Farmers, dressed in every kind of headgear from old billycocks to deer-stalker caps, flocked to it from miles around. Every man had a bottle in his pocket, and, as the day progressed, the libations poured to the Scottish god of whisky would have made a decent-sized "spate". To even respectable, sober farmers, who never touched a drop of spirits for the rest of the year, the day was not merely an excuse but a necessity for getting drunk. Fights were frequent, and in an empty cattle pen I saw a scrap between four drunks which lives in my memory far more clearly than any prize-fight I have ever witnessed. Rather frightened yet driven forward by an irresistible curiosity, Rufus and I crept to the edge of the ring of spectators and supporters. They made no attempt to interfere. Breathlessly we watched the awkward lunges of the staggering men and heard unknown oaths which stuck more readily in youthful minds than Latin nouns and Greek verbs.

Fortunately, although blood flowed freely, the men were too drunk to do each other much harm, and presently the police arrived and arrested them. At the approach of the Law we fled, returning cautiously to follow the staggering procession to the Police Station in the neighbouring square.

Getting home was another adventure, for cattle, including prize bulls, wandered unattended about the streets while their owners stopped at every bar from the *Grant Arms* to the *Strathspey* for the final dram which was to make their journey home a miracle of self-preservation. These scenes made an indelible impression on my imagination. Even then I vaguely connected this staggering helplessness with Balmenach whisky and wondered if my grandmother's conscience was ever troubled by the same thought.

I had not then appreciated the special virtues which have elevated so many distillers and brewers to the British peerage. Nor, having seen something of the effects of Prohibition in the United States, do I hold to-day any strong views about the regulation of strong drink, believing that a raging thirst, like most other temptations, must be fought by each man in single combat. For centuries whisky has been the national drink of the Highlander, and there are few Highlanders, and, indeed, few Lowlanders who do not like to think that their ancestors were reared on whisky and oat-meal.

In the early days at Balmenach, my great-grandfather's huge family of sixteen sat down daily to the breakfast of porridge and whisky which was then the staple food of every class of the population. My mother's family owes much to whisky, and, as it has helped to pay my debts, I am under a similar obligation.

Nor am I alone in this debt. The great Highland land-owners, who rely for their Scottish income on letting or selling their moors and fishings, have found their best clients among the brewers and distillers. During my lifetime the best "lets" and sales in Strathspey have been to Basses, Walkers, Haigs, Edwards, and Ushers.

But what whisky has given with one hand, it has taken with the other, and there is not a family in the Highlands which has not its alcoholic skeleton in the cupboard. Al-though they were men of magnificent physique, most of my Macgregor grand-uncles died comparatively young from over-indulgence in whisky, and I could quote numerous examples of similar ravages among their friends. In the days before rapid communications the long Highland winter afforded temptations which few could resist. The country doctor, driving miles in his trap to some lonely shepherd's cottage to attend a child-birth case, was paid in whisky, and many a brilliant young minister of the Kirk, deprived of the intellectual conversation to which his education and training had accustomed him, found consolation in the bottle. Before the big sales to the south were organised, my great-grand-father sold his whisky locally. The Highland lairds were good buyers, but the account books of those early years show that the best client was the parish minister of Cromdale.

Although whisky still figures to excess in most Scottish smoking-room conversations, the whisky era has passed, and since the war Grantown, like the rest of Scotland, has so-bered, preferring more civilised, if less virile, recreations to the pleasures and expense of hard drinking. I went to the Cattle Show a year or two ago. It was not entirely a temperance meeting, but I saw few "drunks".

Two factors have contributed largely to this improvement of social conditions. They are the huge excise duty on whisky and the advent of the motor car. The high duty has put whisky beyond the reach of the average Highland purse, and with this forcible removal of temptation the local farmer has learnt to forget the need of whisky. I cannot say that he has lost the taste. At the Dulnain Bridge Coronation celebrations the free gift of a case of whisky, given of course by a visitor, produced unexpected results, including the premature firing of the bonfire.

The motor car has banished the loneliness of Highland life. It has had another curbing influence. In the old days the drinking capacity of the Highland farmer was greatly facilitated by the possession of a horse that Mr. Bertram Mills or any circus proprietor would be glad to possess. This Highland horse was more than human. He took the farmer to the market town, stopped mechanically at the necessary refreshment halts, and waited patiently until the drinking bout was over. Then the farmer's friends or the hotel-keeper strapped the farmer into his seat in the trap, and the faithful horse took him home. No genius of modern science has yet been able to devise a car which will perform this useful service, and to-day, when every farmer has a car of sorts or, at least, a motor bike, he thinks of his driving licence even while he drinks. Thus, by methods which, however far they may fall short of the standards of the civilisation of ancient Greece, have nevertheless proved efficacious, modern man can point to progress.

But the Cattle Show was an isolated incident in a drab holiday. In Grantown we were much more under our parents' control than we were in the country, and nearly every day we were dragged off to tea-parties or bazaars, which then rivalled concerts as a means of raising money for local charities. It was at a Grantown bazaar that I saw and shook hands with Marie Corelli for the only time in my life. She was then at the height of her popularity as a writer and took herself very seriously. When she drove down the High Street with her large picture hat, her ponies and her Pomeranians, she made Grantown take her seriously. Perhaps that is why, although she inspired in me no desire to write, she gave me the mistaken impression that authors were not only rich but very important people.

At the bazaar Miss Corelli who, I remember, flouted local opinion by stating that white heather brought ill luck, spoke at considerable length on many subjects including drink, but I am afraid that her earnest exhortations did not succeed in altering the course of my life. Speeches are unfair ordeals for boys on holiday, and a surfeit of bazaars and afternoon teas drove me, for want of a proper escape, into mischief. Prompted by two boys home from South Africa, I formed a smoking club. Its headquarters was the thick pine wood between Grantown and Spey Bridge, and here we consumed innumerable cigarettes, smoking them to the very end and using a pine needle as a holder when they burned too low to be held by the fingers. Ogden's Guinea Gold, at ten, I think, for threepence, was our brand, and for some weeks all our pocket money went to swell the Ogden millions.

This smoking craze, which lasted for several weeks, ended abruptly. My grandmother had a reinforced sense of smell. One evening, when she was dining with my father and mother, my brother Rufus and I came in to say goodnight. Rufus bent forward to kiss the old lady. She, too, bent to meet him, but it was a short-lived bend. With a faugh she pushed him away, and with great presence of mind my brother looked down at his shoes to see if he had stepped into some cattle dung. But the old lady's eyes were stern.

"Boy," she said in a voice that rang with the wrath of the prophets, "you've been smoking."

She made an imperious gesture with her hand towards my mother.

"Florrie, smell your second son."

The unfortunate Rufus was passed round for inspection, and, the verdict being unanimous, was led away by my father for immediate execution. I escaped his fate by having taken the precaution to eat some "sugar alley", a villainous-smelling sweetmeat made of liquorice.

Strangely enough, this was the only holiday during which my brother and I ever smoked until we left our public schools. Stern moralists will stress the beneficent effects of corporal punishment. They may be right, but I prefer to point the moral by referring the reader to the opening paragraph of this chapter. That summer holiday in Grantown was the last which we ever spent as boys in a town.

The next year we returned to the Cromdale area and discovered the Delliefure district on the opposite bank of the Spey. And to Delliefure we remained true, not only until I went abroad, but until all my four brothers and my sister had gone out into the world.

It became in a very real sense my mother's home, not a home of walls and leased houses, but the other home of moors and hills which, after years in the South of England, was all that she asked from life. Like Catriona she loved the place and the roots that grew there, and the name of it made all of her rejoice. Here came to her, as though fate had recognised her choice of home, the chief joys and sorrows which constitute the intimate drama of all human existence. Here she received the news of the successes and failures of her sons; and here, surrounded for the last time by all her family, for the place was a rallying ground for exiles like myself and my brother Rob who is in the Indian Army, she celebrated her silver wedding. Here too, in 1915, came my brother Norman to spend his last leave before going back to France, where he was killed at Loos a few days later.

In this district there were only three houses, Tomvaich,

Lower Delliefure and Upper Delliefure, and we leased them all at various times. Upper Delliefure I liked best, because it was the most remote. It stood on a wide stretch of moor at the foot of a wooded hill. To the west lay the woods of Castle Grant. From the front we could see the chimney of Balmenach, the Cromdale hills, and the wide crest of the Cairngorms. By the door flowed a burn, full of plump trout and in those pre-motor car days rarely fished, and within easy walk was a glorious stretch of the Spey with a grass path leading down to the famous Pollowick, where on warm nights the salmon could be seen leaping in scores.

We had a permit to fish for trout, and if our flies and casts were too strong for trout, and a salmon or grilse made a mistake, there was no one to say nay. The late Mr. McCorquodale, most fanatical of salmon fishers, had not then extended his grip on the Spey beyond the Tulchan stretch. The salmon generally broke us, and in any case fly-fishing never did serious harm to any water. It was the same with shooting. There were rabbits in plenty on the farm, and the Castle Grant keepers had no objection to honest rabbit-shooting, and, if occasionally we added a grouse or a blackcock to our bag, keepers are kind to boys who know how to be polite and how to give them an opportunity of airing their knowledge of bird and fish life.

From childhood I was brought up to regard the Highland keeper as the finest man on God's earth which to every right-minded Scottish boy is of course Scotland. I think the same to-day, but I have been slightly disillusioned by the knowledge that even in the Highlands some of the best keepers are Lowlanders. Still, Highland or Lowland, keepers are a fine body of men. They are well-read and have evolved a philosophy of life which has given to them a remarkable strength of character as well as of limb. I have often marvelled at their forbearance with the vulgarity and ineptitude of many a modern shooting and fishing tenant. I should not call the average keeper a great fisherman, but, when he is asked to provide a fish for the table, he can always get one and get it quickly. After all, he has a life-long experience of the methods of poachers.

Increasing experience added ingenuity to our own fishing prowess. At Delliefure there was a dam with a mill below it. By releasing the water from the dam and letting the mill-wheel churn it up, a very fair imitation of a "spate" could be made. Having made the "spate", Rufus and I would then run down the burn and, casting our worms into the muddy water, would land our reward in the form of an extra large trout.

These artificial "spates" were summarily ended, not by the farmer's wrath, for we always took care to try our experiment when he was absent, but by an accident. On one occasion the mill-wheel refused to operate, and my young cousin Ian, my uncle Jim's eldest son, climbed on to the wheel-boards in order to make the wheel go round. His effort was only too successful, for the wheel started suddenly and he was carried round until his arm was wedged between the wall and the wheel. Fortunately, we managed to extricate him before he was seriously hurt. But the experience gave us a fright and put a final stop to our praiseworthy attempts to improve on Nature.

From this period of my life dates my passion for looking down on water from bridges. Below the house at Delliefure there was a wooden bridge over the burn, and here I would stand for long intervals, keeping very still and watching the voles and the moorhens as they swam between the banks. But it was the fish that commanded my main attention. Primarily, I suppose, I was intent on their future capture, but their movements always chained me to my observation post.

It fascinated me to see how the trout took up their line in order of physical superiority, with the biggest fish commanding the best feeding. If he left his place for one second on some predatory expedition, the next biggest would automatically move up. Then the big fellow would return and fiercely drive away his weaker rival. Occasionally a huge eel, for the burn contained some monsters, would wind his way out of the weeds. Then all but the biggest trout would dart under the weeds, leaving a shadowy trail of sand behind them.

Like most anglers I have a dream river. It runs between the Ewe and the Broom on the north-west coast of Ross-shire. It has a little island-studded bay to itself, and at its mouth there is a charming lodge. No other houses are near it, and provisions have to be brought by a steam yacht. It is, of course, a rich man's river, and therefore I shall never fish it. But even if I could I doubt if to-day the fishing of it would give me as much lasting pleasure as my study of Nature from bridges.

For many years now I have developed this study into a kind of game. The big trout at the head of the bridge pool is Britain. The rivals who are always waiting to take his place are Germany and Italy. The little trout who lie cautiously behind and who indulge in the same tactics only when the big fellows are resting under the bank are the small nations of Europe. The sinister eel is Russia or the greater menace, remote more in distance perhaps than in time, which threatens Europe from the Far East. I understand why every man of culture hates war. I cannot understand why so many biologists are pacifists. The ways of fish and of most animals are not very different from the ways of mankind.

As far as our house at Delliefure was concerned, the centre of our life was the apology for a tennis court which we turned into a tiny cricket ground. Here for hours on end, when the sun was too bright for fishing, we played cricket with passionate zest. My brothers Rob and Norman were now old enough to be pressed into these matches, and without respite we went through the English county championship in miniature.

Norman, my fourth brother, played with me against my second and third brothers, Rufus and Rob. There was a certain fairness about the rules. Both sides fielded, and no bowler could bowl more than one over at a time. Even then my brother Norman showed promise as a fast bowler, and if ever he began to lag could nearly always be roused to fresh energy by my fierce shout of "get fizzy".

In this manner the two younger brothers had at least some share in the game. But to them it must have been more like work than play, for they were subjected to stern discipline, and any slackness was punished with a cricket stump. Tears, therefore, watered the pitch on many occasions, and Rob has since told me how Norman and he hated those games and how one day they plotted to incapacitate me by digging a trench and filling it with stones at the bottom of a hill down which they knew I must ride my bicycle.

Poor Rob! Doubtless he vastly preferred riding the farm horses and drilling the farm hands, for even then he was soldier-mad and wanted to be a General. But the games drilling which he received from me did not impair his own zest for games. He became the best footballer in the family, and even as a big boy used to cry gently as a relief to suppressed fury all through the game. His chances of an international cap were destroyed by the grimmer international contest of the Great War. But he has gone far towards realising his martial ambitions, for at the age of forty-two he is now commanding a brigade in India.

To these early Delliefure days belongs the cycling craze which captivated us as it captivated most people at a time when, railway trains excepted, the bicycle was man's fastest means of transport. Rufus and I regarded it chiefly as a Heaven-sent convenience for extending our fishing area. We rose with the dawn, and sometimes before it, in order to reach remote burns, and, travelling thirty or forty miles, returned home with marvellous baskets of trout which we proudly distributed among my parents' friends, especially those who tipped well. In this manner I made my first visit to Tomintoul, travelling partly by cycle but mainly on foot across the rough hill road, then little more than a track, from Grantown. The highest village in the Highlands, it lies in the romantic valley of the Avon, and, although no longer as inaccessible as it was, has so endeared itself to my heart, as much by the natural beauty of its surroundings as by the link with Macgregor associations, that for many years it has been the shrine of my annual pilgrimage north. Its old hotel, the *Richmond Arms,* can be recommended for the best poor man's salmon fishing in Britain, and its proprietor, Duncan McNiven, an Argyllshire man with Campbell connections, is the best all-round fisherman that I have ever met.

The bicycle did more than extend the range of our angling expeditions. It opened up new tracks for historical exploration. Both my father and my mother liked cycling, and with them we made many excursions which took us as far afield as Elgin, Lossiemouth, Culloden, Inverness and Glen Affric. If my memories of our first trip to Elgin are more vivid, not merely because in that city we saw the famous Wild West show with Buffalo Bill himself performing on horseback wondrous feats with a rifle, but also because, while coasting down the long hill at Carron, I ran over a large collie, and nearly lost my life, this does not mean that my interest in more serious matters has left no permanent impression. From these days dates the beginning of what I may call my Baedeker mania—and I doubt if any one possesses a larger collection of guide books than I do—and also of my passionate and still unsatisfied desire to soak myself in the atmosphere of the "Forty Five". The romance of that lost cause gripped me against all reason, and the logical arguments of my father in favour of the Lowland attitude merely roused my resentment and increased my devotion to the Jacobites. With priggish obstinacy I used all the Jacobite names in preference to those long since adopted by Hanoverian-minded historians, calling Prestonpans Gladsmuir, and never referring to Culloden except as Drummossie.

It thrilled my pride to read that one of the seven outlaws who protected Prince Charlie in Glen Moriston, when the English had set a price of £30,000 on his head, was a Macgregor; and my first visit to Culloden, then the loneliest and loveliest of battlefields, so stirred my emotions that I vowed that I should never visit it again except alone. I have revisited it many times and have broken the vow only once, when in 1936 I made a technical study of the ground with my soldier brother Rob.

In his admirable book on Scotland Mr. H. V. Morton describes Culloden as "almost the only unspoilt battlefield in Britain". But it is spoilt to-day. Two tea houses and a filling station look down on the former solitary grandeur of the memorial cairn, and rude advertisements for oil and petrol shriek their vulgarity to the sky. In other countries such desecration is forbidden. Is there no newspaper in Britain, no member of the House of Lords, to bring the petrol and the oil lords to book for this Philistine irreverence? They do not tolerate advertisements on their own mansions. Have they not made enough millions to spare Scotland and all beauty-lovers this insult?

For the view from Culloden is still as fair a sight as any that Scotland has to offer. To the south lie hills and the valley of the Nairn; to the west, between the Moray Firth and the long glorious line of the mountains, the rich cornfields of the Black Isle glisten in the same sun which on that fateful April day of 1746 went down on the hopes of the Stuarts.

My latest visit to Culloden brought other shocks than tea houses and petrol signs. Small boys hawked souvenirs, and, wishing to discover whether the locals pronounced Culloden with a shut or an open "o", I questioned one of them. He did not know, his own pronunciation being something between the two. His name was Macgregor, and for the family connection and the pains which he had taken I bought a small life of Prince Charlie from him. I opened the book at Culloden and at the end of the chapter I read: "Foremost among the remorseless instruments of Cumberland's vengeance was the shameless General Hawley, and the names of Lieutenant-Colonel Howard, Captain Scott, and Major *Lockhart* are also to be handed down as worthy of everlasting execration." So there had been a Lockhart on the other side. Even in these days when I take my Jacobite devotions much as an ambassador takes his glass of port, that is, as a rite to be performed regularly but not to be allowed to affect one's judgment, the information gives me a mild shock. But I accept it as a salutary reminder that Jacobite enthusiasms are compatible with a comfortable double allegiance, and that in Scotland and, indeed, in all Britain there are no such rough and ready divisions as Gael and Saxon and very few "pure" Celts or 100 per cent. Scots whose heredity would stand for a moment the test of serious investigation.

Our trip to Lossiemouth, I fear, was purely a pleasure expedition with golf as its main objective. I had not then heard of **Mr.** Ramsay MacDonald, for he had not yet reached that pinnacle of fame which was later to make his name honoured or held in execration in his native town in accordance with the conflicting political views of his fellow citizens. Less than a decade before my first visit to Lossiemouth, he had been a pupil-teacher in the neighbouring school of Drainie. A friend of mine, to-day a famous doctor in a British Dominion, was a pupil in Mr. MacDonald's class.

"Was Mr. MacDonald a good master?" I asked him once.

The doctor, himself now a stern and exacting professor, smiled beatifically.

"He didn't last long," he said with pride. "He couldn't keep order for toffee."

Mr. MacDonald is not the only great man who has failed to keep boys in order, although, doubtless, his experiences at Drainie helped him later when he had to control the unruly boys of the Labour Party.

At about the same time that Mr. MacDonald was teaching at Drainie, a future colleague of his and a sterner disciplinarian was living further up the Spey at Rothes. This was exciseman

Philip Snowden, later Lord Snowden and first Labour Chancellor of the Exchequer of Britain. A few years before his death, I discussed with him more than once his experiences at Rothes. From his early youth, I think, he had always held teetotal principles, and his work in the Speyside distilleries certainly did nothing to weaken them.

At Balmenach I naturally met various excise officers. They were mostly very pleasant fellows who were always ready to put their fishing lore at my disposal. They led such pleasant lives that until the age of fifteen or sixteen I had fleeting ambitions of becoming a "gauger". If they established good relations with the distillery owner or manager, they could arrange their work to suit their own convenience. They had thus a considerable amount of free time for fishing, and, as the history of modern Scottish literature has proved, also for the writing of books.

Both the talented Mr. Neil Gunn and the popular Mr. Maurice Walsh are, or were, excise officers, and although neither, as far as I know, was ever stationed at Balmenach, Mr. Walsh knows the Strathspey district well and has described it with great charm both in *The Key Above the Door* and in *The Small Dark Man*.

CHAPTER FIVE

IF THESE HOLIDAYS at Delliefure now glow in retrospect like the radiance of a Highland sunset, our bliss ran in short cycles of six days. At the end of each cycle was the seventh day in which rest meant for us a long walk to church and the same strictures on play as were parentally enforced at Broughty Ferry.

It is true that the rigours of our Highland Sabbath could sometimes be softened, for, wearied by a week's hard tennis and golf, my father occasionally slept on Sunday afternoons, and then we could steal up to the burn, look at our night lines, and hide any captures under the moss until the next morning. But these minor relaxations were more than redressed by the extra length and grimness of the church services.

Moreover, our orthodoxy was subjected to further fluctuations. At Broughty Ferry we were Episcopalians; in the Highlands we were Presbyterians. Here the denominational pea was split still further. The Cromdale Parish Church was the old church of the Macgregors. Here my Macgregor forbears are buried, and here my Macgregor grandfather and grandmother worshipped with their dog Joey. For the Macgregor dog always went to church, taking his place in the family pew and listening to the sermon with greater attention than most of my uncles.

But there had been a dissension. In the Presbyterian church the congregation chooses the new minister by votes, generally after listening to a series of trial sermons by the various candidates. Some years before, there had been a vacancy at Cromdale, and, as the Balmenach Distillery was by far the biggest concern in that small parish, my grandmother's wishes had a commanding influence on the votes of the local congregation. Unfortunately, owing to some oversight, the members of the neighbouring parish of Advie were still on the Cromdale register. The candidate whom my grandmother did not favour secured these outside votes and obtained the nomination.

This was too much for my imperious grandmother, who was always at her best in the hour of battle. She led a Cromdale revolt, and, taking a large part of the Cromdale congregation with her, including, of course, the big Balmenach contingent, she left her old church. A new Free Church and a fine manse were put up less than a mile away, with an exclusive back pew for the Macgregor family.

Loyalty to the Macgregors dictated that we should worship at the new church. But my father, as independent in family matters as he was in his church allegiances, preferred strong sermons, and truth compels me to admit that Mr. McCowan of the Parish Church was a more forceful preacher than the amiable Mr. Dykes Lang of the new church. To the Parish Church, therefore, we went, and in spite of our grandmother's disfavour my brother Rufus and I approved our father's choice.

The Parish Church was almost a mile nearer our house. Through the open window we could hear the Spey running by the graveyard wall and even an occasional salmon splashing in the Minister's Pool. And to Mr. McCowan we owed one debt. Until he came to Cromdale, the Gaelic service had always been held first, the English service not beginning till after midday. Mr. McCowan reversed the order, and in this way we were spared the ordeal of having to wait until three o'clock for our Sunday dinner.

At first the novelty of the service attracted us. In those days the church had not even a harmonium, and the singing was led by a precentor. The proceedings began with a tuning fork which the precentor tapped frequently in frenzied attempts to strike a note that was not too high or too low. When at last the right "ah" had been sounded, the precentor waved his finger, and the choir broke into "All people that on earth do dwell". The congregation, nervously trying to find the key, lagged behind, and the first line was always taken at a snail's pace. This used to worry the precentor, who would then accelerate with an American pick-up, and, while the congregation were still dwelling on the "dwell", the choir would get off "Sing to the Lord with cheerful voice", almost in one breath. The effort frequently made us giggle, and if the giggling were noticed we spent an unpleasant afternoon.

Mr. McCowan's extempore prayers provided another inspiring diversion. A fine-looking old man with a venerable beard, he had a gift of oratory which commanded our undivided attention because Rufus and I always had a competition to decide whether he would say conscience or mercy, which he pronounced "cunscience" and "mur-rcy", more often.

His sermons, however, were very long and difficult to follow, and soon we suffered from fidgets and pins and needles. There was only one remedy, and it worked only once. After wriggling about for a few minutes we pleaded physical distress and asked to leave the hall. Then we sneaked out on tiptoe and, swaying on the suspension bridge, tried to spot the fish in the river below. But my father was too much of a schoolmaster to be taken in by such obvious subterfuges, and after the first success we received strict orders to come back within two minutes if ever nature compelled us to withdraw. And with this our continence returned.

When my father finally accepted the bicycle as a legitimate Sunday means of transport, we went once or twice to the Seafield Memorial Church in Grantown. This church had a sentimental attraction, for my parents' marriage was the first ever celebrated in it. When we were at Dulnain Bridge, where we spent one summer, we went to the Duthil Church. Here in two mausoleums the Earls of Seafield are buried. At that time the church had a local fame on account of a body called "The Men of Duthil". They were not a sect but a kind of self-constituted committee of control which sat in judgment on the minister. They met on Sunday afternoons and discussed the sermon and other weighty matters. A former Grantown merchant was a prominent member. He brought the keg of whisky.

Alas! for the uncompromising sternness of that great age. The "Men of Duthil" have long since passed away, and a weaker generation knows them not. In Cromdale there are no more Gaelic services. My grandmother and Mr. McCowan are dead. Their remains rest beneath the great beeches in the graveyard by the Spey, and with the union of the Scottish churches the community has gone back to the old Parish Church.

I paid a visit to Cromdale during the great snowstorm of 1937. The manse which my grandmother built was empty. It was bought cheaply by an Aberdeen banker who uses it as a holiday home. Her church has become the village hall. As I stopped to go in, I saw a notice on the door: "Saturday, March 6, Whist Drive and Dance".

I felt a pang of regret and remorse. There was a symbol in the conversion of that church into a dance-hall. It marked the end of a generation of men and women who, however narrow their views may have been, were self-reliant and as severe to themselves as they were to others. They set themselves a high standard of frugality and hard work, and from this standard they rarely departed. Theirs was a life which seemed to yield little, but I wonder if they were unhappier than a generation which wants more from God and man and gives less to both. The union of the churches is a necessary and eminently desirable step forward, but I doubt if the Church of Scotland has as strong a hold to-day on the people as it had in that stern age when it was torn by dissensions of pin-point principle. These dissensions are perhaps the greatest weakness of the Christian churches, but in one sense they make for vigour and vigilance.

I have always felt that a state-established church lacks some of the virility of a free church. And who shall say that the Free

Church of Scotland lacked vigour or had ever to complain of the lukewarm support of its adherents! To this day I remember my father reciting to us the old Free Church jingles:

"The wee Kirk, the Free Kirk,
The Kirk wi'out the steeple;

The auld Kirk, the cauld (cold) Kirk,
The Kirk wi'out the people."

Even the bells of the two churches were supposed to sound the greater virility and energy of the Free Church. The Established Church bell, heavy and sonorous, droned out:

"Cauld kail hot again; cauld kail hot again",

a refrain which I feel was an unfair reflection on the sermons of the Established Church ministers. The Free Kirk bell ran more briskly and said: "collection, collection, collection, collection." And certainly the Free Kirk supporters put their hands deep into their pockets.

Nor do I think that to-day the United Church of Scotland is finding it easy to replace the old type of minister, who had all the virtues of his generation. To these virtues he added a humaneness and an understanding of life which those who knew him only from his sermons never would have suspected. No Scot, whatever his religious denomination, can honestly belittle what the ministers of the Scottish churches have done for Scotland. Nor must I forget their wives. Even if they failed to follow in their fathers' footsteps, are not nearly all Scotland's great men sons of the manse?

My friend, Mihail Sadoveanu, the great Rumanian novelist and lover of Scott and Scotland, tells a good story of the creation. The nations of the world assemble before God to receive their special racial qualities. First come the Jews. For the crucifixion of Jesus they have to suffer, but in compensation they are given the gift of money-making. Then come in turn the Germans, the English, the Turks, the Serbs, and the

Russians, and all are given a special characteristic in life, the quality of hard drinking being bestowed with some injustice on the Russians. Last of all come the Scots, the Transylvanians, the people of the mountains who live by the land and are a race apart. They have come too late, because everything has already been given away. But God loves them and he gives to them the priceless gifts of contentment, beautiful and sturdy women to maintain their race, and the violin and the bagpipes to gladden their hearts.

Speyside was the home of the Strathspey, and its most famous reel, "The Reel of Tulloch", was composed by a Macgregor. The dance notice on that Cromdale village hall was a symbol of a new generation which, in spite of all the efforts to revive Gaelic song and dance, was being relentlessly conquered by the mass production music of the gramophone and the radio. It is a generation which is not content with what it has and which no longer lives by the land. The men and women of my grandmother's generation had possessed in full measure the three gifts of the mountain people, and with their passing something of the glory of Scotland has departed for ever.

This is not mere nostalgic sentimentality. Acre for acre the area which lies between the Findhorn and the Deveron has produced more self-made men than any other part of Britain. The list includes two post-war Cabinet Ministers in Mr. Ramsay MacDonald, first Labour Prime Minister of Britain, and Lord Strathcarron, a fine Celtic scholar who will always be best remembered as Ian Macpherson. Both these men were of humble birth but not so humble as that of Donald Smith who built the Canadian Pacific Railway and became Lord Strathcona. He may well be called the Morayshire Homer in that several Morayshire towns and villages through which he more or less begged his way now contend for the honour of having been his birthplace. Forres, by dint of her size, has established the noisiest claim, but there is considerable weight of tradition in favour of Grantown-on-

Spey, and as the Strathcona family itself has no documentary proofs the matter is never likely to be settled.

Lord Mountstephen, Strathcona's cousin and collaborator in Canada, was born in Glen Rinnes. Publishing is represented by Alexander Elder of Banff and a lad, Smith, from Elgin who founded the famous house of Smith Elder, and journalism by James Gordon Bennet, who was born at Enzie and lived on the banks of the Spey until he emigrated to America to start *The New York Herald*, and by Archibald Forbes, the most famous of all war-correspondents. In the world of letters the district claims, among many more or less important figures, Dr. Gordon Stables, the Scottish Henty, whose *On To The Rescue* pointed my brother Rob's way to India, and A. G. Macdonell whose forbears, like my own, came from Tomintoul, while music is represented by William Marshall, whose reel tunes Burns admired so much that he wrote his well-known *Of a' the airts* to the music of one of them. Exploration and discovery have distinguished representatives in Gordon Cumming, the first of the great lion hunters, and James Augustus Grant, the companion of Speke.

To the services rendered by natives of the district on foreign battlefields both the Catholic and the Protestant graveyards of these Highland glens bear ample testimony. There is not a cemetery where the lettering on the stones will not take the reader on a journey round the world. Pipers and V.C. privates lie beside majors and generals, and the juxtaposition is surely not merely because in death there should be no distinction but also because most of them sprang from the same peasant stock.

Although the list of generals includes names famous in the military history both of Britain and of foreign powers like Russia, I shall mention only one military representative. This is Major Wilson, whose name will be remembered as long as the British race survives as the hero of "Wilson's last stand" in the Matabele War of 1893.

I have already said that Andrew Lang's *Red True Story*

Book was a favourite of my childhood. There was no story in that book which stirred my emotions so deeply as the account of Wilson's death when, surprised by an overwhelming force of Matabele warriors, he fought on after his handful of followers had been killed, and then, when his ammunition was finished, stood, silent and alone, to await the final thrust of the Matabele spears. I hope that the story has not been forgotten or expunged from boys' books by muddle-minded moralists.

Wilson was a native of Fochabers, and the last photograph taken of him in Scotland shows him in the typical tweed knickerbocker suit of the Strathspey farmer of those days. The expression on his face shows the same rugged determination which formerly characterised the inhabitants of this district.

I have mentioned only a small list of men whose names are known throughout the British Empire. To them must be added the scores of crofters' sons who left the home farm to seek and make a fortune overseas. I shall give two instances which have some connection with my own youth. The farmer-tenant from whom we leased our home at Delliefure was a man called James Grant. He had a brother, and their history is typical of many a Strathspey home. James, a farmer's son, became in the natural course of heredity a farmer. The younger son, Robertson Grant, was employed as a footman at Tulchan. One of the Basses, then a tenant of this famous shoot, gave him a steerage passage to the Argentine, and there the crofter's son made a fortune. His son Ned I remember in my youth as one of the first racing motorists. The contrast with our landlord James was complete. James, a big man with a huge red beard, remained a rough, impoverished farmer. When we knew him, he was a pathetic figure and had become a whisky addict. He had a pony which took him home after his drinking bouts, and many a time did I meet him on the Grantown road swaying from side to side in his phaeton with the urchins running after him and chanting

"Reid (red) Jimmie's drunk again". Providence and the pony kept him safe, but one winter he fell from his seat into a snowdrift. The next morning he was found frozen in, and everyone thought that Red Jimmie had taken his last dram. Highland physique, however, can conquer many hurdles. He was thawed out, and, awaking from his Arctic sleep, seemed none the worse for his experience. But he died long before the war.

My other example is also of a family of Grants who had the Garvault farm near Advie. There were several brothers, one of whom in due course took over the farm from his father. Another became a mason and married Lily McLean, my first nurse. The third went to the Argentine and prospered exceedingly. For many years now he has rented Muckerach, a former property of the chiefs of the Clan Grant with an excellent grouse moor and an ancient castle which is said to date from the time of the Romans. He now figures in the list of proprietors and tenants of Scottish shootings as Mr. A. D. Grant of Santa Fé. Fortune has continued to smile on him. During the post-war slump in the Argentine when it was difficult to export money from that country he won a large prize in the Irish sweepstake, thus providing another illustration of the eternal truth that to him who hath shall be given.

These successful Highland boys owed something to the Highland schoolmaster who, in the old days at any rate, was a splendid type, teaching his little well and sparing no pains in the literal sense to ensure that his pupils both learnt and understood it. They owed even more to their parents and, most of all, to their frugal upbringing. Their home environment taught them that hard work is the only road to success, and, up in the morning when city folk slept, they set high store by an education which richer boys regarded as a drudgery. Their lean, well-knit frame, able to support fatigue almost beyond the limits of human endurance, was no fairy's birthday gift. It came from their simple diet of oatmeal and hard walking. From the first they knew the value of money, and when they went abroad they took their frugal habits with them, spurning the temptations of even modest comforts and saving something from whatever they earned. In this way they husbanded their resources. Thus, when the opportunities of the New World presented themselves, they were able to seize them with that curious mixture of boldness and foresight which has always been the chief characteristic of the Highland pioneer in foreign countries. Doubtless, some of them were harsh and even unscrupulous men; but there were others who gave away generously what they had earned so hardly. In *Nicholas Nickleby* Charles Dickens modelled the Cheerybles, surely the kindest-hearted business men in literature, from two Grant brothers who were born at Knockando on the Spey.

In those days of my youth there was another Strathspey celebrity who, not having been born in a crofter's cradle, had not been forced to go abroad to seek riches and high station. This was Caroline, Countess of Seafield. She was then a widow of seventy and marvellously like Queen Victoria both in appearance and in character. Rumour said that in her youth she had enjoyed her full share of the good things of life, and rumour was supported by her early portraits, which showed a woman of remarkable charm and beauty.

Her life, however, had brought its fill of sorrows. After her husband's death her love was concentrated on her son, the 8th Earl, who suffered from the Highland failing of intemperance. His mother did all she could to help him, even to the extent of smashing up the wine-cellars at Castle Grant. He died, however, at the age of thirty-three, and the title went to his father's brother. But the estates remained with Caroline. They had been heavily encumbered by the stepmother of the 7th Earl, an Irish lady with a passion for gambling, and on the accession of Caroline's husband the entail was broken in order to pay off his two brothers. Caroline was therefore sole mistress of the Seafield fortunes with the right to dispose of them as she wished.

Having buried her husband and her son in a magnificent mausoleum at Duthil, she settled down at Castle Grant and at Cullen to devote the rest of her life to good works. She carried out her duties as a great landowner and as chieftain of the Clan Grant with scrupulous attention to detail. She visited all her tenants regularly and, by patting their children on the head and listening to their troubles, identified herself with their lives. In Grantown, where every stone belonged to her and every house and shop paid her a feu, she opened bazaars and lent her name to every charity. By these good deeds she was known to the whole countryside, and in summer there were few visitors who did not see her driving out in her carriage to visit the sick or who had not heard from some gossiping "local" the tragic story of her sorrows.

It is true that these sorrows had been embittered by Highland pride and dictatorial proclivities. During those years she was much harassed in heart and mind by thoughts of the future. The 9th Earl, her husband's brother, who had never reigned at Castle Grant, had died and had been succeeded by his son. This son, having no money, had emigrated to New Zealand and, after working there as a railway porter and a rabbit-trapper, had married and also produced a son. The father never came home, dying in New Zealand as an earl without an earldom, and it was his son, Caroline's grand-nephew, who was then the Earl of Seafield.

When he succeeded in 1888, Caroline did what in the eyes of the clan was the right thing. She wrote to his widowed mother offering to bring him home and to educate him as his exalted position befitted. This generous offer carried with it one condition: the mother was to give up all rights over her son. The offer was not accepted. The young Earl grew up in New Zealand and became engaged to a doctor's daughter. Again the Countess intervened. On this occasion she wrote to the young Earl himself, begging him to come home for a year and promising that if at the end of that period he was still of the same mind, she would not oppose his marriage. This time the offer was accepted, and the young Earl was about to step on the steamer when he was recalled by a telegram announcing his fiancée's illness. He stepped back on to the quay, and this time the old Countess hardened her heart for ever.

The Earl eventually came to Europe with his wife, but he did not go to Castle Grant. Caroline gave him a small allowance, but it was so small that for several years the Clan Grant was much exercised in its mind lest she should leave the estates away from the rightful heir.

Again the Countess did the right thing. She left the estates in the line of succession, but she made a will which ensured that the grand-nephew who had flouted her wishes should never enjoy more than a strictly limited allowance and which deprived his heir or heiress from entering into the full rights of the estates until the age of forty.

This brief account of an involved family history does but scant justice to a lady who in her own way was the most remarkable woman in the Highlands and whose virtues can be appreciated only with full knowledge of the times in which she lived. Undoubtedly she was imperious, regarding her wishes as law throughout her domains. She had a sturdy contempt for governments, and, when the Great North of Scotland Railway wished to run a line through part of her property near Cullen, she fought both the company and the government to the last ditch. When the line was eventually made, she never used it on her journeys to Grantown, preferring the more distant Highland Railway station at Portessie. There is a local legend that the only time she rode on the Great North of Scotland Railway was when she was carried in her coffin from Cullen to Castle Grant. The story is not correct. It is, however, true that the Highland Railway was so pleased by the Countess's feud with a rival railway that they built her a private platform near Castle Grant, and this platform she always used on her journeys between her two residences.

Occasionally there were rash spirits among her subjects who questioned her infallibility. There was one old minister who, greatly daring, would give out such texts as "the earth is the Lord's and all that therein is", and would then deliver an hour's sermon on the difference between heavenly and earthly landowners in the fulfilment of their duties. But by the vast majority of her tenants she was loved with much the same veneration and pride as the British public lavished on Queen Victoria in the closing years of that great widow's life, and because of her devotion to her own and her tenants' interests she enjoyed a respect which the absentee landowners of to-day will never know.

She was the last of the great feudal chiefs. Long before her death in 1911 she herself had been conscious of the fact, for beside the great mausoleum which held the earthly remains of her husband and her son she had built a second mausoleum to house weaker and less worthy Seafields. James, the 9th Earl, is already buried in the new mausoleum. This ingenious distinction is not a novel idea. Two years ago, when I was visiting the tombs of the Sultans in Djokja in Java, I noticed a curious grave which seemed to be built half inside the temple and half outside. I asked the reigning Sultan's equerry who was with me to explain this strange monument. It was a grave. It had been built in this manner on purpose. It sheltered the remains of a former Sultan's son-in-law who had rebelled against his father-in-law and had therefore been excluded from the full privileges of royal burial.

Caroline herself was buried beside her husband and her son, and the mausoleum was then sealed for such earthly time as granite will endure. Her grand-nephew, a shy, pleasant man who made himself very popular, did not live long to enjoy his reign at Castle Grant. In the war he was a captain in the Cameron's and was killed in France in 1915 while walking beside my cousin, Ian Macgregor. He was succeeded by his daughter Nina, who is now Countess of Seafield in her own right, although she will have to wait ten more years before she is entirely free from the restrictions of the old Countess's will.

During those years in the Highlands I met more exalted personages than members of the peerage. Our various houses in the Delliefure district were close to the main road to Tulchan, where King Edward VII and King George V used to come to shoot with the Sassoons. My brother and I saw them several times, and long before we were in our "teens" we ran straight into King Edward driving into Grantown in an open carriage. The road was deserted, and, as he passed, we stood at attention with our fishing rods sloped like rifles. As he acknowledged the salute, the King smiled broadly, thus making two small loyalists more loyal than ever.

My own loyalty took a curious form. When he came to Tulchan, King Edward always used to order a suit of Highland tweeds from A. C. Grant, the local outfitter, who took a pride in pointing out to his clients the material chosen by the King. It was this material which I selected when my grandmother generously offered to pay for a new knickerbocker suit. I was bitterly disappointed when my mother, a safe judge in such matters, insisted on a more sombre pattern.

Tulchan, too, was the scene of a narrowly averted tragedy in one of the great ducal families of England. It was while he was staying with the Sassoons that the late Duke of St. Albans went salmon fishing in the Spey below the house and was swept off his feet by the current. The river was in semi-flood, and his Grace, clad in breast waders, was being rapidly carried bottom upwards to his doom, when, the stream fortunately bringing him near the edge, the present Earl of Rosslyn, then a young man with a strong arm and a good eye, neatly gaffed him by the posterior and with little loss of blood brought him safely to the bank.

The Sassoons, who lived at Tulchan, have long since gone to their last rest. The famous house is now being pulled down, and the shooting and the fishing have been let on a long-term lease to Sir Ian Walker, who is one of the most popular shooting-tenants in the Highlands.

But of all persons, great and small, who flitted across the stage of my Highland life the one who made the greatest impression on my mind and on my heart was my grandmother. She belonged to that breed of women of whom Neil Munro wrote: "It's milk o' your mother that fills ye wi' steel."

She herself was made of steel. She had sailed for New Zealand on the day after her marriage and had been held up on the way by a mutiny on her ship. She had roughed it with her husband among gold diggers and sheep shearers, and her first child, as she liked to tell her grand-daughters, was born in a bullock-cart.

She had her hard side and other faults as well. Her business ability, which was strongly impressed on my youthful mind, was, I realise to-day, exaggerated by her flatterers. But she had an indubitable genius for money-making and for taking risks. Until her death she wrote the clearest of hands, and she knew her Bible as well as any Presbyterian minister. She had no sense of aesthetic values, but she faced adversity with rock-like courage and without complaint. As a mother and a grandmother she was an imperious autocrat who had her favourites. She had, however, the rare merit of remaining faithful to them. She paid an exaggerated worship to success, and her joy was supreme when her favourite son, Alister, who had been much criticised by the family for his extravagance, made a substantial fortune for her and for himself as a pioneer of the plantation rubber industry. I can see her now sitting on her chair in her Edinburgh home and unburdening her soul to me: "My boy, I have been much criticised. But what I say is this. Where should we all be now but for Alister?" It was the triumph of the punter who, after a long series of failures, has at last pulled off a successful double and whose gambling sins are thereby hardened beyond redemption.

I was, I think, her favourite grandson, and, during my

brief months of glory in Russia, I too enjoyed the full measure of her favour and of her generosity. She died when I was entering the difficult post-war period of my life. From my own point of view it was perhaps for the best. She would not have approved my choice of popular journalism as a career.

I owe her much, and of all the host of my relations she remains in my memory as the outstanding personality and strongest character. She was nearly eighty-four when she died. Her mother lived to ninety-six and her sister, my grand-aunt Mary, who is still alive, is now in her ninety-sixth year.

The Highlands of those days produced a hardy stock, and those who survived the perils of infancy might reasonably expect to exceed four score. Among the Grants and Macgregors who lie buried on both sides of the Cromdale hills there is one family grave which bears the names of a father and mother and their four children. The inscriptions run as follows:

Donald Grant	aged 80
Sarah, his wife	aged 86
Charles	aged 75
Helen	aged 92
Cuthbert	aged 89
and Grace	in her 101st year.

Charles, the eldest son, was the only member of the family who did not reach the age of eighty. Perhaps his brother and sisters were conscious of some stigma in this early demise, for after the 75 opposite Charles's name appear in brackets the explanatory words "after thirty-six years in the West Indies".

CHAPTER SIX

IT IS IN the nature of the Gael to regret the vanished days. All too willingly he lets his mind linger in a past which to generations of Highlanders since time immemorial has always seemed more glorious than the present. It is this tendency to repine and to regret that has given him the reputation of being a mystic and a poet, and, if these things be the essence of poetry, then every Gael has poetry in his soul even if he lacks the words to express it.

This passion for the past is a weakness of all Highlanders. It is a weakness of my own which I have never sought to deny. I yield too readily to the influence of the sunset instead of concentrating on the glories of the sunrise. Sometimes I wonder if the Highlands ever had a sunrise, and then in an examination of conscience I try to analyse the motives which impel me and other Scottish exiles to return year after year to the same harbourage of our own imagining. To many of us the motive of escape from toiling for the foreigner is strong, for, in spite of his vaunted independence and material success, the Scot is always a servant in a foreign land, and nowhere more so than in England. How large a part has vainglory played in this return of the native? I have met the vain Scot who likes to return to the croft where he was born, to see his relations left behind in the struggle for material prosperity, ploughing the fields or reaping the hay with handscythes, and to glory openly in his own strength which has raised him to higher things than these. But the glory-hunters are few. Nor does their vanity bring more than a momentary reward. Highland sentiment has one great weakness. It is grudging to success. And it rightly resents the son who has gone out into the world and who returns to try to play the laird over the companions of his youth.

There is, however, a far stronger motive than these. It is perhaps best expressed in the old Celtic saying that in the end life returns to the beginning. As we grow older, the yearning to go back to our beginnings becomes peremptory and all-compelling. It is strongest of all in the hour of sickness or of approaching death, and there can be few Scots who have read Mr. Cunninghame Graham's *Beattock for Moffat* without reacting to the feelings of the exile for whose lungs the smoke of London has been "ower muckle" and whose last earthly hope, as the train carries him up the high incline to Beattock, is to see his native town before he dies.

In my own case, I have been too great a wanderer to have a real home, but since the war I have gone back almost yearly to find my beginnings in Tomintoul. The village is the high-est in the Highlands, but it does not always commend itself to visitors. In her famous Journal Queen Victoria described it as "the most tumble-down, poor-looking place I ever saw —a long street with three inns, miserable dirty-looking houses and people, and a sad look of wretchedness about it". Perhaps the Queen was in a bad humour on the day of her visit, although I have heard a young Englishman, who mea-sured happiness in shillings and pence, express a similar ver-dict only a year ago. Everything depends on one's angle of vision, and mine is nostalgic from the moment that I leave the train.

On my way from some distant station, generally Avie-more or Grantown, for the village has still no railway, I pass the farm where more than a hundred years ago my Macgregor forbears wrested their simple living from the soil. It stands on a little plateau overlooking the river Avon as it emerges from a gorge clad with silver birches. Although every tree and stone belongs to the Duke of Richmond, and shooting lodges control the fishing rights of most of the river, the water here is free. To the south there is an unim-peded view of the green glen through which the river twists and turns in its fierce course from the Cairngorms, and the distant scene is dominated by the pimply crest of Ben Avon, forming what more than one unbiased writer has described as the greatest picture in the Highlands. Away to the north-east stretches a rolling panorama of heather and bleak hill-side leading to the Lecht and to the pass through the mountains to Braemar.

It is a country such as Shakespeare described with great accuracy in Macbeth. He may even have seen it with his own eyes, for it is known that his company of players travelled as far north as Aberdeen.

Behind the farm there is a pine wood to shelter the house from the winter blasts, and to the west the eye looks on the broad vista of the hills of Cromdale with their two cairns dominating the horizon. One of these cairns I helped to erect for King Edward the Seventh's Coronation and from the Balmenach side climbed the hill by night when my uncle's elder daughter Ena, then a child of ten, lit the Coronation bonfire. Small wonder that my great-grandfather left his Tomintoul farm to cross this range, for of all the mountains which impel a man to climb and see what is on the other side, I know none which are so inviting as these brown hills of Cromdale.

And always when I come to Tomintoul, every morning and every evening I walk the few hundred yards from the village to the farm to watch the green corn waving in the wind and the sun shining on the gorse with the racing clouds tracing dark shadows on the heather. It is a corner of quietness which the cars passing on the road above do not disturb, and never does it fail to induce in me a rapture of mind inspired as much by the beauty of the scene as by the spirit of the past which lingers over it.

Nor is this enchantment a mere passing glory of the summer. It is present in all seasons, and its charm is perhaps greatest when a heavy fall of snow covers the ground and the mountains, wraith-like and seemingly twice their real size, assume the ethereal grandeur of the Himalayas. The fir trees cast a bluish light on the snow-clad moor. The river, losing its silver colour, twists like a black thread through a great field of white, and the strange silence of the snow is more stimulating to thought than the warmest tints of the Mediterranean.

These are holy moments, but I keep them to myself. The villagers may know that I have some vague connection with Tomintoul but they have no idea what that connection is. The farm is my secret. It is nearly a hundred and fifty years since my forbears left it and in a Highland village a hundred years are already beyond the bourne of time and memory.

Quietly I amuse myself by trying to gather the scraps of folklore which can still be picked up from the old men. Less than a hundred years ago Macgregor was the commonest name in the Tomintoul district. Macgregor families were so numerous that they had to be distinguished by nicknames. To-day, not one is left. But the name lives in legends which are fanciful and in stories which have departed little from the truth.

Within the memory of living man there was one Macgregor who was known as Warlock Willock. His title of warlock or wizard came from the possession of a healing stone, which had come down to him from an ancestor. It had an amazing history. In those days a kelpie, the horse-shaped sprite which inhabits Highland streams and lochs, had enticed several people to their doom by inviting them to a ride on its back and then plunging with them into the depths of the water. Then came the Macgregor forewarned and forearmed. When the kelpie gave its usual invitation, the Macgregor drew his sword and cut off the kelpie's bridle. In order to get it back, the water-sprite offered him a magic stone which would heal anyone except himself.

So much for the legend and now for the truth. My Macgregor ancestor, who was alive until seventy years ago, had a healing stone which he used to his own advantage. One of his rules was that the stone would not operate without a fee; his other rule was that the amount of the fee must never be disclosed. He had numerous clients. They included farmers with sick cattle and sterile women who came from centres as distant as Aberdeen.

This Macgregor is described in a private pamphlet of those days as a gentleman in that he kept a pair of staghounds, did no work, and drank whisky. He also made whisky—of course illicitly. On one occasion when his farmhouse was full of kegs of newly distilled whisky his wife, who was keeping watch, announced to him that Gillespie, the preventive officer, and six soldiers were coming over the brow of the hill.

It was impossible to move the whisky. But Warlock Willock was a man of resource. The village tailor happened to be with him at the time, so Warlock bribed him with a sack of potatoes to take off all his clothes, creep into bed, and pretend that he was dead.

In a few minutes Gillespie arrived at the door, where Warlock Willock met him with a long face. His brother had died of smallpox. The preventive officer must not come in. He himself was taking snuff every minute to ward off any risk of infection.

"Warlock," said Gillespie, "I did not know you had a brother."

"Yes," said the Macgregor. "He's been in the South for years. But he came back last week, and now we have this terrible tragedy."

"Where's your snuff-box?" said Gillespie. Warlock produced it, and, taking a large pinch, Gillespie walked over to the bed, pulled back the sheet, and sprinkled the snuff under the tailor's nose.

Up sprang the tailor, and Gillespie, roaring with laughter, called in the soldiers.

"Look, lads," he said. "I'm a greater man than Warlock. He can heal the sick. But I've raised a man from the dead."

He was so pleased with his joke that he went off to tell the tale to the neighbours, quite forgetting to search for the whisky. When he came back, Warlock Willock had removed it to a safe hiding-place.

To-day, Warlock Willock's stone has disappeared, and local experts differ regarding the place and even the stream in which the kelpie lived. But below the old farm of my own immediate Macgregor ancestors there is a deep pool with a strong under-current which a year or two ago dragged a boy down into its depths. As far as I know, it has never been called the kelpie pool. It is a long way from Warlock Willock's old farm. But, although it is a favourite lie for salmon, I never fish it.

Since the Creation, the sound of running water has gladdened the heart of man. But those Highland rivers have many moods, and the roar of Spey or Avon or Dulnain in flood will strike terror into the hearts of all but the bravest. It is, however, at night that they enter into the full majesty of their mysterious charm, and only a wholly unimaginative man can return alone from an evening's fishing without feeling around him the enveloping presence of the supernatural. The mist which rises from the river-bed twines itself into shadowy, spiral wraiths. The great granite boulders, springing to life in the half-light, assume eerie human shapes until one can almost see Finn and his wife tearing the waters apart with giant stride.

Even the stranger to these parts yields to this spell of the uncanny, and Highland superstition has invested these stones with a wealth of legend. Above Tomintoul there is a curious boulder. According to local legend it marks the place where in a sterner age a priest was burnt for making advances to a girl. Another stone by the roadside bears a half-obliterated date. It may have been a boundary mark; it may shelter the bones of a favourite dog. But to the water bailiff it is the tombstone of a Highland officer who was stabbed to death by his own men for cowardice after the Battle of Cromdale.

Farther south the hills to Carrbridge have a sinister reputation for the cloudbursts which they bring down. Scientists explain this spouting of the heavens by the peculiar mineralogical properties of these hills. But never a bridge is carried away but local superstition recalls the witch who was put to death over two hundred years ago and who, at the stake, vowed as a proof of her innocence to sweep Carrbridge from off the face of the earth. She has not yet established her innocence, but twice within my lifetime she has unloosed the skies to spread destruction over the countryside and to hurl a train into the roaring flood below.

Those who dwell in cities will smile at these interpretations of natural phenomena. But I believe with Lorenzo de Medici that a man who has no hope of another life is already dead for this life, and here by these Highland rivers I realise as nowhere else the fulness of my insignificance in the presence of higher things.

I had a curious experience of the effect of environment on the imagination. After the war I first revisited Tomintoul in 1919, and, eager to recapture the joys of my youth, I set out for a long day far up the Conglass burn which rises in the narrow neck of the Lecht pass. It is a grim and lonely valley, but it has been the scene of more than one drama in history. Through its defiles Montrose marched his men, and after the "Forty-Five" one of Wade's officers built the inevitable road which helped to keep the Highlands in subjection. The valley contains deposits of iron ore and manganese, and more than two hundred years ago mad-dogs of Englishmen from York formed a company to smelt the ore and to transport it over fifteen miles of roadless hill and moor to Abernethy. Their spirit of adventure was greater than their judgment, and, although they worked the mine for some years, they ran it at a loss and finally decamped. And until comparatively recent times the valley provided a safe shelter for the illicit distillation of whisky.

At the time of my visit the Lecht road had not been made passable for motor cars, and I fished the whole day without seeing a living soul. As I rested towards evening, I was interested in a lonely, uninhabited cottage which stood at the corner of the entrance to a dark glen. My fancy took wings, and that night I sat down and wrote a short story called *The Mask*. In it I described my meeting with an imaginary inhabitant of the cottage. He dodged me all day, but in the end I made friends with him through his dog. He was an officer who had had his face shot away in the war and who had found in this silent glen a shelter where he could hide his shapeless ugliness from the sight of his fellow-creatures.

Within a year the cottage was to be known all over Britain. In May of 1920 an out-of-work Englishman came to Tomintoul. He was modest and pleasant in his manner. He was fond of music. He described himself as an ex-Service man, and the hospitable villagers were kind to him. With their help he obtained work on the deer-forest at Inchrory. But hard work was not to his liking, and presently he was found occupying my lonely cottage up the glen. Again the villagers, sorry for an ex-Service man down on his luck, made no attempt to interfere with him, and here he lived unmolested for some weeks until he began to tear down the nearest farmer's sheep-pens for firewood. This was too much for the farmer, who, wanting to stop this destruction, went off to consult Mackenzie, the Lecht keeper, who had nominal control of the cottage, which had been built originally as a watcher's shelter. The two men then enlisted the village policeman and all three set out for the cottage.

It was evening, and, candle in hand, they made their way across the burn to the cottage. They went in. The man had a bed drawn across the door and was lying between the bed and the fire. Although the policeman had no intention of taking any further action than giving the man a warning, he assumed a stern look as he asked the uninvited tenant his name.

'Williams," answered the man quietly.

"Well," said the policeman, "you've no business here and you've no right to burn other people's wood. You'd better come along with me to the village."

Again the man betrayed no nervousness, but asked politely

if he might collect his belongings from a back room. The permission was granted. As he disappeared into a narrow corridor, the others followed him. Then, turning suddenly and pulling out a revolver, he fired a series of shots point-blank at the three men.

The farmer was badly hit in the side above the hip. Mitchell, the policeman, was shot through the left shoulder. By some miracle Mackenzie, who had been holding the candle, was unhurt.

Meanwhile, the Englishman had made his escape, and the last Mackenzie saw of him was when he stopped to light a cigarette before mounting his bicycle and riding off over the Lecht pass to Braemar and the south.

The man was Percy Toplis, the English Dillinger, who had been wanted for some weeks for the brutal murder of an Aldershot chauffeur whose car he had then stolen.

Toplis ended his life as fiercely as he had lived it. A few days after leaving the cottage he was shot on the hills near Penrith after a running fight with the police which ended only when he ran out of ammunition. He was the first of the English gangsters of the American type, and he lost his life through typical gangster vanity. He had among his belongings a diary in which he had chronicled all his misdeeds, and this diary, if found, would have sent him straight to the gallows.

It is a lesson which as a lifelong diarist I should, but shall not, take to heart.

CHAPTER SEVEN

I DO NOT wish to give the impression that my interest in the Highlands is purely egotistical or confined to incursions into the past. It is the poorest of God's creatures who has no zest for the present and the future, and I have no wish to be labelled with my own definition.

I have an insatiable curiosity about the lives of the people around me, and apart from this curiosity the people of Tomintoul have a special claim on my interests and pre-occupation. I have studied their problems with the same scrutiny and, I hope, the same detachment that during my official career I brought to bear on the economic and socio-logical problems of foreign countries. And as the problems of Tomintoul are in miniature the problems of all the High-lands they should go deeper below the skin of every Scot and, for that matter, of every Englishman than the problems of Moscow or Berlin or Rome or Valencia. For they con-cern, not the preference for a particular system of govern-ment, but the survival of a race which is dying on our own doorstep.

Books on Scottish villages are of two kinds. One kind, and it has had a long run, wallows in the slush of sickly senti-mentalism. The other tries to imitate the stark brutality of *The House With The Green Shutters* in which that wayward genius, George Douglas Brown, supplied a fierce and neces-sary correction to the kail-yard school. It would be easy to write in either vein about Tomintoul. For a village is very like a public school. It is a microcosm of its own. The longer one lives in it, the more one loves it and exaggerates its vir-tues or the more one hates it and distorts its faults. And if the truth lies halfway, one must steer a middle course between naive idealism and jaundiced realism in order to find it.

In Tomintoul the summer visitor sees only the virtues, for the Gaels like the Slavs wear their graces on the surface and keep their vices deep down. He is delighted to learn that the population, once predominantly Catholic but now equally divided, has no religious differences. He hears Catholics extol the musical prowess of the Presbyterian minister, and he is indeed a great musician. From Protestants he hears a eulogy of the gentleness of good Father Auer who, since his name at once suggests Pater Noster, is known to the whole village as "The Lord's Prayer". He is not told that the Presbyterian minister's Catholic-Presbyterian Highland choir broke up because of the same apathy that has overtaken all the Highlands, nor does he learn that sometimes on Saturday nights youths in their cups will start a religious discussion which ends in quarrels if not in blows. He does not see that, through indifference and lack of fixity of outlook, the youth of Tomintoul has lost the faith of its fathers, that the Presbyterian Church is almost empty on Sundays, and that, if the Catholics still come to hear Mass, the winter club for young men is neglected, the young men preferring philandering and gambling to the innocuous diversions of billiards and ping-pong.

He sees a vast group of happy children gathering in the square to listen to the strains of some itinerant band and, happy in himself because he is on holiday, he concludes that all is well with Tomintoul and that here is one blessed Highland village on which the curse of depopulation has not fallen. Unless he is of an inquiring mind, he will not discover that this infantile army is composed of orphans from the slums of Glasgow and Edinburgh, that this army now constitutes about a quarter of the total population of Tomintoul, and that the "locals" are eagerly glad to receive the weekly eight shillings and sixpence which the Corporations of those cities pay for each child's upkeep.

In the evening, while he watches the setting sun flooding the hills with light, he will see men still working in the shadows of the valley below and children driving the cattle home, and his heart will be gladdened by the contemplation of this honest toil. He will not know that every enlightened farmer who tries to introduce any form of co-operative agriculture is up against a brick wall of obstinacy, and that, if three farmers agree to sell their honey at a fixed price, one of the three will immediately try to steal a march on his fellows by offering his honey for less.

Indeed, in the summer the villagers are too busy making money out of the tourist to have time to reveal their weaknesses. It is in the long winter, when there is little to do, that parochial narrowness asserts itself and that they wrangle among themselves over such weighty matters as Sunday golf and the uses to which the Memorial Hall is to be put.

These are faults which are not confined to Tomintoul. They are common to every agricultural community and, indeed, to all small units including most families. They weigh heavily or fall lightly off the back according to the depression or buoyancy of individual temperament.

In this respect Tomintoul is rather better than most villages. There is a deal of kindness and much that is lovable in the character of its inhabitants, and on the whole Catholics and Presbyterians, especially when the priest and the minister are men of common sense, mix more amicably than one might expect in a country with the religious traditions of Scotland. The blight which has settled on it comes from deeper-rooted evils. They are the decline of agriculture and the inertia and lack of initiative that has come with it.

For many years now the failure to give adequate protection to agriculture has drained the Highlands of its best human stock. Less than a hundred years ago, in the one glen between Inchrory and Tomintoul alone, there were four hundred and fifty people living by the land. It would be vain to pretend that they lived luxuriously. Meat was a rare treat and tea an unknown luxury. Their fare was mainly milk, potatoes and oatmeal, and, if they lived frugally, they were affluent not because they possessed much but because their wants were few. Were they unhappier because they had no radio and no dance hall? I doubt if any young man in Tomintoul would admit that he was satisfied to-day. And they, at any rate, made few complaints. Their physique was good. A Tomintoul man, writing home from the south seventy years ago, does not seem to have found happiness there. At all events he compared his Highland compatriots more than favourably with the town folk of the Sassenach. "For bodily strength and endurance of hardship", he wrote, "they might be backed against an equal number of the best men, reared on roast beef, that England could produce."

Of the four hundred and fifty souls who once inhabited this glen only a score are left to-day, and they include the proprietor of the deer forest and his keepers. With depopulation has come a new curse. The young men will not work on the land. As the older men die off, farms go back to waste or are amalgamated with others for pasture, and the young men, unable or unwilling to emigrate, hang about the village. And the same story can be told of every glen in the Highlands.

In my own boyhood in the Highlands I heard much talk about Canada and Australia and New Zealand, and there was similar talk in most Highland farms and crofts. And because they knew the secrets of the land and of hard work, men went out to the Dominions and made good. To-day, no one speaks of the lands overseas. There is a magnet nearer home which now attracts the young men, and it is a perverted magnet, for it points south to London. Ambitions do not aim high. They do not reach beyond cigarettes, a girl, an easy job, and, of course, noise and garish lights, and at the present moment the two most delectable careers in the minds of Tomintoul youth are those of lorry-driver and asylum attendant, because two Tomintoul lads wandered to London and found employment as a lorry-driver and an asylum warder. The politicians may talk glibly of emigration schemes, but even if the Dominions could take the whole population of the Highlands, the men would be little better than the rejected misfits of the cities. Not only will they not go back to the land; they have forgotten how to work it, and in the village school agriculture has no place in the new education.

I believe firmly that it is the duty of every Government to protect its people from starvation, but I cannot help contrasting the Highland spirit of the past with that of the present. Forty years ago there were men in all these districts who would have gone to any shifts rather than seek parish relief. To-day, the old spirit of independence is gone, and the smartest lad in the village is the one who gets on the "dole" quickest. It is not a difficult problem, for in these parts employment in the distilleries and on the roads is largely seasonal. And here the unemployed man lives comparatively well. In the great cities he has to spend most of his benefit on rent. But here in the Highlands rent is a minor consideration. If a youth pays his parents five shillings a week for his keep, they are content, and he has ten shillings for Anzora cream, a second-hand motor bicycle, and his fares to football matches and dances. The wages of an agricultural labourer are little more, and the village Aleck is smart enough to appreciate the advantages of leisure.

Many remedies have been suggested for a state of affairs whose grimness and bleakness have long been recognised by every Scot who puts the interests of his country before his own. Successive Governments have been blamed for their failure to promote by every means in their power an agricultural revival, and, indeed, it is hard to absolve Governments which have never been able to make up their minds whether they really wish to increase home production or to let it decline and die in order to avoid trouble with foreign governments over the import of foreign foodstuffs. It is perhaps the greatest weakness of democracies, that, with their system of vote-catching, they are unable to force through any long-term policy which may affect adversely the pockets of the immediate generation. Yet only a long-term policy can save and restore agriculture.

There are many who rail against the great landowners. They are accused of shutting off large areas of hill-land which were formerly used for sheep, and, by the restrictions which they impose on tourists, of preventing the Highlands from being converted into a second Switzerland. There is some truth in these complaints. The old land-owning families who understood their tenants are rapidly disappearing. Many have become de-nationalised. Some have been taxed out of existence. Others have squandered their substance by their own extravagance. To-day, most of the land between Perth and John o' Groats is owned by the insurance companies who find it hard enough to collect the interest on their mortgages. In some cases the old landowners have been replaced by the new plutocracy, and the change has not improved the relations between owner and tenant. There are landowners, especially among the industrial magnates who have recently acquired Highland estates, who become property-mad. They erect fierce notices stating that they have stocked their lochs at great expense and that they will defend their rights with the utmost vigour. They offer large rewards for information which will lead to the conviction of anyone tampering with their notice boards. They put gates across existing rights of way and wage bitter feuds with the local villagers. The feud is taken up. The villagers repay arrogance with dislike. But it is not the natural dislike of the toiler, who wins a precarious living from the soil, for the idle aristocrat who does nothing but collect his rent. It is the rancour and the envy of the idle "have-nots" for the idle "haves".

Such unpleasantness, however, is comparatively rare. Most of the shooting tenants are Englishmen or Americans. Like Queen Victoria they regard the Highlands as a magnificent and romantic background for a holiday provided that a proper seclusion is guaranteed. But they pay generously, and the Gael, if he does not respect them, accepts their money with a subservience that is as degrading as it is inevitable. It is true that during the holiday months of August and September most of the mountain peaks of the Highlands are barred to the tourist. But even if free access were given, I do not see what the conversion of the Highlands into a vast and prosperous tourist centre would do for the preservation of the once characteristic virtues of the Highland race.

There are also critics who blame the Highlander himself, holding that any hope of revival must depend in the first instance on Highland effort and Highland self-assertion. This is a truism, but the root of the evil lies deeper. When all is said and done, it is the Scot who is primarily responsible for the present state of the Highlands and, indeed, of Scotland itself. It was the industrial revolution and the selfishness of the Scottish industrialist which caused the decline of agriculture. It was the Scottish industrialist who imported cheap Irish labour and who insisted on cheap food in order to maintain the advantages of low wages. And now that industry has begun to move southwards, many Scots engaged in industry and in the financial operations connected with it have marched south too, in mind, if not in body, in a scramble for personal security. Not only do they successfully close their eyes to the problems of their own country, but—and I think this is not an over-statement—they are often ready to assure English politicians that these problems are non-existent or, at least, not so serious as some of their countrymen suggest.

They are the first, too, to shudder at the mere mention of even the mildest scheme of decentralisation, and more than one has said to me: "Man Lockhart, I thought you had more sense than that. If I believed for one second there was any chance of daftness like that going through, I'd cross the Border and become an Englishman." And their misgivings are natural. They are afraid lest, given the opportunity, the monster of ugliness which they have created will rise and devour them. The religious wars which rent Scotland during centuries may have a modern counterpart in social wars.

Every Scot is a nationalist at heart—which is not the same

as saying that he is a member of the Scottish National Party. I am not a member of that Party and, as I do not like political parties, I do not suppose that I ever shall be. But I admit that I have found it a useful pin-prick to my own complacency. I think that it can serve the complacent consciences of many other Scots in the same capacity. My own creed is a simple one. I am not a Conservative, because I dislike class privilege and the tyranny of money and also because I know too many Conservatives, who, when they talk of the necessity of conserving order, are thinking only of the conservation of their own order. I am not a Socialist, because my reason rebels against the domination of the conduct of the nation's affairs by the lowest common denominator of intelligence and also because Russia has shown the world that with the abolition of capitalism the exploitation of man by man does not cease. I do believe sincerely and passionately that agriculture is not even partly an economic question. Its major aspect is or should be the aspect of race survival. I believe that this is a fundamental truth which, like Christianity, nearly every man acknowledges in his secret heart. Since the beginning of historical time no race has survived without a healthy agricultural population to replenish its wasted human stock. In Scotland the life-blood of that healthy population has been the farmer, the shepherd and the fisher. And when I see the Highland farms falling in year after year and the empty shepherds' cottages; when I hear the Morayshire fishermen praying to God for the deliverance which the Government denies them, I register a solemn vow not to vote for any Parliamentary candidate who will not pledge himself to the full protection of our Scottish agriculture and our Scottish fishing rights.

The Anglicisation of Scotland is manifest in many forms. But I think that it strikes me most forcibly in Tomintoul. For there a process of regimentation is taking place with staggering rapidity. The solid reading which was once the mental fare of the Gael is a thing of the past. The old books on theology and philosophy have disappeared. Their place has been taken by English thrillers and English detective stories, and on Sundays large crowds of young men and girls wait outside the postmaster's shop for the cheap sensationalism of the English Sunday newspapers.

In my youth the Highland games, now sadly artificial, did something to encourage local piping and local dancing. To-day, the last local piper has put away his pipes, and his son plays the saxophone. In the dance halls the young men and women sway to the languorous notes of a modern waltz, and in the square the boys whistle *Goodnight, my Love* and the Broadway tunes of the previous year. In my boyhood everyone in Tomintoul spoke of the River A'an and the Brig o' Broon. Now all the young people say Bridge of Brown and something which sounds like Avven, and no two people agree whether the river should be spelt Avon or Aven. I doubt if there is a man in the village who can read Burns without a glossary, and already in the village school the children mouth their reading lesson in the mincing accents of a B.B.C. broadcaster. Soon they will be talking cockney. The agents of this uniformity are the radio and the gramophone, and, although he cannot be held responsible for what is happening, I cannot refrain from stressing the singular fact that Sir John Reith is an Aberdonian Scot.

I cannot believe that Scotland or, for that matter, the British Empire has anything to gain from this gradual suppression of local individuality and local customs. The charm and some of the strength of the old Germany can be attributed directly to the twenty or more different capitals and free cities, each with its own university, its own theatres and museums, its own traditions, and its own culture. What Nazi-ism with its creed of mass-uniformity has done to destroy local culture in Germany, the mass-civilisation which radiates from London is now doing in Scotland. Edinburgh, the most beautiful capital in Europe, has long lost the atmosphere of a capital city, and of all the numerous Scottish ministers of the Crown there have been few who have shown any more interest in Scottish affairs than that of an ordinary English Member of Parliament.

It is the North—and for my North I shall take here not only the Highlands but all the area north of the Trent—which has given to Britain her pioneers, her inventors and her men of bone and muscle; and with the increasing spread of London culture and London civilisation there has come an inevitable loss of virility.

By many peoples the Scot has been praised for his adaptability. In the Dominions and the United States he is accepted readily as a worthy citizen when the Sassenach is all too frequently dismissed as a "bloody Englishman". I sometimes wonder if adaptability is not the Scot's greatest curse. It may bring him material success in England or overseas, but it signifies national subservience and a lack of national self-assertion which bode ill for his own country. There is a fine national individualism about that "bloody Englishman", and I should feel happier about the future of Scotland if the epithet were applied more frequently to my own countrymen. For too long we have followed the advice of the prophet: "Arise, get you unto the wealthy nation that dwelleth without care."

I admit that the new post-war age has brought a certain prosperity even to the Highlands. The people are better fed. The children no longer go ragged. There is a higher standard of life. But this partial sufficiency is sustained largely by spoon feeding, by subsidised lack of work, and, in many cases, by a subsidised indolence which must lead inevitably to moral stagnation and decline.

Only by the constant assertion of its will-power can a nation hope to survive, and to me the saddest thing in Scotland to-day is the decline of the national will-power. Indeed, the state of the Highlands and probably of all Scotland has gone far beyond such individual remedies as Government schemes for agriculture, smallholdings, electric power and new home industries. It demands a national revival which only a long and united national effort can create. Although I have too much of the Loti temperament in me not to regret a past which is gone beyond recall, I am not wholly pessimistic. It is to educated Scottish youth that I look for the regeneration of the Scottish people.

If the immediate post-war generations were—not entirely through their own fault—unsatisfactory, I see signs of promise in the young men and women who have come of age during the last few years. Certainly they are better equipped and better educated than the youth of my day, and I cannot believe that they lack either the courage or the staying power of their forbears. I like to think that they have been inspired by the post-war revival in Scottish art and literature, and I am certain that from their efforts will come a cultural nationalism which will mean something more than Burns nights, whisky, and the raucous shout of "Feet, Scotland, Feet" at Murrayfield.

I hope that they will be truly national and not parochial, that they will be mindful of Scotland's place in the Empire, that they will remember that we are a mixed race and will therefore resist the narrowing influences of party politics and religious dissensions, and that they will root out from themselves the canker of intellectual snobbishness which is the greatest evil of modern education.

I hope that they will conceive boldly and that they will be always ready to drive their chariot through difficulties. For this is the task and the privilege of youth, and there are too many brilliant men in our Civil Service who are all too adept in providing the politicians with well-reasoned objections to the best of schemes.

Above all, I hope that they will be creative and boldly empirical and that they will not dissipate their energies in destructive criticism and unhealthy introspection. For the surest sign of decadence in a nation is when criticism usurps the place of experiment. It is a pretty good maxim that you get out of life what you put into it, and to-day there is an unhealthy tendency to think more of material standards of living than of moral standards of life.

The future of Scotland is theirs for the asking. It is not the English whom they have to fear but the old and the middle-aged men in their own country who, like the "over fifties" in all countries, put personal security before all other interests. The English are a tolerant people who are a hundred years ahead of the rest of the world in political understanding and political instinct. They will never make the mistake of creating a Sinn Fein movement in Scotland, and to reasonable national demands expressed with united determination they will yield not only with grace but with wise counsels. If hitherto they have neglected Scottish affairs, it is because the Scots themselves have never insisted on a closer attention.

I have only two excuses for these general observations of a Scot who has been too long an exile from his own country. The first is that every man learns his job by experience, and in so far as I have had any training at all, it has been as an observer. The best years of my life have been spent in studying the political, social, and economic trends in various foreign countries, and I find it both natural and seemly to apply the experience I have thus acquired to my own country. Although I should be foolish as well as immodest to claim any prescience or special skill, there are, I think, occasions when the general observations of an outsider are nearer the truth than the data of expert statisticians, who are often too busy counting and measuring the trees to see the shape of the wood.

Were I the counsellor of a foreign government and were I asked to write a confidential report on Scotland, I should have to paint my picture in black colours. I should underline the lack of unity among the population. I should refer to the danger of Scotland becoming little more than the fag-end of the depressed areas of England. And I should be compelled to point out that the Scots have now the poorest physique of any race in Europe. Moreover I know that such reports have been written in such colours by unbiased foreign observers. There is one experienced diplomatist who has compared the post-war Scotland with post-war Austria—a land that has lost faith in itself and now lives on the foreign tourist.

I hope that the picture is exaggerated. But if I were asked to give an example of the decline of survival will-power among the Scottish people, I should cite the case of the road bridge across the Forth. I shall be told that the bridge, like most bridges, is not an economic project. I can give only one answer. I do not believe that there is a single country in the Balkans, in the Baltic, or in South America, whose national dignity would not have had that bridge built long ago. Only this summer in the hotel in Tomintoul I saw an Englishman, a relation of Sir Maurice Hankey, watch a peat fire struggling to burn. He rang the bell and asked for some paraffin. The Highland maid who came in looked at him scornfully. "It's patience you want for peats, not paraffin." To-day, when I see the holiday crowds at North Queensferry waiting in a long queue for the ferry-steamer, I wonder if the Scottish virtues of thrift and patience have been too dearly bought.

My second excuse is the innate love that I have for the land that bore me. There are few Scots who are not bound, however loosely, by this chain and whose own thoughts do not at some time or other in their life echo Rob Roy's confession: "Were I to lose sight of my native hills, my heart would sink and my arm would wither like a fern in the winter's blast."

To most of us our "native hills" mean the one hill or the one range of hills, which, varying hourly in its light and shade, yet ever constant, has looked down on all the changing shadows of our own lives. If to me the hills of Cromdale and the Cairngorms are the very heart of Scotland, it is not because I claim for them any boastful superiority of scenic beauty, but because I feel myself anchored to them, and to the people who dwell in their glens, by the fellowship and heritage of the past.

BOOK IV
THE LAST TERM

"TELL ME, Mr. Wren, what school would you recommend for a boy who has to make his own way in life?"

CHAPTER ONE

HAVING WRITTEN A schoolmaster's homily on the Highlands, I must now go back to my own school days at Seafield. I was just over twelve when I began my last year there as a preparatory schoolboy, and by this time I had reached the stage of being a little "blood". I was near the top of the school; I was a prominent member of the football team, and I had been two years longer in the cricket eleven than anyone else.

I had also made an important advance towards manhood in my home life, for my brother Rufus and I had now been given a study of our own. It was, I think, the biggest study that I have ever had, not excluding the palatial room which I occupied in St. Petersburg when I was Head of the British Mission in 1918. As the school had increased in size, my father had converted some of the large cellars into living rooms, and one of them, a long barrack-like hall large enough to stage an indoor cricket match, had been set aside as our private den. It had a stone floor and very little furniture, and in winter the cold was bitter. But there was a good fireplace in one corner, and here we warmed ourselves by brewing cocoa and roasting the sparrows that we shot with our air-guns.

The cooking was a simple matter once the sparrow was plucked. The only utensils that were required were a plate of melted fat, a spoon, a nail and a piece of string. The nail was hammered into the mantelpiece, just above the centre of the fire. One end of the string was attached to the nail and the other to the sparrow's legs. We then gave the string a few twists so that the bird spun slowly before the red-hot fire. One of us held the plate to catch the gravy that fell from the roasting bird, and the spoon was used to keep on pouring the mixture of fat and gravy over the sparrow until he was ready for eating. I have eaten many tougher and less palatable pheasants, not to mention the stringy chickens of Malaya.

Actually, this craze for cooking sparrows came, I think, a year later. At any rate we learnt the trick from a delicious book which for several years accompanied me not only to the Highlands but to school. It was by a Winchester master called Hewett and its title was *The Open-Air Boy*. It dealt with bird-nesting, butterfly-catching, caterpillar-rearing, and of course the whole menagerie of a boy's pets. There was a fine poaching spirit about it. The chapter on angling taught you how to "sniggle" pike with a pole and a wire noose and the chapter on rabbiting and ratting how to set snares, how to handle ferrets, and how to make a catapult that would shoot as straight as a gun. The hints on cooking supplemented the chapter on camping out, which was not then the national hobby that it has now become. Every page was written in a manner, half-instructional, half-reminiscent, that made you itch until you had put every experiment to a personal test. I have no hesitation in describing it as the best open-air book for boys ever written, and I am surprised to learn that it has been out of print for some time. Unless the modern boy has altered in character, I feel sure that a new edition would be a small gold mine to any publisher in the English-speaking world.

The greatest treasures in our study, however, were the bureaus which my father had specially designed for us. They stood about six feet high and were divided into three parts. The top was a bookcase with three shelves. The middle was a folding writing-desk which could be shut and locked without disturbing the papers inside. The bottom was a large cupboard with two partitions. Solidly made, these bureaus descended in due course to my brothers and my sister, have since been used by my second brother's children, and will, doubtless, serve a third generation as well. They were not things of beauty, but they answered a boy's requirements perfectly, and, although I have no strong possessive instincts, I liked mine better than any personal piece of furniture that I have ever bought or that has ever been given to me.

Like most preparatory schoolboys who rise to these intox-icating heights of self-importance, I was entirely devoid of self-consciousness. This means, of course, that I was blissfully and innocently bumptious. In a very simple way my life had run on smooth and harmonious lines, and I saw no reason why this harmony should ever be disturbed. I had no thought for the future, and my father, too busy perhaps, and in any case always inclined to postpone decision, made little attempt to jog my mind. It is true that at one time he threw out vague hints about the Navy. Gordon Walker, one of my Seafield friends, had just passed into the *Britannia*, and his example was held up to me as one worthy of emulation. At Christmas dances, young Troup, now Admiral Troup, resplendent in his cadet's uniform, was pointed out to me as the best-mannered and most self-possessed boy in the room. Prospectuses of Stubbington House, the naval crammer, and pictures of the *Britannia* lying at anchor in the Dart, were dangled before my eyes. The *Britannia*, however, reminded me of the *Mars*, and, after toying mildly with these oblique suggestions, I side-tracked them by meeting my father's indecisive enthusiasm with a more deliberate indecision. As for public schools, I doubt if I had any ideas about them. I was only twelve. In those days, most boys did not go to their public school until they were nearly fourteen. Fondly I imagined that I should have two more years at Seafield and then I should be captain of football and cricket and head of the school. The decision about a public school could easily be left for another year.

During the Easter holidays of 1900 my complacency received a rude shock. One day my father sent for me and announced that in the coming summer term he had arranged for me to go up for the foundationer competitive examina-tion at Fettes College, the leading Scottish public school. These foundationships were reserved for poor boys, and there was a special urgency for my father's decision. His going to Seafield had been a mistake. Scottish parents were not then accustomed to the idea of a preparatory school, especially a boarding school. My father's concession to local peculiarities in taking day-boys and weekly boarders was another handicap, for the few parents who had any experience of preparatory schools rightly regarded Seafield as an unsatisfactory compromise and sent their boys to England. The school, therefore, made little or no profit. My father had then no capital. Owing to the failure of coffee in Malaya, my maternal grandmother had had to finance my uncle Alister all over again in his new and uncertain venture of planting up his coffee estates with rubber and was then in the throes of one of her periodical monetary crises. In any case, she had an army of her own children to support, and the same may be said of my paternal grandfather, who had just added to his financial burdens by marrying for the second time at the age of sixty-nine.

Preparation for the examination did not interfere with my normal life. I was given no special "cramming" for the very good reason that I was still young enough to compete again the next year, and even my father did not regard this first examination as more than a trial experiment. Dressed in a new knickerbocker suit, I made the journey to Edinburgh by myself, and, taking a cab at the Haymarket Station, made my first of many descents from the Dean Bridge, then famous for its suicides, down Comely Bank to the great grey building standing in its own grounds and looking more like a French château than a school. I was impressed by its grandeur, but I had no feeling of awe, regarding my visit as an exciting new adventure and as a pleasant interlude in my Seafield life.

My father had arranged for me to stay with John Salvation Yeo, the most popular of all Fettes masters and then house-master of Carrington. He made me feel almost too much at ease, and that night he had to reprove me and two other examination candidates, with whom I shared a room, for "ragging".

The next morning we were shepherded into the school gymnasium which, for the occasion, had been turned into an examination room. Here I met some forty other boys of all shapes and sizes, and as we stood about waiting to be shown our places I felt sheepish and dejected. Some boys with big heads on frail bodies looked very clever and some, who had brought their own pens, pencils, compasses, and even pencil-sharpeners, I thought must be very efficient. Others again looked very poor and were shabbily dressed. Regarding my own chances as less favourable than ever, I suffered no nervousness. Indeed, the examination itself presented no great difficulties and, as there was a generous time allowance for each paper, I had ample opportunity to study the gymnasium with its bridge ladder, its array of bars, and its large platform with wooden tiers behind it. It seemed a very inferior gymnasium to the one at Broughty Ferry. I did not know then that it also served as the school hall for such celebrations as Founder's Day, and that I should one day be sitting on the platform as a member of the school orchestra and choir.

From time to time during the examination boys would be sent for and would leave the room for ten minutes or so by a side door. My own turn came in due course, and I was taken into a small room where I shook hands gravely with a short, squat man with long hair and a straggling profusion of sidewhiskers. He had a high forehead, a fine aquiline nose, and very white hands. His hair was black; his eyebrows and sidewhiskers were black; his high-cut coat was black; his trousers were black; his gown was black. The only relief to the general blackness was provided by the white collar and the heavy gold chain across his waistcoat. He smiled pleasantly, but in his smile there was a sadness which was further reflected in his care-worn expression. He looked a little like a black penguin. Presently he sat down at a small table and turned over a sheaf of papers. Then he asked me a few questions which came deep down from the back of his throat.

The questions seemed inconsequent. They were mostly about my father and Seafield. I realised instinctively that he was Dr. Heard, the headmaster, and that I was in the presence of a personality of whom I should always stand in awe.

I was glad when this ordeal was over, but it was not the most painful experience of that first visit to Fettes. The disaster which overtook me was unforeseen and unavoidable, but it had a profound effect on my character. The examination lasted two days, and, as the gymnasium was close to the cricket field, we spent the intervals between papers in practising cricket at the nets which were arranged in an even row stretching almost the whole length of the huge field. One of these intervals unfortunately coincided with a school interval, and, while I was batting, a crowd of Fettes boys assembled behind the net. It was the First Eleven net, and the boys applauded every stroke. Thinking that they were genuinely impressed by my prowess, I began to concentrate on style. With my left foot well across I leant forward to off-drive. I late-cut with the quick turn of the wrists which I had learnt from our English masters at Seafield. I ran out a couple of yards to drive a half-volley to the railings, and the clapping became a well-timed chorus! I felt elated. Then the skies of heaven fell in. As I bent down to pick up a ball and throw it back to the bowler, a big boy said contemptuously "bumptious little tick" and walked away. Only then did I understand that the applause had been a huge joke, organised by some ragster in order to enliven the short interval. Realisation killed stone-dead my innocence and my trust in the world, and tears of shame welled up in my eyes. Nevertheless, I continued my knock at the nets, and to my relief the boys soon went back into school.

That evening I discussed the examination papers with the two candidates who were staying with me in Carrington. They seemed to have performed brilliantly, and apparently many of my answers were wrong. I felt more subdued than ever and returned home a changed boy. Even as a child, man is full of vanity. It is not the big things in life which hurt. It is the petty humiliations to our pride which leave the enduring sting of bitterness.

Two weeks later my father received an official intimation that I had passed in second out of twelve successful candidates. The two boys who had shared the room in Carrington with me had failed. The announcement filled me with a vague apprehension.

Fortunately, normal boys do not brood over their minor chagrins, and a score of seventy-nine for the Boarders in the cricket match against the Day-boys did much to restore my self-confidence. There was, too, all the fun of a last term in which one had the satisfaction of having done well and the knowledge that those who presided over our destinies were pleased. Something of the sadness of regret was there as well. Several other boys with whom I had been in daily association for the last five years were also leaving. It was an upheaval of a small but stable world, and, as the upheaval approached, all personal quarrels and animosities were forgotten. All boys respond to the emotions of a leave-taking, and small boys perhaps more readily than big boys. At the prize-giving on the last day, my father read over the list of the term's successes. When he mentioned my name, he stumbled, and I felt a lump rise in my throat. Afterwards we sang "Auld Lang Syne" and then with many professions of lasting friendship we said our goodbyes.

There is no greater fallacy than the sentimental belief that one makes one's life friends at school. The truth is that friendship depends entirely on environment and the association of common interests. Boys who have been boon companions go out into the world, and their courses run in all directions. If they become jute manufacturers, their life friends will also be in jute. If they become diplomatists, they will wander over the face of the earth, making close friends for a few years and then losing them. School friends who meet after a separation of many years dine together and spend one happy evening in talking over old times. If they go their separate ways the next morning, all will be well. The sentimental affection will remain, and at Christmas-time each will remember the other over his glass of port and say perhaps: "By Jove, I must send old 'Snookie' a brace of pheasants." But, if by some accident of fate the reunion is prolonged, disillusionment is inevitable. The two men have drifted too far apart. Their interests and their friends are different, and after that first exchange of reminiscences they find that they have nothing to say to one another.

Since leaving Seafield I have seen almost nothing of the boys who were my companions in those preparatory school days. They were a hardy, efficient band, and, if few have achieved fame, most of them have done well in life. The most distinguished is probably Sir George Cunningham, who, after captaining Oxford and Scotland at rugby football, passed into the Indian Civil Service, was political secretary to Lord Irwin during the latter's difficult period as Viceroy, and is now, at the age of forty-eight, Governor of the North-West Frontier Province. An even better-known name, because it appears on nearly all the picture-postcards of Scottish scenery, is that of W. P. S. Valentine, whose family founded the famous firm of photographers. Journalism is represented by W. Harold Thomson, who is to-day Dundee's press lord. Others are prominent Dundee jute manufacturers, and of these, one at least is in the millionaire class. Others again are liberally distributed among the various professions. For so small a school the list of athletic distinctions is a long one, and includes two Scottish rugby internationals, several trial internationals, half a dozen Oxford and Cambridge rugby Blues, four golfers who have appeared with distinction in the amateur championship, and a Cambridge cricket Blue.

Even longer is the list of greatest honour. In March of 1937 I went back to Seafield. It was my first visit for over twenty-five years. The place seemed to have shrunk. The

greenhouses and the fine old copper beech had been removed. But the sun was shining with the first warmth of
spring. It shone most brightly on the terraced garden plot
above the cricket field. And there in the centre of the rose-
beds stood a little monument dignified by its simplicity and
with its grey stone already softened by the rain and the sea
mist. On its sides were engraved the names of those young
friends of my boyhood who had fallen for the preservation
of a poorer generation and the worst of their own. Among
these names were those of two Cunningham brothers and of
my own brother Norman who, having been by the accident
of my father's various changes of residence at three different
preparatory schools, appears on three different war memorials.

At Seafield I had led a sheltered existence. Now I was to
go out into a new world in which I should have to fend for
myself against new temptations. It was not until far on into
September that the thought in any way troubled my mind.
By a fortunate dispensation boys possess the knack of being
able to divide their school-life and their holidays into water-
tight compartments, and visions of Fettes were not allowed
to obtrude themselves into my dreams of fishing and
shooting in the Highlands. There was, too, all the vain-
glorious excitement of ordering and trying on my school
kit. It gave me my first experience of long trousers, and, to
accustom myself to these strange garments, I wore my
school suits several times in the holidays. As my legs were
woefully short, I must have cut a comic figure. Even my
own sense of dignity suffered from the Eton jacket and top
hat which formed the full-dress attire for the small boys at
Fettes, and I endured with bad grace the chaff of my parents
and of my brothers. But there was compensation for injured
vanity in the magenta and brown jersey and blazer which,
by their shrieking ugliness, stood out prominently in the pile
of clothing laid out on the beds of an empty dormitory.

Soon, I reflected, I should be wearing the colours of the most famous "rugger" school in the world. My proudest new possession, however, was the umbrella which figured in the school list of indispensable articles. True, it would be used for every purpose except sheltering me from the rain. But through my promotion to this new dignity I felt that I had become a man, and, indeed, during my time at Fettes the boys always referred to each other as "men".

Realisation that the holidays were drawing to an end was forced on me by a new habit of my father. He would march me off for a walk by myself. He would talk in general terms of the new life that was opening before me. Although he seemed unable to come to the point, I felt instinctively that he was trying to say something more definite, for, while he talked, he gripped my arm fiercely as though he were afraid of losing me.

He *was* going to lose me, as every father loses his son in the inevitable gulf which comes between them when a boy enters the age of puberty. For even in the age of innocence there are certain things which a boy does not reveal to his father. They increase in number when the boy discovers the secret of sex, and the gulf is never entirely bridged until both father and son have reached an age when passion is spent and sex can be discussed objectively. This barrier is pre-ordained by Nature and is created by the instinctive respect which every son should feel for his father.

Although at the time I had no inkling of my father's difficulties, to-day, as a parent, I suffer from the same restraint in discussing sex matters with my own son. I now feel strongly that this task of enlightenment and of warning should be entrusted, preferably to a sensible doctor, but almost to anyone rather than to the father or mother.

In my own case, I was completely innocent at the age of twelve. School life at Seafield had been clean and healthy. We were taught to work hard and to play hard, and little or nothing was done to stimulate any latent sense of the aesthetic. If I knew that people painted pictures, I did not know the name of a single famous painter; and in a general knowledge paper set to the whole school one boy who afterwards won a scholarship gave as his list of well-known British artists, Florence Nightingale, Queen Victoria, and Prince Albert. There were few feminine influences to soften our Spartan standards. I had then no sister, for I was twenty-one when my only sister was born. Although Christmas parties and juvenile dances were a prominent feature of Broughty Ferry life, and my mother insisted on our going to them, twice as many boys as girls had to be asked, for the very good reason that most boys disliked dancing. I hated it, and, when I was not spending my time in the supper-room or at the buffet, was a sulky wall-flower. I had been only once to the Dundee theatre, and then my father was not present.

His absence was perhaps fortunate, for the play was a musical comedy and provided one family joke which my father might not have understood. In one act the funny man made an appalling retort with a double meaning in answer to the question: "Are there any more at home like you?" It was received in horrified and stony silence by the stolid Dundonians. This silence was broken by a loud and prolonged roar of laughter from my brother Rufus, who, as became a future headmaster, even then took his humour slowly. At first, my aunt, who had given us this treat, was shocked until she discovered that my brother was laughing at something which had happened two minutes previously and which he had suddenly realised was funny.

Minor vulgarities there had been in our Seafield life. Of vice, however, there was none. When, therefore, on my last day at home, my father, bracing his courage, took me into his study and warned me of the dangers to come, everything he said seemed so vague and nebulous that beyond a hazy feeling that somehow Fettes would be different from Seafield, I understood nothing.

CHAPTER TWO

THERE ARE, I suppose, few boys who do not remember their first day at a public school more vividly than any other event in their subsequent career. It is not merely that the experience is sufficiently terrifying in itself to remain clear-cut in the memory. The sense of loneliness which overcomes a boy during those first few hours when he is left to find his own feet makes his mind peculiarly receptive to these first impressions of his new surroundings.

Yet I doubt if the first day of one's first term is as un-pleasant as the first day of the second term. Curiosity is the mainspring of a boy's life, and during the first term there are so many new things to learn that one has little time to feel homesick. At the beginning of the second term, the sense of novelty has been blunted. It is then that the small boy realises to the full both the completeness of his own insignificance and the necessity of conforming to one accepted standard. A public school is a sausage factory. Its job is to turn the product boy into as many similar sausages as possible, and, whatever great headmasters may say at their annual con-ferences, this sausage-making process is the strength and the weakness of the public school system. During his first term a boy is scarcely conscious of the process. If he happens to dislike sausage, it is during his second term that he suffers most from this forcible feeding.

In my own case, I remember only the beginning and end of my first day at Fettes. One afternoon towards the end of September, 1900, my father took me by train from Broughty Ferry to Edinburgh. We drove down to Fettes in a four-wheeler. As we drew up at the main entrance, my father paid the cabman and handed me three half-crowns, which, in addition to my weekly allowance of a shilling, were to be my pocket money for the term. He asked for the hall-porter. Guided by the bearded Skinner, we walked up two flights of stone stairs and were led to a green baize door. We went in, and my father introduced me to my house master. Then, fearful perhaps of his own emotions, he left me abruptly.

I looked timidly round the room while "Johnnie" Coast asked me a few questions and tried to put me at my ease. He seemed almost as nervous as I was, and, indeed, he too was almost a new boy in the sense that he had only recently become a house master. Then there was a knock at the door. Another parent and another new boy entered, and I was turned out into the long stone corridors.

My sense of loneliness was complete, but of the next three hours till prayers I remember nothing except the dank smell of soft soap from the wooden floor of the "prep" room which was to be my home until I reached the dignity of a study. Furtively, like a dog that has just recovered from an attack of hysteria, I watched the older boys as they strolled about arm in arm and exchanged uproarious greetings. Occasionally someone would ask me my name. Sometimes the question would be supplemented by a further request for information. Had I ever played "rugger"? But as soon as the answer was given, the big boy turned away, and I was left severely alone. No one, however, was unkind to me, nor was I subjected to any leg-pulling.

The end of the day was not so pleasant. With two other new boys I was placed in "B" dormitory, a long, narrow room with rows of cubicles on each side. One of these cubicles was to be mine for the rest of my stay at Fettes. It contained a small bed, a washstand, a tin hip-bath, and a narrow recess window with two long drawers beneath it. It was not much bigger than a large dog kennel, and the fitful light of an open gas-jet two cubicles away made reading in bed if not difficult, at least bad for young eyes. But the window faced south and, being situated high up, commanded a superb view of Edinburgh. As I undressed, I watched the lights of the city, friendly yet so distant, with much the same feeling as I have watched the lights of a port from my ship's cabin. Then I crept into bed.

I was, however, not allowed to sleep. Presently a prefect came along and hauled me out for inspection. He had a hair-brush with a handle in his hand. As I stood with the two other new boys in a row, he gave me a hard crack on the cheek with the bristle side of the brush.

"Does that hurt?" he said with a sardonic grin.

In spite of all my efforts to control myself, the tears came into my eyes. I therefore said "yes", and received another crack for crying. Then he transferred his attention to a sturdy red-cheeked boy with broad shoulders and a splendid chest. Crack went the hair-brush. Again there was the grunt of "does that hurt". This time the answer was "no". There was a fiercer blow followed by the same question and the same answer. Then in quick succession the cracks were continued until tiny pearls of blood began to form on the broken skin. But with lips compressed, the boy held out and still said "no."

The new boy, who at once became my secret hero, was Moir Mackenzie. Afterwards he became one of Fettes' and Scotland's greatest forwards. He was a terror on the "rugger" field and in a rough match always gave as good as he got. Rumour has it that there was, later, almost a price on his head in Wales. If there was, it was never collected.

Moir was, and still is, a Sandow of a man. But neither at school nor elsewhere did he ever use his strength unfairly. Indeed, off the football field he had a marvellously kind and cheerful disposition, and I doubt if, even as a prefect, he ever beat a small boy. His courage was proved on a sterner field than Inverleith or Cardiff Arms Park. During the Great War he took part in the Ostende-Zeebrugge raid. He has made a success of life, has a string of six letters after his name, and as Empire Director of the Federation of British Industries is a deservedly popular figure in London and in the capitals of the Dominions.

To-day, I count him as one of my best friends, but I have never admired him so much as on that first night at Fettes when his Highland obstinacy refused to surrender to brute force. Three years after that incident one of the senior boys recited, at Founder's Day, Browning's "An Incident in the French Camp". I did not know the poem then and I listened inattentively to a trying performance until suddenly four lines arrested my attention:

> "So tight he kept his lips compressed
> Scarce any blood came through.
> You looked twice ere you saw his breast
> Was all but shot in two."

Suddenly I saw the whole scene of that first night enact itself before my eyes. And it is of Moir that I always think whenever I hear that poem to-day. The prefect who made Moir compress his lips was a brilliant scholar, and I admit readily that I remember no further instance of rough treatment at his hands. But his genius must have been as wayward as his cruelty; for he fell on hard times, and not very long ago applied to me to help him to obtain employment.

I do not wish to create the impression that in my time Fettes was a hot-bed of bullying. It was not. Indeed, I think that on the whole big boys are less cruel than small boys. There were one or two sadistic fellows in my house, but they were rare exceptions. Nor were they given much opportunity of exercising their minor tortures. There was a wild Irishman who invented a game called "perfect confidence". It consisted in making a small boy stand stock still against a wall while the big boy delivered a series of right-arm punches which he tried to land as near the small boy's nose as possible without touching it. Like a German student in a Mensur duel, the small boy was expected not to flinch. Occasionally the big boy over-shot his mark, and once a small boy's nose was broken in this manner. This martyr suffered in a good cause. After this incident the game was stopped.

There was, too, a thoughtless English boy who, having learnt to flick a wet towel like a whip, practised his new art on the behinds of small boys. He was in my dormitory, and on one occasion was engaged in flicking a group of small boys when the head of the house walked in.

"Let me see if I can do that," he said quietly.

Then he made the big boy undo his pyjamas, and, taking the towel, gave him a good dose of his own medicine. The big boy, at heart a very good fellow, bore no malice. He realised that justice had been done, and afterwards we were left in peace.

And here I should like to pay a tribute to our house prefects. Our house having more than fifty boys, there were generally seven or eight prefects, and their powers and privileges were considerable. They had their own room. They had tea by themselves. They had their own list of special fags and could claim the services of the whole Lower School indiscriminately merely by shouting "fa-ag". They shared with the house-master the duty of superintending the preparation of those boys who had no study, and in the dormitories they were in sole charge. They could give "lines" as a punishment to almost anyone in the house. But no prefect could beat alone. A prefect's caning had to be sanctioned by the head of the house; the permission of the house master had to be obtained, and the execution was carried out by the body corporate of all the prefects, each prefect in turn delivering one stroke of the cane on the victim's behind. It was, in fact, a solemn ritual and was always celebrated after evening prayers. The whole house knew when the sacrifice was going to be performed, for on those occasions the hymn at prayers was always "Through the night of doubt and sorrow".

This system of corporate castigation was an excellent safeguard and in my time was never abused. I was a lazy boy, much addicted to "ragging". Yet during my five years at Fettes I suffered only twice at the hands of the prefects. My first beating was for showing up bought "lines" as my own for an imposition which I had received for "ragging" during preparation. This trick could generally be worked successfully on the less vigilant prefects, but on this occasion, unfortunately for me, the writing bore no trace of similarity to my own. The prefect who reported me was the good-natured A. Y. Campbell. He was a brilliant scholar who, even at school, gave many proofs of the talents which were afterwards to bring him fame as a poet. Like most poets he was not a very strict disciplinarian.

On this occasion I was dealt with very lightly, and the cuts which I received caused little discomfort. My second offence, however, brought sterner retribution. I missed a call-over and, wishing to avoid a tiresome imposition, I persuaded a smaller boy to say "here" when my name was called. Call-over was taken by A. V. Rooth, who was head of the school as well as head of the house. He was a strict but scrupulously fair disciplinarian. The small boy stumbled over his answer and was immediately detected. An explanation followed, and I was hauled up for cross-examination. As I was then a bigger boy, Rooth regarded my offence as a serious one, and this time I had to bite my hand in order not to wince.

As a class of men prefects are like schoolmasters. Some are born to exercise authority and discipline, and their influence lasts beyond their own time. Others are just averagely good and are therefore colourless. Some again have favourites and some indulge in too much sarcasm, and these are rightly unpopular. There are always one or two who, because they are too sensitive and too self-conscious, are physically incapable of maintaining any kind of order. Small boys have a devilish knack of being able to divide schoolmasters and prefects into their separate categories at the first glance. They know instinctively what liberties they may safely take, and woe betide the unfortunate individual who is unable to establish his ascendancy over them in the first hour.

During my period at Fettes the prefects in "College", as my house was called, were a remarkably level-headed lot. Occasionally there would be one whom the exercise of authority would endow with an irritating and hypocritical smugness. But he was the exception. Abuses of power and privilege alike were remarkably few. As fag-masters prefects were tolerably lenient, and fagging itself was light, consisting mainly in making toast for prefects' tea, dusting one's fagmaster's study, and lighting his study fire. During preparation they could be relied on, for they were scholars, to help one over a difficult construction in one's Latin or Greek translation. Indeed, the gentle A. Y. Campbell, if properly approached, would sometimes translate the whole passage set for the next morning, thus sparing the small boy much unnecessary trouble and leaving him free to spend the rest of preparation in reading a book surreptitiously balanced on his knees beneath the desk, or in that vacant idleness which is his special attribute. Other prefects were not to be imposed on in this manner, and firm disciplinarians like John Stevenson, now Canada's leading journalist, Geoffrey Gowlland, a future Scottish "rugger" international who passed high into Woolwich, and A. V. Rooth conducted preparation with more strictness and efficiency than most house masters. They were strong men, efficient and impartial in all they did. I do not remember any of them committing an injustice; and there was no abuse, no case of bullying, with which, if they came across it, they did not deal severely.

Although there are cranks who object to the prefect system, it worked admirably at Fettes or, at least, in "College". Indeed, the only bad feature of the house administration was the toleration of a self-appointed body of sub-prefects who were called "dooks". They were mostly big boys who, through laziness, stupidity, or other defects, had been passed over in the selection of prefects, and in minor ways they exercised an illegal and sometimes tyrannous authority over the small fry in the house. Although I became a "dook" myself, the system had nothing to recommend it. Since the war it has very wisely been abolished.

If fagging was not burdensome and bullying almost non-existent, there was no slacking and no mollycoddling. While I was at school, I remember reading an article in the Loretto magazine, in which Fettes was compared with Athens, while Loretto allocated to herself the rôle of Sparta. If the comparison be confined to the school buildings, it is fair enough. For even in a city so rich in architectural treasures as Edinburgh, Fettes stands out both by the slender grace of its outline and by its commanding site, whereas a visitor to Musselburgh might pass through the town without being aware of Loretto's existence. But as far as régimes are concerned, there is or was little to choose between the two schools.

Certainly life at Fettes was Spartan enough compared with English or even Scottish school standards. New boys had to do a circle on the bar within their first three weeks. Like everyone else they had to take a daily cold bath, even if they had to crack the film of ice on it. And in winter ice did form, for there was no central heating, and by a rule rigidly enforced we slept with open windows. Dormitories in "College" were on the top floor of the main building and were fully exposed to the onslaught of the weather. And when the east wind whistled round the great tower no supplement of rugs and greatcoats could protect one from its penetrative iciness. Winter and summer there was an hour's school, followed by chapel, before breakfast. Form-rooms were large and were warmed by a single open fire. Masters kept out the cold by wearing thick woollen waist-coats, by standing before the fire, or by stumping the room as they taught. Small boys were denied the comforts of these privileges, and if they sat far away from the fireplace they shivered in silence. Games were compulsory, and no in-clemency of the weather was ever severe enough to prevent one from changing into football kit. If the heavens descended in buckets to turn the football field into a quagmire, we went for a "run", coming back like drowned rats to wash the mud from our knees in cold water.

Other minor afflictions reserved specially for new boys were singing and learning how to shout "Fettes". The shout was the school cry at inter-school matches and had to be sustained in order to lend support to the school fifteen in a long scrum. Even when dragged out into two long syllables of "Fet-tes" the word does not lend itself to penetrative vocalism and as a battle cry is not to be compared with Loret'-to-o-o or even Merchi'-sto-o-one. I imagine that the first Fettesians were conscious of this defect, for, by tradition, new boys were carefully rehearsed in the cry before matches. It was a trying test, for most boys including myself were overcome by self-consciousness. On the other hand, if our combined efforts failed to produce sufficient volume of sound, we had books thrown at our head until we could satisfy our torturers.

The affliction of singing was also connected with football. New boys had to learn a song and sing it before the house and the prefects after the first victory in a school match. As the first school match was against Glenalmond, the victory was nearly always forthcoming. This victory paean was an unpleasant experience, for performance was individual, each new boy having to sing by himself. He could choose his own song. If he were wise he selected some innocuous ditty with not more than two verses. Then, after a few comments such as "awful", "rotten", he was allowed to sit down in peace. A popular favourite was "The Fish Ball' with its chorus of "The waiter roared across the hall, You can't have bread with one fish ball." But as a rule comic songs were dangerous, for the singer ran the risk of being accused of "side".

This ordeal by singing provided the only occasion on which I ever saw Moir Mackenzie discomfited. His voice, I think, had just broken. At any rate he disliked singing and, standing up on his bench in Hall, asked if he might tell a story instead of singing a song. The permission being given, Moir asked blandly: "Do you know the story of the empty box?" Believe it or not, there was a shout of "No; get on with it".

"There's nothing in it," said Moir and promptly sat down. This impudence from a new boy brought a swift punishment, and a volley of breadcrusts and pats of butter brought home to the unfortunate Moir the enormity of his offence.

On this régime we throve. At games we more than held our own with other schools. I have made a careful analysis of all matches against other schools at cricket and football until 1905, the year in which I left, and I find that Fettes has beaten every other school at both games more often than it has been defeated. At work, especially in classics, we stood and stand pre-eminent above the other public schools of Scotland.

"College", which, as at Eton, contained nothing but foundationers, was essentially the house with the highest standard of work. All Collegers therefore were poor boys who had to work not merely because they had to make their own way in the world, but also because they had to satisfy the authorities. Otherwise, they ran the risk of being deprived of the benefits of a free or almost free education. They came from nearly every walk of life except commerce. Among them were sons of doctors, schoolmasters, civil servants, and officers. Some were orphans, and others had widowed mothers. There was a certain proportion of English boys and of boys whose parents had settled in England. But by far the largest group was composed of sons of Scottish ministers and English clergymen. During my time these sons of the manse numbered twenty-four, and since the school was opened in 1870 Fettes must have educated many hundreds of them. Both in games and in work they rank high among the school's most distinguished alumni and they include Sir John Simon, although he, having won an Open Scholarship, did not go to "College".

In the circumstances, the standard of work was higher in "College" than in the other houses, although they too have furnished some fine scholars, including perhaps a greater than Sir John Simon in Sir Sidney Rowlatt, who at Cambridge won almost every classical prize that the University has to offer. "College", however, provided most of the Sixth Form. In my first year the head of the school was an English boy who was in Carrington, but during my next four years, every head of school was a "College" boy. It is to "College" and to the existence of so large a number of foundationers that Fettes owes its great reputation for scholarship. The reputation was early established. Within ten years of the school's creation, Wren, the well-known coach for the Indian Civil Service examination, was consulted by a father in search of a school for his son. "Send him to Fettes," said Wren. "The education there is perhaps the best that I know of."

If the foundationers were the brains of Fettes, they were the very essence of its origin. The school takes its name from its founder, Sir William Fettes, a Kincardine wine and tea merchant, who rose to be one of the great merchant princes of Scotland, had his portrait painted by Raeburn, and achieved the dignity of a baronetage. On his death he left the bulk of his fortune for the establishment of a Trust endowment "for the maintenance, education, and outfit of young people whose parents have either died without leaving sufficient funds for that purpose, or who from innocent misfortunate during their lives, are unable to give suitable education to their children."

Whether Sir William Fettes ever meditated the creation of a public school run on English lines has sometimes been doubted. But he was a wise and shrewd man, and in his will he gave his trustees almost unlimited powers for the management of the trust. Of these trustees, the greatest was Lord Justice Clerk Inglis.

If Sir William was the founder, Inglis was the creator of

Fettes, and it is to him that Edinburgh owes its first public school in the sense in which the word is understood in England. The national spirit was then stronger in Edinburgh than it is to-day, when many Edinburgh parents prefer to send their boys to English schools, and at first there was considerable antagonism to the introduction of English methods and especially to the top-hat and Eton jacket or morning coat which formed and still form the Sunday and "up town" dress of every Fettes boy. Inglis subsequently became Lord Glencorse, and his name is perpetuated in the Fettes house which has given to Scottish rugby football two famous pairs of brothers in the Sivrights and the McLeods.

Although the original regulations provided for fifty boys on the Foundation and fifty non-Foundationers, thus assuring absolute equality between Foundationers and other boys, this equality was not maintained for long. When I went to Fettes the number of Foundationers had not changed, but the non-Foundationers had more than trebled. Since the war I have heard one or two old "College" men complain rather bitterly of the attitude of the other houses towards "College". In my time there was no difference. I do remember the son of a Glasgow wine merchant once making a sneering remark about "College keelies", for even in those days Scotland had become so far Anglicised that the money standard counted for more than it ought to count. Possibly, a sensitive boy might have taken the remark to heart. But most "College" boys were far too healthy and full of their own prowess to brood over such trifles. We won nearly all the Governor's prizes and most of the scholarships at Oxford and Cambridge. And in those days the winning of an Open Scholarship was rewarded with an extra half-holiday. Moreover, and this probably counted for more in the eyes of youthful Fettes pride, we had produced more "rugger" internationals than any other house.

In the Fettes life of my day there was no snobbishness, and "side" in any form was severely discouraged. Manners were rough and awkward, and few boys would have shone in a drawing-room. But there was a sturdy spirit of independence among the boys, and never at any time was there any desire to imitate other schools. Indeed, during the whole period of my Fettes career, the great English public schools were rarely, if ever, mentioned.

Writing with some experience of other schools, I am convinced that the inter-house spirit at Fettes was infinitely better than at most schools. Although inter-house "rugger" matches were played with traditional vigour, the vigour itself never survived the afternoon's battle and never degenerated into the feuds which in other schools have sometimes marred the harmony of school life for years on end. In their first two years Fettes boys kept very much to their own houses. But as one went up the school there was more mixing, especially if one were good at games, and one at least of my best friends at Fettes was in Glencorse.

CHAPTER THREE

ALTHOUGH TO-DAY HEADMASTERS insist on taking boys at as early an age as they can catch them, it is, I think, a mistake for a boy to go to his public school when he is younger than most of his companions. In these circumstances the first year is generally a wasted year, and, in addition, the boy loses all the advantages of an extra year at his preparatory school.

In my first term at Fettes I was the youngest of the new foundationers and was placed in the Lower Fourth. Had I spent another year at Seafield, I should have entered a higher form at Fettes, and my work and my chances of promotion would almost certainly have benefited. For the Lower Fourth was not merely a difficult place to work in but also a difficult form for a small boy to escape from on account of the system of "ca' canny" and mutual assistance in work which prevailed. It was presided over by the Rev. G. H. Lenox-Conyngham, who was the first Old Fettesian to become a master at Fettes. He was then a man of just over forty and was clean-shaven and sallow. His expression, even when he smiled, was rather lugubrious. He was careless about his dress, and had anything but an athletic appearance. He was known to the whole school as "Flabby".

Kind and gentle in manner, he had a high sense of duty. But he was absent-minded, and, although, when irritated by insubordination, he beat fairly often, he was a poor disciplinarian. I doubt if he really understood boys. Moreover, although he was truly eloquent as a preacher, he had a high falsetto voice and a habit of moistening his lips before he spoke which invited and of course received imitation. He could generally be relied on to be late for early school, and, although we were supposed to keep quiet until his arrival, pandemonium was rendered safe by a device which, I suppose, is still in use. A hole, cut slanting in the form door, commanded a long view of the corridor, and here a small boy was posted to watch for the first sign of "Flabby's" approach. The boy then shouted "kish", and before the master reached the door the form were in their places and deep in the study of their books. This duty of watching through the loophole was known as "keeping kish".

"Flabby" must have been a great believer in community singing. At any rate the great feature of his form was the chanting in chorus of the paradigms of Greek verbs. It was a thrilling and amusing performance. At the word of command the whole form broke into a rhythmic chant of

$$\text{``}\lambda \bar{\upsilon}\omega, \ \ddot{\epsilon}\lambda \bar{\upsilon}o\nu, \ \lambda \bar{\upsilon}\text{-}\omega, \ \lambda \bar{\upsilon}\text{-}o\iota\mu\iota,$$
$$\lambda \hat{\upsilon}\text{-}\epsilon, \ \lambda \bar{\upsilon}\text{-}\epsilon\iota\nu, \ \lambda \bar{\upsilon}\text{-}\omega\nu\text{''}$$

It began like the first sound of thunder, with a low rolling murmur. Then it gradually swelled. Bolder spirits like Norman Moncreiff, an incorrigible ragster who was beaten more often than any boy who has ever been at Fettes, kept the time with their feet. With "$\lambda \hat{\upsilon}\text{-}\epsilon, \ \lambda \bar{\upsilon}\text{-}\epsilon\iota\nu$" the pace quickened and the volume rose, and the "$\lambda \bar{\upsilon}\text{-}\omega\nu$" ended in a shout which in summer must have been heard in Princes Street.

There were other delectable moments. On Sundays we had a divinity lesson in the afternoon, and "Flabby", who was a great Biblical scholar, had a pleasant habit of taking a text and explaining it to us. On occasions he would open his Bible and begin reading. He would pause to moisten his lips and begin again, the high falsetto drawl lingering over some particular word before he completed the passage. This was frequently too much for the innate vulgarity of small boys, especially if the word, as sometimes happened, had a double meaning, and every bench in the room shook. "Flabby" could not have noticed, for later, after one such unfair strain on our risibility, he used the same text for a sermon in chapel. It was another matter when he caught Moncreiff, oblivious to everything but the perfection of his performance, in the act of delivering an imitation of the sermon and of the text. For this offence Moncreiff, who met a soldier's death in France, added another caning to his long list.

I should not like to say that I learnt nothing in the Lower Fourth. Even if I forget every word of Greek that I ever learnt, I shall remember those paradigms until I die. And the same is true of the Latin gender rules. Certain fragments of Old Testament history which are imprinted almost textually on my mind owe their retention in my memory to "Flabby's" reiterative inspiration. Nor as a master was he lacking in conscientiousness. When he detected slacking, he rarely failed to inflict punishment. Except for one occasion, I was successful in avoiding his not too acute vigilance. Then I was caught indulging in school hours in a cricket game, played with a pencil and paper squares and invented by an English boy called Burt who, coming from Hove, was a cricket fanatic. This was the cause of the only beating that I ever received from "Flabby". It was, however, a memorable one, for that morning I had already been beaten by Mr. Broadrick, my French master, for failing to deliver an imposition at the appointed time. I mentioned this previous beating to "Flabby", and he consulted my house master. As a result of their deliberations, I was offered a day's grace in which to allow my wounds to heal. I chose immediate execution, and my preference was wise, for "Flabby" let me off lightly. Still, the fresh cuts on top of the old stung painfully.

These two canings on one day were the only beatings I received from masters at Fettes. With the two beatings from the house prefects they made a grand total of four. This average of less than one a year was not excessive and might have been increased with advantage to myself.

There were certain drawbacks in "Flabby's" form which only a boy of exceptionally strong character could overcome. The form had many bigger boys who cared little or nothing about promotion. As far as work was concerned, Trades Union principles prevailed, and anything in the nature of "swotting" or "sapping" was severely discouraged. Cribbing, not to gain marks but to avoid punishment, was widespread, and in this atmosphere it was not easy to work hard. As a boy I was always anxious to curry favour, and all too willingly I failed to surmount the minor difficulties of the situation. At the end of my first term the Headmaster set a Latin sentence paper for the whole school except the top forms. I came out first. For me it was a disaster, for I never again finished in the first fifty. My success earned me my only good report from the Headmaster, who commented on my promise in a note in red ink. Never afterwards did he fail to draw attention to my subsequent failures in his sentence paper, and "has ability, lacks application" became his favourite text to my address. Worse still, when the first term order for the Lower Fourth came out, I was well down on the list and therefore missed my remove. To the detriment of my chances of a scholarship at Cambridge—and this was my father's ambition for me—I stayed stuck in the Lower Fourth for a whole year.

Provided that he is not given to bumptiousness, and has no idiosyncrasies of manner or appearance to render him a butt to other boys, a youngster in his first year at a public school can efface himself successfully. He is too small to make any mark at games, and the chief pleasures of his life are gastronomic. At Fettes I lived mainly for Sundays, or rather for every third Sunday, for then we were allowed leave "up town" from after early chapel until four-thirty to visit relations or friends in Edinburgh.

The ordinary school Sunday was a tedious day. In spite of three religious services and a Scripture lesson, time lagged heavily and was therefore an invitation to mischief. No games were allowed. Even the swimming baths were closed. In summer small boys went for rather dreary walks. In winter they "brewed" cocoa with Nestlé's condensed milk, known vulgarly as "Swiss piss", and ruined their digestions with cake and sweet biscuits. For morning church service two-thirds of the school went to St. Stephen's, the Presbyterian church half-way between Fettes and Princes Street, and the other third to the Anglican church of Holy Trinity beside the Dean Bridge. At Beith I had been a United Presbyterian. In Broughty Ferry I was an Episcopalian and during the holidays continued to visit the Episcopal church. But at Fettes I returned to the established church of my paternal ancestors and attended St. Stephen's. My wishes were not consulted in the matter. This somewhat erratic direction of my religious faith was prescribed by my father.

At St. Stephen's the services were long and scarcely suitable for small boys. A master on duty and a row of prefects guaranteed good behaviour. But the church was large and, after one had finished inspecting the clothes of the Edinburgh congregation, it was quite safe to read a book under the shelter of the pew-front. In this way I read most of Anthony Hope and Stanley Weyman. Mr. Grant, the St. Stephen's minister, was a dignified and erudite figure with few mannerisms, but comic relief was provided on rare occasions by visiting preachers.

I remember one earnest missionary who, in the broadest of Scottish accents, gave an eloquent exhortation against the evils of alcohol. His naive text, "don't drink and you will never be drunk", provoked a smile even from the staid members of the grown-up congregation. It appealed to my imagination in a curious manner. Next door to St. Stephen's was the Tivoli, a cheap Edinburgh music-hall, which, according to school rumour, was the scene of Saturday night orgies when the Scottish Rugby Fifteen visited the place after a victory in an international match. While the missionary preached, I saw visions of burly Scottish forwards dealing roughly with the chucker-out and wondered how the good man would have fared if he had delivered his sermon next door.

Services in the school chapel were altogether different. Simple in character and inspiring by their surroundings, they were an escape from school life and an outlet for emotions which had been suppressed during the week. I followed them devoutly and at the benediction made many good resolutions. Most of all, perhaps, I was moved by the singing. With the exception of two terms, when my voice broke, I was in the choir during the whole period of my school career. I began as an alto and soon learnt to read music with tolerable ease. There was generally an anthem, and on these occasions, having learnt my part at choir practice, I panted my little lungs out "as the hart panted after the water brooks", not only to please my music-master whom I liked, but because I felt emotionally exalted.

The sermons, too, commanded attention, and, if Dr. Heard had an uninspiring delivery, his addresses at any rate were addresses for boys. Occasionally one of the masters preached, and once a term there was a sermon by a distinguished visitor. These visiting preachers were rarely successful, either talking above our heads or committing the more damning error of talking down to us. Afterwards, we criticised them freely and generally adversely. There was one old theological professor from St. Andrews who saved himself from anathema by an unrehearsed and quite unconscious touch of humour. He began his sermon with a vast bundle of small notes which he had probably scribbled out in the train on his way to Edinburgh. They were quite unmanageable, and almost every sentence that came from his mouth was preceded by a lick of the thumb and a noisy turning over of his notes. The general effect was irksome and boring. But it was summer and the windows were open, and suddenly a gust of the freshening wind swept down on the lectern which served as a pulpit and carried off his little sheets of paper, strewing them in scattered singles before the masters' desks. For a moment the poor professor looked nonplussed. Then, taking off his pince-nez and smiling, he said:

"What the Lord hath given it hath pleased Him to take away. I shall now continue without my notes." He became immediately human and brief. We took him to our hearts and, although I do not remember a word of his sermon, we voted him a success.

It was in the Fettes chapel that I heard the most inspiring preacher to whom it has ever been my lot to listen. This was the famous Dr. Almond, the founder and first headmaster of Loretto. I had heard of him often from my father, who admired him greatly; and he figured in my mental book of deeds as the man who had refereed the first "rugger" international between Scotland and England and who had caught what then ranked as the largest trout ever taken on a fly. I had pictured him as a muscular Christian combining the virtues of Dr. Arnold and Charles Kingsley, and, although I had no personal knowledge of him, I think that this description fits him. He was an old man when I heard him preach at Fettes, and his white beard gave him the appearance of an Old Testament patriarch. But there was a magnetism in his voice and in his eyes which held me spellbound. It had the same effect on the other boys, and during his sermon not a cough or a shuffle of the feet was heard. His words made a lasting impression on me and almost made me wish that I had gone to Loretto. Since then I have compared all subsequent preachers with him and have always found them wanting. The gift of oratory has not been given generously to the English or to the Scots, and bad preaching to-day is far too prevalent in both England and Scotland. A Dr. Almond in every church would do more for the revival of Christianity and of church-going than a thousand bishops' conferences. The services in chapel are among my happiest memories of Fettes, and in those memories the dim incandescent lights shining on the venerable figure of the Loretto headmaster stand out as the symbol of the unfulfilled aspirations of my youth.

On the Thursday before each third Sunday in the term I

nervously approached both my house master and my form master with my Sunday-leave form in my hand. If both signed it, I was free soon after half-past eight on Sunday morning. Then, arrayed in my "topper" and Eton jacket, I set out for Merchiston where both my maternal grandmother and my paternal grandfather had houses. I arrived in time for breakfast, and in my case Sunday leave meant mainly feasting and church-going.

Indeed, at my grandfather's I was nearly always in time for morning prayers, which were *de rigueur* for the whole household. This miniature service included a hymn and a chapter read by my grandfather from a wonderful old Bible. It had full-page illustrations, and I can still see a very hairy Nebuchadnezzar shovelling grass into his mouth with long, unkept nails. By this time my grandfather had married again, and at her own request my brother and I called his second wife "Aunt Lottie". The difference in years was considerable, and from being a marvellously young old man my grandfather became suddenly aged and ailing. Morning prayers did not release me from going to church. Both my Macgregor grandmother and my Lockhart grandfather were persistent churchgoers, and in this way I visited most of the leading Scottish churches in Edinburgh and heard the best Scottish preachers, including Mathieson, the blind minister, who composed the hymn "O Love That wilt not let me go". This hymn was my mother's favourite, and the last verse

> "O Cross that liftest up my head,
> I dare not ask to flee from Thee.
> I lay in dust life's glory dead,
> And from the ground there blossoms red
> Life that shall endless be."

is engraved on the memorial tablet to my brother Norman, who lies buried somewhere in France.

By parental instructions I had to divide my Sundays between my grandmother and my grandfather, but I preferred going to my grandmother's, for she understood better how to feed small boys and she never failed to give me a tip. Indeed, when I went to my grandfather's I generally made a point of calling at my grandmother's on my way back to Fettes in order to collect the customary ten shillings from her. When my uncle Alister was at home I usually got a second tip, for, after my grandmother had done her share, he would fumble in his pockets and then say: "Mother, lend me ten shillings." The old lady was noble. She always found the extra ten shillings nor did she ever reduce her own contribution on account of this extra levy.

On most Sundays I stayed with my relations till the last moment and then raced home by cab for afternoon school. But sometimes, when my grandfather or my grandmother had to go out, I started my homeward journey earlier and, leaving the cab at the West End, walked, making my way by the side streets until I came to Stockbridge.

It was in those days that I developed the habit of exploring Edinburgh, which to-day is one of the chief pleasures of my life. It was then, too, that, in order to spur me to greater industry, I made a point of going back via Castle Street and passing the house where Scott lived in the days of his financial distress and where revellers, returning home in the early hours of the morning, saw on the blind the shadow of the Wizard's hand writing indefatigably in an effort to pay off the huge burden of his debts. To-day, when after seven years of toil I have paid off the burden of my own debts by writing, I never visit Edinburgh without making a quiet pilgrimage to the house in Castle Street and paying a silent vow of thanks to its former occupant for his inspiring example. The house is now the office of a New Zealand mortgage company.

For the walker, Edinburgh stands alone among cities, excelling even Rome, because her history has been written within a square mile. Indeed, Edinburgh never fails to yield new discoveries, and one of my latest is Nicolson Square. It is named after a direct ancestor of Harold Nicolson. For some strange reason most people regard Harold as an Ulsterman. His family is of purely Scottish origin and comes from Skye. His forbears were called McNicol, were staunch Jacobites, and after years of exile changed their name to Nicolson when they came to Edinburgh to study law. Harold is a good Scot, and so was his father—the famous ambassador and Under-Secretary of State for Foreign Affairs. Indeed, Lord Carnock, as he subsequently became, always professed never to be able to understand Englishmen. Talking of Sir Edward Grey (afterwards Lord Grey) he used to say: "It is an extraordinary thing that, although Grey comes from just across the Border, there is a gulf between us which I can never bridge."

Looking back to-day, I realise that the seeds of my passion for the Queen of Cities must have been sown in my first summer term at Fettes. My cubicle window commanded a superb view of the city. Indeed, I know only one better, and that is the distant view from Gullane golf course, from which the city can be seen nestling behind Arthur's Seat at the end of the glorious estuary of the Forth. But I do not recommend it to tourists, for golfers are a selfish and soulless race and resent any invasion of their sacred precincts. My dormitory window was a safer vantage point, for it was private, and its glory was at eventide. Then the last embers of the June sunset would cast a fairy light on the castle long after the hideous slums below had been submerged by the tide of advancing greyness. Away to the right was the rolling brown mass of the Pentlands, turning black as the fading light receded. They were not the Cairngorms. In their stern and rugged outline there was something which suggested the grimness of their Presbyterian history. The very names of the hills and villages, Black Hill, Scald Law, Martyrs' Cross, and Rullion Green, conjured up visions of Covenanters' tabernacles, of slaughter, and of fleeing men. But they were very satisfying to a boy who has always liked the voluptuousness of solitude and who found the deprivation of privacy the greatest hardship of his life at school, and in summer I would linger at my cubicle window over a scene which provided a greater cavalcade and pageant than any theatre or present-day cinema.

I remember places by the moods which they invoke. To my mind Port Dickson suggests infinity and timelessness and eternal longing. Aden, with its glaring whitewash and its burning rocks, is the symbol of savage heat and tropical death. Moscow provokes a conflict of two opposing wishes: the hankering to return to see the end of an experiment at whose birth I assisted, and a fearful anxiety to blot out all memory of the Russian period of my existence. These landmarks in my life are now extinct volcanoes and the moods they invoke are passive. But the Pentlands are active and vitalising. And to-day, when I know them well, they still inspire me with the desire to be up and doing and to go out and discover what lies beyond them.

They are associated in my life with Stevenson. Like Stevenson, I spent part of my boyhood beneath their slopes. During one period of my life at Fettes my grandmother had a house at Colinton where Stevenson's grandfather was once the parish minister, and, like Stevenson, I spent my Easter holidays there. Later my uncle had a house and a small property near Martyr's Cross, and here I spent many happy weeks shooting grouse on the steep moorside, fishing the corporation reservoirs, and climbing the hills. Within easy walk of the house was the battlefield of Rullion Green, where on a cold November day in 1666 nine hundred Covenanters, ill-armed and untrained, withstood for several hours the onslaught of three thousand trained troops led by Sir Thomas Dalzell, who because of his service in the Russian army has gone down to history as "The Muscovy Brute".

To-day, I never think of Edinburgh apart from the Pentlands. I know them now from every side, and after the Cairngorms they are to me the hills of home.

Like most boys at Fettes I liked the summer term best and the Easter term least. But these preferences did not establish themselves during my first year. I was fond of cricket, but at Fettes the game was not supervised with the same zeal as rugby football, and a small boy in his first year had little chance of getting out of the ruck of junior games which were badly organised and dominated largely by big boys who disliked the game because they were no good at it. My first summer term was therefore a disappointment.

On the other hand, my first Easter term provided me with one memorable thrill. This came from Scotland's two "rugger" internationals against Wales and Ireland which were played in Edinburgh. Inverleith, which was then the Scottish Rugby Union's international ground, was only a few hundred yards distant from Fettes, and of course the whole school went to the matches. Most boys stood among the crowd on the terraces, but, as my father was a member of the Union, I went with him and sat among the gods. Not only did I see the greatest Scottish Fifteen of all time win two dazzling victories over Wales and Ireland, not only were there two Old Fettesians among the eight irresistible Scottish forwards, but my father's position as a selector gave me a brief moment of reflected glory.

When I returned to "College" on the Saturday evening, a prefect who was a member of the school fifteen came up to me during preparation and asked me what my father thought of the game. Having by this time learnt the importance of self-restraint, I thought that my leg was being pulled. Like most small boys, I was afraid of parading my parents before other boys, and on Founder's Day suffered agonies lest they should commit some solecism which would make my life miserable for the rest of the term. I was especially fearful on account of my father, who had a knack not only of engaging the sacred person of the headmaster in conversation in front of the cricket screen but also at football matches of walking up to the even more sacred person of the captain of the fifteen and asking him questions about my football abilities. When, therefore, the prefect asked me about my father's views on the match, I hesitated not from ignorance but from caution. I soon saw that the prefect's desire for knowledge was genuine, and for a few minutes we discoursed gravely and quietly on the virtues and vices of the Scottish team. Boys are not entirely lacking in the human quality of self-interest. Nearly every member of a Fettes fifteen indulged in dreams, very often justifiable dreams, of a Blue or of a Scottish cap, and in his eyes a Scottish selector was a more important person than an archbishop or a duke.

I remember my first Easter term for an incident which still strikes me not only as a flagrant miscarriage of justice but also as curious in connection with a Scottish school. On Boat Race day, mainly, I suppose, because the masters were almost exclusively Englishmen, the whole school wore Light Blue or Dark Blue rosettes. Probably more than half the boys had no connection with either Oxford or Cambridge. But this anomaly made no difference. The rosettes were provided by the matrons in the houses, and we put them in our lapel before early school. In Glencorse there was an American boy called Lawson. He was a youth of talent and originality, being an Open Scholar and a member of the school rugby fifteen. As he was going to Cornell, he owed no allegiance to either Oxford or Cambridge, and, in order to maintain a strictly American neutrality, he bought himself two rosettes, one Dark Blue and the other Light, put one in each lapel, and thus adorned trooped into chapel.

He was promptly spotted by his house master, K. P. Wilson, who is known to generations of Fettesians as "K. P." A great athlete and a most inspiring teacher, he disliked anything in the nature of impudence from big boys. Lawson's two rosettes were regarded as an offence against modesty and, perhaps, tradition, and, although he was then in the Upper Sixth and a prefect, he was given a hefty imposition. Incidentally, he must have been the first American that I ever saw, although I have vague memories of American tourists, coatless and with belted trousers, "doing" the sights of Edinburgh with characteristic thoroughness.

Psychologists, I suppose, would say that the most important event of my first year at Fettes was the discovery of sex. To most schoolmasters morality is a fixed quantity, and any deviation from it is punishable with various recognised penalties. A school where sex obtrudes itself is dismissed as a bad school. Where what are called sex abuses escape detection, the school's reputation is frequently higher than it deserves to be.

I am far from denying the necessity of differentiating between good and bad schools. But the difference depends far more on the masters than on the boys. What I do think is that the dangers of sex in schools have been exaggerated and that if the whole problem were treated rationally it would be regarded as an inevitable stage in a boy's development. It is true that in public schools the discovery of sex is sometimes forced on a small boy. It is also true that cases of abnormal vice are very rare. On the other hand, self-abuse and mutual assistance in committing that abuse are common to every school, and the schoolmaster who denies the existence of this abuse is either a fool or a hypocrite, for he has been a boy himself.

I am not criticising the schoolmaster's attitude towards "vice" or protesting against the severe penalties with which he treats it. His job is not to save the erring sheep but to keep his whole flock as free from contamination as he can. The subject is one which can be discussed fully only in a medical treatise. But parents, I think, should realise that a boy's curiosity is insatiable and that, when he discovers sex, as discover it he must whether he goes to school or not, he will satisfy that curiosity in some form or other. Indeed, the best medical opinion puts the figure of boys who do so at over ninety per cent. And this ninety per cent must therefore be taken as affecting the normal boy. Anxious mothers, however, may be comforted by the knowledge that the normal boy throws off this so-called "vice" as easily as he discards his clothes before bathing and that he suffers less from it than he would from an unnatural suppression.

Nor do I think that the public school system produces more sex evils than any other form of education. Before I went to the Sorbonne, my father sent me for a few months to the house of a French professor of literature at Douai. Among the places where this professor lectured was the local lycée. Although I was then nineteen, he arranged for me to attend his literature classes at the school, and in this manner I got to know the bigger boys. Most of them had mistresses among the working-class girls of Douai. Some may say that this outlet for sex is healthier than that which the English system enforces, but I remember my rage when the Douai school football team, which I helped in its cup-ties, was deprived of the services of one of its best forwards owing to venereal disease. Such cases were not merely fairly common but were the subject of coarse jests.

At Fettes the discovery of sex was forced on me, but I was far too keen on games and on athletic fitness to debase my physical currency. And this, I think, was true of scores of other boys.

Of the effect of sex discovery on my character I am perhaps not the best judge. Like most boys between the ages of fourteen and sixteen I was incorrigibly lazy, but there was, I think, nothing abnormal in this laziness. Most boys and, for that matter, most men work best under the stress of necessity. Not counting the Sixth Form, I was under four different form masters during my Fettes career. Two of them, K. P. Wilson and Johnnie Coast, made me work because the consequences of not working were too unpleasant. In their forms I won the form-prize, and these were the only prizes I ever obtained at Fettes.

Although I am not sure that it had any connection with sex, the greatest change was in my home life. I looked forward to the holidays with all the eagerness of the normal small boy. When I returned to Seafield, my relations with my brother were unaltered. We resumed a natural companionship. We collected stamps together. We opened our butterfly boxes and compared the ravages which dust and invisible worms had wrought on fragile wings. Our likes and dislikes, which had always coincided, had not changed. I boasted of Fettes prowess at games. But of my private life at school I told him nothing. There was, too, a new restraint in my attitude towards my parents. I was intolerant of criticism. I nursed imaginary grievances and developed temporarily a sulky temper, imagining myself misunderstood. Like a vixen's cub which has learnt to fend for itself, I was resentful of authority and wanted to be on my own.

There was this difference, and it applies to many boys: the vixen's cub can provide its own food and its own shelter. The schoolboy whelp, while asserting the same independence, lives on his father and mother and often continues to do so until long after his student days. Between the ages of fourteen and eighteen the average boy is an unattractive animal.

CHAPTER FOUR

WHEN A MAN looks back on his school life, it is the masters that he visualises more than his own boy contemporaries. This is as it should be. Boys are at an unformed and uninteresting stage of their development. The master is, or should be, in his prime, and, since after parents, nurses, and other primary influences he is the most important factor in moulding a boy's character, it is right that the man-boy should remember him with contemplative self-interest and even with gratitude.

As the son and the brother and the uncle of schoolmasters, I flatter myself, perhaps wrongly, that I know something of the caste. At any rate I have met more schoolmasters than most men who are not schoolmasters. I have heard them discussed *ad nauseam*. And I have had the advantage of being able to study them at close quarters and yet from the outside.

Their faults lie on the surface. Accustomed from the first day to be regarded as oracles on all subjects, they become dictatorially didactic. They acquire fixed views and set ideas and, rightly rebutting argument from boys, are inclined to resent it from grown-ups. In the public schools the profession suffers from the number of men who, having gone up to Oxford or Cambridge with no definite career in view, drift into schoolmastering as the easiest means of providing an immediate salary to a man who has taken a fair degree and is tolerably good at some game. Schoolmastering, in fact, is the only career in which a man can step straight into a remunerative post without any previous training. And this is perhaps its greatest weakness as a profession.

On the other hand, I admit readily that schoolmasters, like diplomatists, suffer from one unfair disadvantage. The ordinary citizen will hesitate to walk into the Bank of England and tell Mr. Montagu Norman how to run the country's financial policy. Still less readily will he give to a scientist a practical demonstration of how to improve shell fuses. He realises that he knows nothing about finance and science. But every man, from a bishop to a butler, thinks himself fully qualified to show Mr. Eden exactly where he made his last mistake and to tell any headmaster what subjects ought to be included in the school curriculum.

I feel that the British attitude towards schoolmasters is lop-sided. The average well-to-do British citizen pays or helps to pay the best doctors £40,000 a year in order to prolong a life which may not be worth preserving. Yet, when it is a question of the more valuable life of his son, the same citizen rates the salary of the best-paid headmaster at about £4000 and grumbles both at the figure and at what he calls "too much education". There is only one cure for "too much education", and that is more and better education. There is only one remedy for bad schoolmasters, and that is to offer greater inducements to better men to enter the profession.

Fortunately, there are more efficient schoolmasters than the public dreams of, and the good schoolmaster is the salt of the earth.

He is the most unselfish man in the world. His interest in boys is comprehensive and for all time, and, if in his heart he does not suffer foolish parents gladly, he is amazingly tolerant of boyish stupidity. What I admire most in him is the unflagging zeal and energy with which he will devote his time and his endeavour to doing the best for, and getting the best out of, one set of boys and then, when they pass on, beginning again with equal enthusiasm the same task with another set. Nor are the boys who leave him forgotten. A schoolmaster's devotion to his school is more selfless than that of an officer to his regiment, and I know several schoolmasters who keep up an enormous correspondence with old boys in every part of the world.

I had an illuminating experience of this zeal and devotion quite recently. One morning I received a long letter from

Mr. Ashcroft, the present headmaster of Fettes, informing me of a fund for some new building scheme and setting forth the reasons why I should contribute to it. It was a personal letter in his own handwriting. I had met him only once before. I knew nothing of the merits of the building scheme. But the fact that an English headmaster had the interests of this Scottish school so much at heart that he could find the time to write a long personal letter to an old boy, impressed me so strongly that although, as usual, I was overdrawn at the bank, I sat down and sent him a cheque.

The Fettes staff in my time included some truly remarkable men. To the average boy, Dr. Heard, the headmaster, was a distant and awe-inspiring figure. He adopted the methods of Stalin in the sense that he rarely descended into the public arena. Homeric figures who had spent several terms in the Upper Sixth spoke admiringly of his sense of humour and of his kindness, but the average boy rarely saw him and felt strangely uncomfortable if he passed him in the corridor. Like most Foundationers I went to breakfast with him during my first term, and, coming out, was badgered with the usual questions about what we had to eat, and what his three daughters had said. I was too nervous to remember what he himself said, and I knew him best as the author of the Greek Exercise Book with which I had to wrestle during the first two years of my career. Although he was called the "Bulge", and occasionally the "Black Beetle", he was held in great respect, and I remember the excitement of the small boys, of whom I was one, when, during a rag performance of a Shakespeare play at the Poorhouse Concert, a Sixth Form boy-actor bending down over an imaginary discovery exclaimed loudly: "It's a black beetle." It is perhaps a tribute to the headmaster's personality that this impromptu was regarded as the height of schoolboy audacity and that for the rest of the evening we wondered what awful fate would overtake its perpetrator.

Two legends about him were current in my time. One was disrespectful and was murmured by the bolder spirits. It was that as an assistant master at Westminster he had been unmercifully ragged. I do not think that even the small boys believed the tale. The other story was that in his youth he had been a champion gymnast. I do not know if it was true. Certainly he did not look like an athlete. But the story was to his credit and was typical of a school which regarded some form of athletic distinction as an essential qualification for popular respect.

Of the three great house masters of those days, John Yeo, D. W. Tanqueray and K. P. Wilson, I saw much more, especially of "K. P." Yeo, a second wrangler and Smith's Prizeman at Cambridge, was then house master of Carrington and was worshipped by the boys of his own house and, indeed, by all who came under his influence. As a teacher of mathematics he was superb, for he could make even the stupidest boy see the light. He had infinite patience, rarely beat anyone, and never lost his temper. He put a boy on his honour, and personal grief when one let him down was his method of reducing one to contrition. He had an infectious laugh, and on account of a cultivated cheeriness was known as "Ha-ha, lads". I feel to-day that he might even have achieved the miracle of teaching me the mysteries of mathematics, but he took the top sets in the various schools and, as I have never been able to make any sum balance, I was under him for only one term. Like all popular masters, Yeo worshipped a little at the shrine of the god of athletics, in winter encouraging the boys to play fives with him, in summer coaching at the nets, and in the first week of August taking a cricket team at his own expense to the Lake District.

Tanqueray, who was known to everyone as "Tink", was house master of Moredun, and in school presided over the destinies of the Upper Mods, a form which provided an easy escape for Laodiceans anxious to avoid the rigours of the Classical Upper Fifth. He was a small man with a little grey moustache, which gave him a slightly pugnacious appearance. He had a fussy manner, was a great stickler for accuracy, and spoke in a stilted staccato voice. He was not an inspiring teacher, and boys in his form spent most of their time taking down notes which they were encouraged to underline with inks of various colours. But he must have been a great house master, for the boys in his house both liked and respected him, and I have since met distinguished old Moredun boys who, with obvious sincerity, ascribed their success in life to the inspiring influence of their house master. With the rest of the school he was less popular, mainly, I think, on account of his fussiness and his rigid insistence on the observation to the letter of the school laws.

"Tink", too, found it necessary to swing his incense before the altar of athletics. "At Cambridge", he would tell his form in expansive moments, "I was called bull-dog, not on account of any physical resemblance to that noble animal, but for my ferocity on the field of play."

Of all the Fettes masters of my time, K. P. Wilson was the one whom I admired most and liked best. Until the term before I went to Fettes, he had been house master in "College" and was, in fact, the reason for my going there. For my father had known him at Cambridge and was much upset when "K. P." was transferred from "College" to Glencorse. Although I missed having him as my house master, he took a kindly interest in my destiny from my first days at Fettes, and towards the end of my school career I spent four inspiring terms in his form, the famous Upper Fifth.

In his Cambridge days "K. P." had been a tremendous athletic "blood", excelling especially at association football and cricket. He came of a famous athletic family and his brother "C. P." had achieved the almost unparalleled distinction of winning an England cap for both "soccer" and "rugger". "K. P." himself was the embodiment of physical fitness. When I went to Fettes, he was already in the early "forties". But he still played "soccer", and in matches for the masters against the school could meet the heftiest Fettes forward in a charge and give more than he received.

But it is not as an athlete that he lives in my memory, nor had he himself much use for the boy who lived solely for games. In sending him to Glencorse, fate had ordained that he should preside over the house which, in my time at any rate, excelled at rugby football and to which rich Glasgow parents sent their boys with the one hope and ambition that their offspring would one day gain a place in the Fettes fifteen. "K. P.", I think, must have suffered a little from the transfer from "College" to Glencorse. At all events he professed to despise "rugger" as a game which not merely exalted brawn but had a deleterious effect on a boy's brains. There was something of pose in this attitude, and doubtless he adopted it as a necessary corrective to the prevalent "rugger" mania which affected ninety per cent of the school. "Rugger" bloods benefited from it. Many a time I remember being put on to construe Virgil or Homer on a winter's afternoon. Not having prepared my translation, I would stumble and hesitate. In the morning such backsliding would have been punished immediately by an "extra". But in the afternoon "K. P." had to have his little joke.

"What have you been doing this afternoon?" he would ask.

"Playing football, Sir," I would reply with a puzzled look.

"Sit down, laddie, sit down."

And down I sat. There was no imposition. Rugby football was sufficient excuse for every muddled head.

As a form master "K. P." was prodigious. Rumour said that he had taken the Upper Fifth from the first day that he arrived at Fettes. There was then no Modern side, and the form was full of "rugger" bloods. During his first "hour" "K. P." had been ragged. His only reaction had been to order the form to come in after luncheon at two o'clock. He had then arrived with a bundle of canes and, beginning with the biggest boy, had carried out an epic execution. This was said to be the origin

of "K. P's" famous "extras", for it was one of the virtues of
this great man that he never gave an imposition for bad
work, preferring instead to sacrifice his own leisure in an
"extra" lesson in which he strove to drive home the neglected precepts of the morning.

What truth there is in this caning legend I do not know.
But I can testify that in my time "K. P's" reputation as a
disciplinarian stood so high that he never required to "beat".
Indeed, I think that he used the cane less than any master in
the school. It is, however, true that certain boys in the
Lower Fifth succeeded in persuading their parents to transfer
them to the Modern side solely in order to avoid the disciplinary terrors of the Upper Fifth. In my view these
terrors were grossly exaggerated. I enjoyed the Upper Fifth
more than any other form at Fettes, almost entirely because
"K. P." made the work interesting. His vigour was immense, and even in his approach there was something
electric. We would watch him coming up the drive from
Glencorse, his head on one side, his well-knit frame rolling
in a jolly swagger, and a red tie easily distinguishable at a
hundred yards. With the first sound of the heavy footsteps
on the stone corridor we would open our books and sit
still. A whistle or a catch of song would float through the
open door. Then "K. P." would burst into the room,
flinging out as he passed a few terse commands: "Latin
conditional sentences. If the army is surrounded, many cap-
tives will be taken." Not one minute of the precious hour
was ever wasted.

If he insisted firmly on proper attention to mental gymnastics, he opened new horizons. History was made to live,
and, although his own views were set and rooted, he never
discouraged opposition, provided that it was expressed
intelligently and with some originality. His English "hours"
were a real joy, and through "K. P." I made my first acquaintance with Conrad. In those days my essays were a
maze of turgid prose and involved argument, and when I

won the form prize, "K. P." gave me a complete set of Browning, informing the rest of the class: "Perhaps Lockhart will understand this stuff, for neither you nor I can."

Generous and full of understanding, "K. P." had his idiosyncracies. Two things he could not abide. One was "side" and the other was obstinacy—a quality of which he had a good deal in his own nature. I remember vividly one great scene when in our last year Moir Mackenzie and I were sole victims of an "extra". As there was a first fifteen practice that afternoon, we turned up at the "extra" in the usual football kit of "bloods": magenta stockings, shorts, a blazer, and a white sweater tied around the neck. I was heard first and got through my lesson satisfactorily. But Moir had hardly started when "K. P." interrupted him. "You great big lump of football swagger," he said. This was his usual address to boys who came to "extras" in football kit and who, because they thought themselves "bloods", assumed that they need not work. Moir, a great stickler for his rights, pointed out that I was dressed exactly as he was, and yet I had not been reproved. The remark was strictly true, but it was scarcely good diplomacy to make it at that moment. "K. P's" eyes blazed. "Write out the first page of the letter 'A' in the Greek dictionary," said "K. P." Moir continued to argue. "Write out the whole dictionary," thundered "K. P." I forget exactly how the scene ended, but of course Moir did not write out the dictionary. Clouds rarely obscured the sun of "K. P's" cheerfulness for more than a few seconds, and he was far too big a man ever to tolerate injustice or to bear malice.

As a master he cared little for the letter of the law, so long as the spirit was properly observed. In this respect he was the very antithesis of Tanqueray, and by the school the two men were not supposed to see eye to eye.

This legend, true or otherwise, probably had its orgin in an episode which was enacted a few years before I went to Fettes. Boys going "up town" were excused "call-over" but had to produce a written leave for their absence. Call-over lists were brought round the next morning to the various form masters by the school sergeant, and absentees had then to give up their "leaves". There was a big boy called De La Cour in Tanqueray's form. One morning, after the boy had been "up town", the list was brought in, and Tanqueray at once spotted the absentee.

"De La Cour," he said, "you were not at call-over yesterday. Have you a leave?"

De La Cour, who was in "K. P.'s" house, stood up and fumbled in his pockets.

"Please, sir," he said, "I had a 'leave' but I changed my suit this morning and I must have left it in my cubicle."

"Well," said Tanqueray, "you must now go to your house master and get a 'leave' for not having a leave."

The same evening De La Cour went to "K. P." and obtained the necessary "leave". The next morning the same scene was enacted.

"De La Cour, have you now your leave for not having a leave?"

The unfortunate boy had again left his "leave" in his cubicle, and again Tanqueray ordered him to get from his house master yet another "leave". De La Cour approached his house master again, but this time "K. P." was irritated and expressed his irritation testily.

On the next day, "Tink", supported by the smiles of the form, asked De La Cour with mincing pedantry.

"Well, De La Cour, have you now your 'leave' for not having a 'leave' for not having a 'leave'?"

Up jumped De La Cour, his face as stolid as an ox's.

"Please, sir, Mr. Wilson told me to tell you that he'd have no more of your fiddle-faddle!"

"K. P." is still alive and lives near my father in Berkshire. His sturdy figure is still as strong as an iron gate. He has the rosy-cheeked complexion of a boy. He still whistles and sings, and thunders against humbugs. He still has a terrier, a worthy descendant of its predecessors at Glencorse. He still wears old clothes. He is still marvellously hospitable to old Fettesians and unostentatiously generous to lame dogs. He is still rigidly Spartan and self-denying towards himself. Only the red tie has vanished.

When I go to see him, I generally find him digging or planting in his garden. He is a great weeder. In his eyes the most noxious weed is luxury, and to-day I see him as a modern Cato setting an example of frugality and sturdy independence to a softer and spiritually poorer generation.

Of the Fettes masters, he was, in my opinion, the outstanding figure of his time, and to him and to William Tilley, my professor in Berlin, I owe the only valuable lesson that I have learnt in life: how to work and the importance of work as an aid to man to rise above the level of his own self-disgust.

"College" itself was ruled by a Duumvirate who enjoyed equal powers. The house master who had special charge of my particular person was "Johnnie" Coast. He was a kind little man who understood boys better than we ourselves realised. He lacked the inspiring breeziness of "K. P" but was a thoroughly conscientious and impartial house master. I liked him, and remember with pleasure and gratitude the Sunday evenings when we small boys who had no studies gathered in his study and munched cake while he read "The Pickwick Papers" to us. I am not a Dickensian, but thanks to Coast I remember my Pickwick. He was, too, an excellent form master and had various devices for making his boys work. On one occasion, when I had been slacking, he informed me that if I did not reach a certain place in the next week's form order I should be beaten. I failed by one place to reach the appointed standard and was given one stroke of the cane. I appreciated the strict impartiality of this justice.

For most of my time at Fettes, the other "College" house master was Harry Pyatt, an old Harrovian and one of the few Oxford men on the staff. A "Double first", he was the best scholar among the masters and took the Lower Fifth. As I spent a whole year in his form, I saw much of him. Himself a poet of distinction, he encouraged originality by organising weekly drawing and verse competitions. I imagine the drawings were better than the poems, but as I could never grasp the elements of perspective I concentrated my efforts on comic verse. Pyatt took great pains to correct these efforts and to suggest improvements, and, although I was too young and too much of a "rugger" Philistine to appreciate the full value of his genius, some vague idea of the importance and the beauty of words remained. As a house master, he remains in my memory chiefly for his conduct of evening prayers which was slightly eccentric. Prayers, as distinct from morning chapel, were held in the houses, and in "College" Pyatt played the hymn on a small harmonium with his back to the boys. Sometimes, if the singing was feeble, he would turn round between verses and exclaim testily: "If you don't sing up, I'll stop the hymn." Naturally these interjections provided amusement. In his first term as a house master, the prefects who chose the hymns had "O Paradise, O Paradise" as often as they dared. On those occasions, the bolder spirits sang "O Pyatt's Eyes, O Pyatt's Eyes".

On John Yeo's death, Pyatt was appointed to Carrington, where he reigned for thirty years dispensing epigrams and hospitality to new and old boys alike. He was succeeded in "College" by A. W. Hudson, a genial and gentle artist who has now abandoned schoolmastering in order to devote his whole time to painting. He has been "hung" both in the Royal Academy and in the Paris Salon. In Fettes history he has a special place as the first person connected with the school to own a motor car. This acquisition was made during my time at school and created a minor sensation. It was, however, not the first car associated with my life. Some years before, my uncle Ian owned the first car ever seen in Strathspey. It was a steam car and the heat from the boiler used to roast the behinds of those who sat on the back seat. My brother and I had our first motor ride in it, and one was enough. After this experience we used to sail past this snorting Billy on our bicycles and cock snooks at our uncle. The first successful car that I remember was Lord Derby's. He was then staying at Tulchan and used to steam past our house at Delliefure leaving a whirlwind of dust behind him. He made a break in our family life, for my mother was so terrified by this juggernaut that she gave up cycling, and our family bicycle picnics, then a popular feature of the summer holidays, had to be abandoned.

After K. P. Wilson, the master whom I liked best and admired most at Fettes was H. V. Phillips. He was a good French and German scholar, but it was as a musician that he commanded my attention and my devotion. He took both the choir and the orchestra and, as I was in both, he must have suffered severely from the false notes of my violin and the raucous harshness of my voice. Better than most men, he could maintain discipline without beating and even without giving impositions. He had a quick and ready wit which, when he was irritated, soon veered to sarcasm, and with a well-turned phrase he could reduce the most turbulent ragster to silence and obedience.

The orchestra and the choir performed on Founder's Day and at the School Concert. Before these occasions, he would make a special appeal to us, and we would do our best to respond. The set piece which I remember best was Kipling's "The English Flag" set to Bridge's music. There was a splendid bass chorus of four lines beginning with "Look— look well to your shipping", and this always produced an impressive roar. But the verse which stirred my emotions almost to the verge of tears was:

"Never the lotus closes, never the wild-fowl wake,
  But a soul goes out on the East Wind that died for
  England's sake."

It was sung pianissimo by the trebles and altos, and the singing filled me with strange longings. Kipling had just entered into my life, and the Boer War lent an added poignancy to tales like *The Drums of the Fore and Aft*. I was something more than a little patriot who was ready to die for England's sake. I wanted to see the world, and, with uncles in Malaya and Singapore sending me home strange stamps with tiger's heads, vaguely I felt the call of the East. I knew all about wild-fowl, but I longed to see that lotus close.

Phillips, a neat, forceful personality with a firm mouth and jaw, left Fettes during my last year. He had been disappointed by the slowness of his promotion. Subsequently, he made a rapid political career, becoming in turn private secretary to Mr. Asquith, a Member of Parliament and, finally, Chairman of the Liberal Party Central Organisation. His departure was a loss to Fettes. He was far too good a master ever to have been allowed to leave.

In those days, the Fettes staff included a man who was to become a greater celebrity than Phillips. This was "Jock" Beith, now known to the world as "Ian Hay". He had been a boy at Fettes, and, when he returned as a master, had been only four years away from the school. As a schoolboy, he had a distinguished career, reaching the dignity of the Upper Sixth and winning as many Governors' prizes as Sir John Simon who, although several years his senior, was at Fettes with him for one year. As a master, Jock Beith took the Remove, a form more distinguished for "rugger" prowess than scholarship. As an old Fettesian, "Jock" understood its ways and managed it successfully. A gentle but firm disciplinarian, he was immensely popular. I remember him best for his fancy waistcoats, his pipe and his versatility as an amateur actor and singer of comic songs. Indeed, at Saturday evening entertainments, the Fettes staff had a versatile trio of entertainers in Pyatt, Phillips, and Beith. Pyatt's singing of "The Magpie" has become a well-established tradition, and

Beith's "Aly" runs it a close second. Phillips' forte was a ditty entitled "I've only one note, my little B flat".

"Jock" Beith had not then blossomed into "Ian Hay" but he was already writing, and his first play, "The Crimson Coker-Nut", was first performed at Fettes. His devotion to the school and, above all, his services to the Fettes O.T.C. have made his name a household word to every generation of Fettesians. Curiously enough, Scottish public schools seem to have the knack of converting their masters into authors. W. J. Locke began his career as a master at Glenalmond, and W. C. Sellar, the author of that successful skit "1066 and All That", was not only a master at Fettes but, like Beith, is a distinguished alumnus of the school.

Of the masters who were unmercifully "ragged", I must write with circumspection. Like most schools, Fettes sheltered a small percentage of these unfortunates, although, in some cases, their stay was only temporary. They were to be found mainly among the teachers of extraneous subjects and included in A. F. Bohuslav Kroupa perhaps the most original character in any public school in Britain. He was the first Czech I ever met and I have already described him fully in my *Retreat from Glory*. Known to boys and masters alike as "B. K.", he taught drawing. Although he had been a lieutenant in the Austrian army and was supposed to have been scalped by a Prussian sabre at Koeniggraetz, he was incapable of enforcing discipline. His drawing classes were a joyful relaxation to small boys, and pandemonium reigned unchecked except on those rare occasions when the Head, alarmed perhaps by some particularly violent explosion, visited the room in order to inspect the budding talent of "B. K's" pupils.

There were other masters who, if they permitted less licence than "B. K.", were more exciting butts because their "ragging" involved a certain risk. I remember one shy and gentle teacher of mathematics and of "Stinks" to whom schoolmastering must have been a nightmare of torture. The school laboratory was far away from the main building, and the windows looked out on a washing-green. Here we were safe from intrusions by other masters, and a favourite trick was to pay an organ grinder to play on the green and to promise him an extra reward if he refused to go away. When the hurdy-gurdy started, the whole class would complain as one man: "Please, sir, I can't work for the noise." The master would listen sympathetically and, when volunteers offered to chase the intruder away, would select the biggest boy. Then, for a quarter-of-an-hour or so we would watch a magnificent sham fight on the green. The boy would advance with a washing-pole. The organ-grinder, playing up magnificently in order to earn his extra five bob, would run round the green with Italian agility. Occasionally, his monkey would take an unrehearsed part in the battle, and then, to our delight, the boy would beat a genuine retreat.

This same master could lose his temper on occasions, but, as he had a soft heart, it was not difficult to impose on him. One hot summer's day, we were allowed to take our coats off, and to add gaiety to this diversion a friend of mine, called Willie McKersie, stripped completely. He was "spotted" and this time the master took a serious view of the offence. Instead of arguing, he announced firmly that he would send McKersie up to the Head. This would have involved unpleasant consequences, and for the rest of the hour McKersie racked his brains to find an excuse that would mollify the master's heart. At the end of the lesson, having cut off a long shaving from the seat of the bench and soaked it well in red ink, he walked up to the master and declared solemnly that he had run a splinter into his behind and had had to take off his trousers in order to get it out. He got off scot free.

Another master, called in temporarily to fill a vacancy caused by death, involved me indirectly in an incident which landed me in the Headmaster's study. This master taught mathematics and, like many mathematicians, was quite incapable of dealing with unruly boys. On one occasion, he kept in a boy called Cassells for an "extra" on a half-holiday. While the master was out of the room, Cassells set a booby trap for him. It consisted of a huge oblong waste-paper basket filled with heavy dictionaries. When the master came in, the trap fell from the top of the door and crashed on his shoulder. Had it landed on his head, he might have been seriously hurt. Frightened and angry, he reported Cassells to the Head.

Cassells saved himself by declaring that he had set the trap for me. I was sent for and had to swear that I had been in the room, and this was strictly true. Fortunately forewarned, I had to add that I had left the room only for a few minutes and was coming back. And this was an elastic interpretation of the truth.

Supporters of a classical education may point out that the weakest masters are always to be found among the modernists. This was certainly true when I was a boy. Nevertheless, ability to maintain order does not depend on the advantages or disadvantages of different systems of education, nor does physique or even prowess at games make in itself for disciplinary powers, although a games-master, by reason of the hero-worship which he enjoys, has generally little trouble with his form. I remember one famous international "rugger" player who, in spite of his popularity as a master, was very weak as a disciplinarian. He was a brilliant scholar. He was not a Fettes master. Realising his own limitations, he consulted one of his colleagues as to how he ought to deal with troublesome boys. He was advised to take out the six biggest boys at the first breach of discipline and to beat them soundly. Primed with this excellent advice, he went into his form-room. The opportunity to act on it was there before his eyes. On his desk was a huge oval-shaped parcel. Obviously this was another "rag". Assuming a stern look, he rapped with his ruler on the desk.

"The boy or boys who placed this object on my desk will stand up at once."

Promptly the whole form stood up. The master was slightly nonplussed, but he did not lose courage.

"Very well," he said, "if you chose to be collectively responsible for this impertinence, you will suffer collectively. The whole form will come in at two o'clock, and I shall deal with you then."

A squeaky voice said falteringly: "Don't you think, Sir, you had better open the parcel first?"

The master untied the string. The parcel contained a magnificent rugby football, made of chocolate, and a card with the congratulations of the form on the master's being chosen to captain his country in the next international. This touching anti-climax scotched finally his attempts to assert his authority. He now devotes his talents and his scholarship to commerce.

Almost as closely associated with our lives as the masters were the school servants who had sometimes to be regarded as enemies, but as a whole were friends, and, on occasions, even allies. They were a fine body of servants, especially the older men like Sergeant Adam, a Crimean veteran, and Skinner, the school porter, who had been at Fettes almost since its opening day. A dear old man, too, was McLeod, who was in charge of the swimming baths. These three were Scots and splendid representatives of their race. But many of the waiters were Englishmen, and, if we mocked them for their Cockney accent, they bore no malice. Very quickly they acquired local patriotism and followed the school's "rugger" fortunes with the keenness of the boys themselves. Most of them could play "soccer" with considerable skill and in their matches against the school generally held their own.

A school servant, and a high one at that, for he was the head steward, was responsible for one of the few unusual incidents of my school life. One night, during my last year, a ghostly figure, carrying a candle, passed through our dormitory long after everyone was asleep and crashed against the partition of my cubicle. I awoke at once and lay for a moment in a sweat of fear. The candle had gone out. Presently I heard a body drag itself along the floor very slowly. Then the door banged, and in the dark stillness the sound of a slow and heavy tread floated back into the room. I ran and woke Moir Mackenzie and together we made our way downstairs to the stone corridor below. Creeping along and thinking of burglars, we saw a light swaying from side to side across the corridor. Then there was another crash and again darkness. We ran forward and nearly tripped over a huddled body. Moir lit a match. Before us lay the prostrate figure of the head steward. He was dead drunk.

The noise of his fall awoke others, for in a moment or two out came Coast, our house master, shivering in a dressing-gown, to join us in our inspection of the body. The next morning the unfortunate steward left, and his departure destroyed any sense of self-importance which Moir and I might have acquired from the part we had played in this mildly exciting drama. Personally I felt a more than momentary remorse in the thought that I had contributed in any way to the ruin of a fellow-creature, and from this first awakening of social conscience dates my moral and physical inability to dismiss anyone in my employment.

Thirty-five years form a whole lifetime in the history of a school. Of the twenty or more Fettes masters who strove to knock some sense into my head, only two remain on the staff to-day. Of the others, some are living in retirement, six, including Dr. Heard, are dead. "Tink", too, has passed on after a career of nearly fifty years, covering Fettes's development from an unknown pile of grey stone into an institution whose name and fame has spread to the farthest outposts of the Empire. When he arrived at Fettes, football was played in knickerbockers, and there were still boys in the school who remembered the years when long trousers were the regulation dress of the first fifteen. He had been a house master for more than forty years and, counting five years as the average period of a schoolboy's life, had sent out eight generations of Fettesians into the world. He had seen two war memorials erected to the memory of Old Fettesians who fell in the two great wars which took place during his period of office. These wars had brought four Victoria Crosses to Fettesians, and of these four, two, awarded for gallantry in the European War, were won by boys who had been in his house.

It was a period of increasing glory which culminated in the Great War. The future may bring still greater glory but it will be a different glory, for the year 1914 made the same break with the past in public schools as it made in other spheres of the nation's life.

For the triumphs won on many fields, much of the credit must be given to the Fettes masters and to the headmaster who selected them. I remember the vast majority of them with respect and admiration, and those who failed to earn my respect gained my affection and, later, caused me contrition for insensitive hurts to what I feel must have been sensitive natures. There is not one to whom I bear even the shadow of a grudge. There was not one who, even under provocation, ever committed an act of injustice or of petty revenge.

They may have had their limitations. They stuck to the established curriculum, never attempting to influence a boy towards Conservatism, Liberalism, Socialism or any other prevalent "ism", but seeking rather to prepare his mind so that later he might be able to reason these things out for himself.

I could wish that the present generation of public-school masters had the same merit of sticking to their last. During the last few years I have seen something of public-school life at first hand. I have been struck by the large number of exotic young masters who worship strange gods, who, having no practical knowledge of the subject, mouth extravagant views on foreign politics, and who, before accepting a post, wish to know the headmaster's attitude towards half a dozen different "isms" including, of course, pacifism. I cannot help feeling that this intrusion of politics into school life is not only wrong but grossly unfair to the boys.

CHAPTER FIVE

DURING MY FIRST two years at Fettes the terms seemed end-
lessly long and the holidays incredibly short, and, if I was not
unhappy, I cannot say honestly that I enjoyed my school life.
I was too young and too small to shine at games, and my
memories of this period are coloured mainly by such extraneous events as Queen Victoria's death, King Edward's
coronation and the visit of Captain Meiklejohn, the first
Fettes V.C.

Queen Victoria's death gave me my first experience of a
funeral service. The whole school went into mourning and,
although on the day of the funeral we did no work, we were
not allowed to play games. The memorial service in chapel
was a sombre ritual. Even the sky seemed to go into mourning. Although I respond easily to any emotional appeal, I
found the service interminably long and depressing. For the
rest of the day I wandered aimlessly about the corridors and
the "prep" room, munching biscuits and afraid to raise my
voice, not so much from respect for the dead monarch as
from fear lest a prefect would reprove me for making a noise.
I doubt the wisdom of enforcing the solemnity of death on
small boys. More frequently than not they are bored, and
where their emotions are affected the reaction is generally
mawkish and unhealthy.

King Edward's Coronation I remember chiefly for the
disappointment of its postponement. It was to have taken
place in term-time, and some weeks before the appointed
date the boys were asked to ascertain whether their parents
wished them to attend the Coronation ceremony or not.
This meant a visit to London and a holiday for three days. I
wrote to my father and was dejected when he turned down
my proposal on the plea of unreasonable expense. This disappointment was mild compared with my bitterness when the
King's sudden attack of appendicitis caused the Coronation

to be postponed at the very last minute. The boys who were going to London to see the ceremony had already left and could not be recalled. But the news of the postponement came in time to cancel the whole holiday which the rest of the school, including myself, were to have been granted. While some of my friends guzzled in London, I had to do an ordinary day's work. My sense of injustice was deeply stirred. Still, we were given an extra week for the summer holidays, and, as this meant more days in the Highlands, I felt later that the compensation was almost adequate.

Captain Meiklejohn's visit to the school roused me to a pitch of emotional ecstasy. A member of a famous family of Fettesians, he had been head of the school and had then entered the army. He had been with the Gordons at Dargai and had won what was generally regarded as the best Victoria Cross in the Boer War. At a critical moment in the battle of Elandslaagte, the Gordons, having lost their leaders, had begun to waver. Meiklejohn, then a young captain, sprang forward and, calling on his men to follow him, led a desperate rush against the enemy. The men rallied, and the threatened break in the line was repaired. Meiklejohn, however, paid dearly for his courage, for, severely wounded in four places, he lay for weeks at death's door. Now that he had recovered, he had been invited by the Head to visit the school in order that we might benefit by this personal contact with bravery.

He was a modest and inspiring hero. I can see him now as he came into Hall to take his place at the masters' table. The whole school rose to him and cheered him for five minutes. He was dressed in mufti, and, although I was disappointed not to see his Victoria Cross, the armless sleeve pinned to his coat told its own story. As he passed between the long tables, I noticed that he blushed as deep a crimson as any new boy.

During luncheon, which was, in fact, our dinner, I did a minor gloat because, as a boy at Fettes, Meiklejohn had been in "College", and was kicked on the shins by other small

boys who were in less privileged houses. But when he rose
to speak at the end of the meal and the cheering was renewed,
these minor exultations were forgotten. Like every other boy
I listened to his address with an attention which I had never
given to any master. He was not very eloquent. He made no
mention of Elandslaagte, but spoke of doing one's job, and
the kind of public service that a school like Fettes could and
did perform. He made some reference to the school motto of
"Industria" and before he sat down he told us that the Headmaster had asked him what he would like the school to do
for him. He then said that, if it did not seem too immodest a
request, he would like to ask for a whole holiday.

I do not think that the Head was over-pleased, for we had
already had a whole holiday for the relief of Mafeking, and
whole holidays at a school like Fettes were rarely granted.
But in the circumstances the request could not be refused,
and I left Hall, my nerves tingling with elation and with a
new determination in my heart to do my own job better
than I had done it before.

I kept my good resolutions for twenty-four hours. But
something of the soldier's speech remained rooted in my
mind. I dislike militarism and hate any form of dictatorship,
but since that day I have never been able to understand
Britain's foolish pride in the volunteer system or why any
citizen should be excused the supreme job of defending his
country by paying someone else to do it for him. Yet the
volunteer system was an even stronger shibboleth than it
is to-day, and Fettes, which sent a considerable number of
her sons into the army, had then no cadet corps.

A year or two before the Great War Meiklejohn died a
death which brought him as much fame as his Victoria Cross.
His mare bolted at a parade in Hyde Park. Handicapped by
the loss of his right arm, he nevertheless succeeded in turning
her aside from a line of troops. The mare, now scared out of
her wits, headed straight for a group of children. There was
only one way to avert disaster from the children, and

Meiklejohn took it without hesitation. He put his mare straight at the Park railings and in this last desperate deed of gallantry both mare and rider were killed.

Towards the end of my second year I began to emerge a little from the state of suppression which, during the early years at school, makes a small boy's life seem so monotonous. I had begun to fulfil some of my early promise as a cricketer and had gained my place quite easily in the "Under Fifteen" cricket team. This promotion widened my horizons, for the "Under Fifteen" played matches against other schools. As a member of the team I travelled as far afield as Musselburgh in order to play against Loretto and derived more enjoyment than I dared to show from this pupillary stage of "blood-hood". It was not, however, until the autumn of 1902 that I became infected with the virus of rugby football. And, to the detriment of my work, this virus was to hold me in its clutches for the rest of my school career.

It would be unfair to blame Fettes for my mania. Fostered by my father's enthusiasm, it dated from my childhood days at Beith and, after a short stage of suppressed quiescence, had broken out again with redoubled violence. At the same time I cannot truthfully say that there was anything in the atmosphere of Fettes life to arrest the progress of this mania. In the eyes of the boys and masters alike rugby football was *the* game to the insignificance of all others, and it was played with a fervour into which entered much of the spirit of Bannockburn and something of the worship of tribal gods.

Fettes prowess at football had been early established. Only ten years after the opening of the school, the Old Fettesians at Cambridge entered for a cup which had been presented for competition between teams from ten leading "rugger-playing" public schools of Britain. Although unable to muster a full fifteen, the Old Fettesians had triumphed over all opposition. The tradition, then established, had gathered momentum with the years, and a long list of Blues and Internationals testified to a supremacy which reached its peak soon after I went to Fettes.

Scotland herself was then as dominant at "rugger" as she is to-day at "soccer". She was well ahead of the other Home countries in victories, and in the decade of 1895-1905, which covered the period of my preparatory and public-school life, had beaten England seven times and had suffered only two defeats. The Scottish capital, too, was the source of Scotland's "rugger" strength, and Fettes was at the football gates of Edinburgh. It is, therefore, not surprising if Fettes boys were football mad, or if a small boy whose father was a member of the Scottish Rugby Union was the greatest of those fanatics.

The game, run by the boys themselves with the assistance of a games master, was taken with grim seriousness. The organisation was thorough and Spartan. Even the lowest game was refereed by a "blood" on Big Side, and special attention was paid to the "Under Fifteen". Courage was the first principle in our "rugger" education, and very soon we learnt that the consequences of "funking" were more unpleasant than the risks of falling on the ball before the feet of advancing forwards. The gods of the game played on Big Side and Little Side which comprised the sixty best players in the school. The rest were organised in "Belows", and two or three times a term the best teams that each house could pick from these "Belows" met in deadly rivalry.

These miniature House matches, generally played on an extra half holiday, were fought out with the fierceness of a real House match. The House "Below" Fifteen had to go into special training. In the evenings the forwards had to "scrum" in the stone corridors against the bigger boys to the detriment of their knees and trousers. Backs like myself were given practice in catching in the dormitories. It took the form of standing at one end of the long corridor while a big boy slung a College tooth-mug, a clumsy china affair with a handle, from the other end. If one missed the catch, the mug was smashed to bits and the breakage was debited to the faulty fieldsman. On the day of days the team was given a preliminary "jaw" by the House Captain. The match was watched by the whole school and was played to a sustained accompaniment of cheering. Defeat was followed by a lecture on our failings and by a warning that in future we must do better. Victory brought such enviable compensations as a hot bath, a special tea, and perhaps a generous proportion of aid in "prep" from a well-satisfied prefect. In this manner the fledglings were prepared for the greater ardours and the greater glories to come.

But far more important in our eyes than our own struggles were the fortunes of the First Fifteen in the School Championship. This was fought out by the six public schools of Scotland and was not decided until late in the season, for each school played the others twice, once in the Christmas term and once in the Easter. The championship was not recognised officially by the headmasters but was accepted religiously by the boys, by the Scottish public and by the Scottish Press. Above all, I should say, by the Edinburgh Press, for the Edinburgh newspapers were, I think, the most harmful factor in exaggerating the importance of schoolboy football. On Fridays both the *Evening News* and the *Evening Dispatch* carried advance notes on the prospects of the match on the following Saturday. On Saturdays the late editions gave a long account of the game, and on the Monday there were further notes on the performances of the individual players. Geordie Howell, the school professional, although himself always sparing of praise, kept these papers with paternal pride, and we used to assemble in his shop in the pavilion to read under headlines of "Schoolboys Astounding" glowing accounts of matches, in which the ball was always referred to as the "spheroid" or the "oblong" and in which the running of schoolboy prodigies like Kenneth McLeod was described as "the poetry of motion".

Doubtless, the intoxication of this reading produced

swollen heads. But as players these schoolboys were, indeed, astounding. Fettes was then entering into the golden age of its football era, when twenty school matches were won in succession and in three years our lines were crossed only twice. In those days, too, there seemed to be less physical difference between men and boys than there is to-day. Club football in Edinburgh was then of a high standard, yet club sides, strengthened by half-a-dozen Internationals, came down to Fettes on Wednesdays and to their surprise and discomfiture went away defeated. In case this statement should raise a smile on the lips of the modern rugby footballer, I point out that of my own actual contemporaries at Fettes thirteen gained international caps for Scotland and fourteen won their "rugger" Blues at Oxford or Cambridge.

I have always been a romantic idealist and have never succeeded in adapting myself to the exigencies of a positive world. If at Fettes Stanley Weyman and H. S. Merriman provided the reading stuff of my dreams, my romanticism found a practical outlet in the arena of the football field. Inter-school matches reduced me to a state of delirious excitement. The east wind, bringing sleet and hailstones in its train, might cut like a knife. The wet turf of Big Side might soak its way through my boots. But I was oblivious to everything except the passionate desire for victory, and my lungs, pumping the air for the incessant roar of "Fet-tes", kept out the cold. And to the heroes of these battles I gave the same devotion as a Spanish waiter lavishes on a matador.

The game entered into and, indeed, almost forced itself into my religion. At evening prayers in "College" we had special hymns chosen by the prefects both before and after school matches. On the eve of the Loretto or the Merchiston match we had "Christian, seek not yet repose", "Fight the Good Fight" or "Forward be our watchword". If Fettes won, and in my last three years she always did, we had "For all the saints who from their labours rest". On those nights Harry

Pyatt had no reason to complain of any lack of fervour in the singing, and the prefects, who walked in last, were cheered by the whole house on their procession into evening prayers.

As far as I was concerned, there was nothing blasphemous in this performance. I took these hymns literally and for some terms always sang "Forwards, be our watchword". It never entered my head that the correct version did not convert the adverb into a plural noun. This form of battle prayer lasted throughout my school career at Fettes, and when I became a member of the school cricket eleven I used, when batting, to mouth a silent prayer before each ball.

Even at Founder's Day, football was not forgotten. The proceedings in the gymnasium, crowded with parents and distinguished Edinburgh big-wigs, were grim enough and included such dreary performances as a cantata by the choir, a suite by the school orchestra and recitations by leading members of the Sixth Form. The only items in the programme which made any appeal to the boys were the school songs, when the old boys in the gallery made the rafters ring with the last "Floreas Fettesia" in a swelling note sustained long after the choir had stopped, and the "Vive-là", a song specially written for the occasion and recapitulating the chief events of the year. In the chronicle of these events, football had several verses to itself, and I remember vividly the cheers and laughter when G. H. Keeton, our Sixth Form master, who was given his English cap while he was at Fettes, was neatly taken off in the following quatrain:

"When Scotland met England the blast of the whistle
　　Proclaimed that the victory lay with the Thistle,
　But I'm told at the start they felt doomed to be beaten,
　When they saw in the enemy's ranks Mr. Keeton."

In fairness to England I should add that for her football prowess, Fettes owes much to her English masters. Keeton himself and, more especially R. F. Cumberlege, an elder brother of the post-war England full-back, revolutionised the tactics of Fettes football, and a large share of the triumphs which the school enjoyed between 1902 and 1914 must be ascribed to their skilful coaching. Their tact deserves as much praise as their technical knowledge. In those days it was not easy for masters, especially for English masters, to enforce new ideas on the minds of Scottish boys like the McLeods, Moir Mackenzie, and several others, who even then were good enough to play for Scotland and, indeed, gained their place in the Scottish Fifteen as soon as they left school. The adoption of novel methods had to be suggested rather than commanded, and by both masters this course was followed, with the result that not only was there no friction, but the school football benefited enormously.

Rugby football was responsible for the one really exciting episode of my career at Fettes. Most novels about public schools have an atmosphere of unreality, for the excellent reason that the actual incidents of school life are too humdrum to provide adequate material for a plot. But the story which I now tell might have gone straight into any novel. During my time, Fettes had a remarkable run of success not only at football but in every other branch of sport. This success owed something to the twin virtues of will-power and team spirit, and still more to the presence in the school of a number of boys with exceptional talent for games. Of these boys the most prominent were the famous McLeod brothers. I was at Fettes with two of them, and Kenneth, the youngest, was my exact contemporary. His full name was Kenneth Grant McLeod, and at school we called him "Grunt". He was, in my opinion, the greatest natural games-player of all time. Every game came naturally to him. He never trained for any game. He excelled at all games. He played "rugger" for Cambridge and Scotland when he was only seventeen and, although he was "capped" ten times, he finished his first-class football career before he was twenty-one. As first string he ran the Hundred Yards for Cambridge against Oxford for three years in succession and was never beaten. He was Long Jump champion of Scotland. He is the only Scottish school-boy who has ever gained a cricket Blue at Cambridge, and I do not think it an exaggeration to say that he could have won a Blue at any game which he cared to take up, except chess.

Perhaps the most remarkable distinction in this unique record was his achievement in getting into the school "rugger" team when he was only fourteen. He was then in the Remove, which was the lowest form on the Modern Side. In those days it was full of rather lazy footballers. Previously it had been taken by Jock Beith who, as I have mentioned, understood its ways. When he left, he was succeeded by a keen young master who, having been at Harrow, probably failed to realise that several rich Scottish parents sent their boys to Fettes mainly to play football, and that these boys drifted naturally into the Remove. He made his form work and, taking exception to the idleness of a boy of fourteen, he kept McLeod in from playing in a match. Although easy-going enough except on the football field, "Grunt" resented this fancied slight to his dignity. Instead of doing his work he sulked and, as his contribution to his afternoon's task, chalked up on the blackboard an impertinent insult to the new master. The actual words were, I think, "—— is a bloody devil."

The master took a serious view of this offence, locked the form-room door, and went straight to the Head. Exaggerating the story, rumour travelled with lightning wings, and by the evening the news had spread through the school that "K. G." was to be "sacked". The Fettes Fifteen were then hot favourites for the Schools' Championship, and feeling ran high.

On the next day the unfortunate master was "taking Hall" and on his way into the dining-room he was hissed. The hissing, started by one or two boys, was taken up by all the bolder spirits. The atmosphere was electric. The master did the only thing that was possible to be done in the circumstances. With face as white as a sepulchre, he left the room and returned presently with the Headmaster. I cannot remember all the penalties which the Head imposed. They were comprehensive, and we left Hall subdued but still defiant.

For the next twelve hours the school was in a state of incipient rebellion. Then common-sense in the person of "K. P." prevailed, and the drama petered out in the anti-climax which was all that it merited. "Grunt" was beaten by "K. P.", who was his housemaster, and made his peace with his form-master. Boy and master became good friends, and for the rest of his time the efficient Harrovian was liked as much as he was respected. He became a "rugger" enthusiast and a great admirer of McLeod's prowess, and I remember an excellent poem from his pen which was printed in *The Fettesian* and is well worth a place in any anthology of sporting verse. He is now headmaster of a public school in England.

To-day, Fettes takes its "rugger" more rationally. The Inter-Schools' Championship is more severely frowned on than ever before, and the Edinburgh Press has been asked to restrain its ardour. The battle hymns have been stopped by a new headmaster who was himself an English "rugger" international. The result of this damping-down process is to be seen in the diminishing number of Fettes boys who find a place in Scotland's Fifteen. No longer does Fettes enjoy a monopoly of Cambridge "rugger" Blues, and three years ago, for the first time for more than thirty years, there was not a single Fettesian in either the Oxford or the Cambridge sides at Twickenham. Gone, too, are the days when mothers of prospective Fettes boys would visit the school and, seeing a House match, promptly withdraw their offsprings' entrance form.

In the complicated age in which we now live it is perhaps
for the best that Fettes football has been reduced to a less
exalted position in the schoolboy scheme of things. The
Fettes boy of to-day has a fuller, richer life than his pre-war
prototype. The Modern Side has become an active force and
now gains scholarships at Oxford and Cambridge for mathematics, science and history. There is, too, a new standard of
comfort, and with the installation of central heating the
freezing terrors of the east wind have been banished. These
are advantages which were unknown to the boys of my
generation, and doubtless the modern boy makes good use
of them.

Yet there was virtue in the former simplicity when boys
worked as hard as they played, and I sometimes wonder if
the new graces have been acquired at the cost of a certain loss
of virility. For whatever its aesthetic defects may have been,
Fettes education in my time was, above all things, virile.
Boys perhaps took the future too much for granted. They
rarely questioned the wisdom of their superiors. They never
doubted the efficacy of the public-school system. But if they
thought more of their bodies than of their souls, they generally acquired some genuine intellectual interest. For all the
school's reputation for "rugger", brawn, except in a few
rare instances, was never cultivated at the expense of brain,
and I know no school to which Kipling's stricture of
"muddied oafs" applied less. The Head of the school was
always the top boy at work. Yet of the sixty Heads of school
from 1870 to 1929 no less than fifteen won Blues at Oxford
or Cambridge. Of the sixty Fettesians who won "rugger"
Blues at these two universities more than one quarter were
scholars or exhibitioners, and nearly half were in the Sixth
Form at school. In 1909 the Oxford and Cambridge "rugger'
captains were both Fettesians. Both were scholars. Both took
"Firsts". One to-day is Governor of the North-West
Frontier Province of India and the other Governor of the
Northern Province of the Sudan.

These figures speak for themselves, and I shall always maintain that rugby football is the best of all school games not merely because it provides the finest training in character and in team spirit, but because it interferes far less with work than cricket.

The Fettes tradition of football prowess and classical scholarship was slightly impaired by the Great War, but it never proved its soundness so convincingly as in that cataclysm. At the outbreak of the War, there were rather less than two thousand Old Fettesians in existence, and of these nearly nine hundred were over forty years of age. Of this small band no less than one thousand and ninety four served in the King's forces and two hundred and forty-six died for their country. The honours gained included two Victoria Crosses, fifty-nine Distinguished Service Orders and a hundred and forty-six Military Crosses. It is both dangerous and unseemly to claim records in connection with war and death, but, for a small school with few great names among its alumni, Fettes's achievement stands extraordinarily high.

I hesitate to claim any special virtues of patriotic duty for rugby footballers, but, as far as Scotland is concerned, their war sacrifice was second to none, and assuredly in the courage and determination shown by Fettesians on the field of honour, there was something of the spirit acquired in the keen struggles of their youth on Big Side.

Last Easter I revisited Fettes during the holidays. The place was deserted, and I stood alone beside the rugged stone figure of the dying kilted Fettesian who holds his arm aloft in a gesture of "Carry On". The memorial faces Arthur's Seat and Edinburgh Castle and stands on a site which every boy must pass daily either on his way to school or to the playing fields. The sides of its base bear the names of the two hundred and forty-six Fettesians who fell in the War. Among them are many of my school contemporaries. But the longest list contains the names of the boys who left school between the years of 1910 and 1915. These were the young officers who as second-lieutenants led the platoons of Kitchener's new armies over the top and all too frequently were the first to fall. The footballers were the natural leaders. Of the Fettes teams of those years more than two whole Fifteens could be formed from the dead.

CHAPTER SIX

I WAS JUST sixteen when I began my third year at Fettes. My first two years had given me little cause for self-satisfaction. As most parents learn to their cost, the years of approaching adolescence are the most difficult in a boy's life. Some boys go through this period with little disturbance. Others undergo a devitalising process which frequently produces apathy, sulkiness and laziness. In my own case I had indulged in both laziness and sulkiness. I had been the most insignificant of small boys, and to that insignificance I had reacted badly. The laziness showed itself in bad work at school. The sulkiness was reserved for the benefit of my parents. I think to-day that the holidays must have released the pent-up suppressions which school life imposes on a sensitive boy. And for all my love of games, I was, I believe, more sensitive than the average Fettes boy.

It was not that I suffered from the awakening of sex. This problem did not worry me unduly. My difficulties were of my own creating. I had one fatal weakness in my character. I cultivated popularity and was always failing because I sought it too eagerly. The self-confidence of my early boyhood had been replaced by a shy and timid self-consciousness.

I was now emerging from this unattractive and unsatisfactory period. During the summer holidays my father had gone to Canada, and in our holiday Highland home I had taken his place as the male head of the family. Although our home life was as simple as ever and I spent most of my time fishing, with my brother Rufus, I had to help my mother to entertain our guests and visitors. In this way my world grew larger. The widening process was maintained at Fettes. The school year of 1903-1904 was to bring me my first athletic distinctions and with them a new sense of my own importance.

The Christmas term of 1903 opened with an emotional

313

shock. I had just arrived in "College" when another boy told me that Broadrick, my French master, had been killed the day before in a climbing accident on Scafell. At first the story was discredited as a rumour. But at prayers that evening we were told officially of his death, and the next morning *The Scotsman* was full of the tragedy. A thoroughly experienced mountaineer who spent all his holidays in Switzerland, he had gone with a friend to the Lake District to spend a few days near the mountains before returning to school. There he had met two strangers in his hotel, and the next day the four men set out to attempt the ascent of the Scafell Pinnacle. Broadrick had been leading and later had changed places with one of the others. Then, when they were more than half-way up the face of the rock, someone fell and all four were hurled to the bottom of the abyss. All were killed, one man with a broken back surviving long enough to give a short account of the accident.

Broadrick had been a good master, not very inspiring perhaps, but abundantly patient, full of understanding and transparently sincere. He was in the literal sense of the word a good man, and in his own quiet way he succeeded in influencing for good all those who came under his supervision. I had been in his set from my first day at Fettes, and, although I had many tussles with him, I liked him best of my first-year masters. With the announcement of his death, all his various acts of kindness surged back into my memory. As I looked round the form-room, still damp with the smell of cleaning, where we had laboured through Daudet's *La Belle Nivernaise* together, I felt suddenly cold and friendless. That night in my cubicle I had an emotional upset and cried bitterly.

Fortunately, death passes lightly from the memory of normal boys, whose minds are rightly obsessed by the trivial activities of their own daily existence. And with the beginning of this term there were more than the usual number of new interests to occupy my mind. As one advances up the school ladder, the beginning of each Christmas term brings its annual surprise. The end of the summer term is always marked by the large exodus of leaving boys, and, when the school reassembles, one wonders how it will carry on without the giants of the past year. Only gradually does one realise that one has become or is in process of becoming a giant one's self.

The school year that had ended had been a memorable one in the history of Fettes's sporting annals. The school had won both the football and the cricket championships. Yet the two ensuing years were to bring even greater successes, and, when the first matches started, I found my name on the school notice board outside Hall as a member of the Second Fifteen. Both the First and Second Fifteens at Fettes wore in matches the famous magenta stockings, the possession of which at one time was an almost certain passport to a Cambridge Blue. I did not keep my place in the "Second", but for one Saturday afternoon I wore the hideous stockings with the same pride as a young subaltern feels when he puts on his first uniform. But I made certain of my place in the Third Fifteen and in due course was given the chocolate cap with white tassel which confers on its wearer the dignity of a minor "blood". Membership of one of the Three Fifteens meant new contacts with boys in other houses and an increased importance in one's own house.

I had succeeded in obtaining my remove from the Lower Fifth and was now in the "Upper Fifth" under the vigilant eye of "K.P.". This promotion entitled me to a study. In recent years I have had numerous opportunities of inspecting boys' studies in English public schools and have marvelled both at the luxury of the fittings and the decorative taste of their occupants. At Fettes there was no such luxury and no such display of artistic talent. One bought or was persuaded to buy the study stock of the previous occupant, and, when one was as poor as I was, one had to be content with these dingy trappings. Some fellows plastered their walls with cheap picture-postcard photographs of popular actresses, for in those days favourites like Miss Edna May, Miss Marie Studholme, Miss Gertie Miller and Miss Gabrielle Ray represented in a very mild manner what Joan Crawford, Ginger Rogers and the Garbo mean to the modern boy. Others again favoured the pretty classicism, reproduced in cheap prints, of Lord Leighton and Sir Alma Tadema. But the commonest form of mural decoration was a many-wired frame in which one inserted the photographs of one's friends. With stiff collar and hair plastered down for the occasion, they looked unnatural and were sometimes scarcely recognisable. The most important piece of furniture, however, was the easy chair. It was known vulgarly as a "soft-arse".

A study meant privacy, and, although there was no virtue and certainly no common-sense in skimping "preparation" for "K.P.", privacy meant the long-desired opportunity for reading. My best friend in "College" was a boy called Black. His mother was a widow, and he was going to be a doctor. He was not very good at games, nor was he particularly interested in them. He had curly hair and was nicknamed "Poodle". But he was a great reader, and because of his interest in books I was in less danger of losing my own love of reading. Even in "College" the standard of reading was not high. Prefects and poets like A. Y. Campbell could browse in the Sixth Form Library whose precincts were to be denied to me until 1905, and what they read I do not know. "A.Y." at any rate, knew his Gilbert, for he parodied him brilliantly in *The Fettesian* in connection with an influenza epidemic. One verse, I remember, ran something like this:

> "For I'm the "preefs" and the dooks and the fags
>   And the waiter who rings the bell,
> The staff entire and the whole of the choir,
>   And the three fifteens as well."

Of the boys in "College", "A.Y." was the only one who gave any tangible evidence of literary taste or talent. If it lurked in the bosoms of other aspirants, they kept it there. The rest of the house was frankly Philistine, and in the House Library the chief "run" was on Kipling and Conan Doyle. Although *The Speckled Band* gave me more than one nightmare, I never became a Sherlock Holmes fanatic. I preferred Doyle's other books like *Rodney Stone* and the Brigadier Gerard series and, more especially, his short sporting stories like *The Master of Croxley*, which I still consider the best boxing story ever written.

"Poodle" Black recommended a man called Wells, and I remember reading *The Invisible Man* with some enjoyment, but with no consciousness that a new star had arisen in the literary firmament. Shaw, who had just written *Man and Superman*, was not even a name to me, and I doubt if his works then figured in our House Library. My romantic mind was captivated by the historical novel, and Merriman's *The Sowers* and *The Vultures*, which I read and re-read, gave me my first interest in diplomacy and in Russia. Scott, whom I had liked as a small boy, had been shelved because boring novels like *Ivanhoe* were used as school text books and were frequently given as holiday tasks. As generally happens, I was put off him, and it was not until I went to Malaya that I returned to him with renewed devotion. In my affections Marion Crawford's *The Cigarette Maker's Romance* shared pride of place with Weyman's *Under the Red Robe* and *Count Hannibal*. *Vanity Fair* was one of my Fettes discoveries. Even then I preferred it vastly to *Esmond*, and to-day its eternal truths have not lost their savour or their power to please.

Taken by and large, however, my first and lasting love was Stevenson. He was not too popular in the puritanical Edinburgh of those days, and my rebellious nature and my capacity for feeling misunderstood made me more than ever his champion and his devotee. My interest in him was stimulated by the fact that 17 Heriot Row, where he lived as a child and which I passed on my way to and from "up town", was next door to the house of old friends of my family. With their assistance I was shown the nursery which was said to have inspired *The Child's Garden of Verses*, and I yielded readily to the pleasant influence of this environment.

I have a passionate fondness for visiting the homes of the great men of the past. Edinburgh is remarkably rich in Scott and Stevenson associations, but it was not until long after I left school that I was able to indulge my passion, to follow the trail of Stevenson's Edinburgh peregrinations, and in the little house in Howard Place to study the first scratchy manuscripts and to inspect the quaint, bent fishing-rods with which he flogged the Scottish burns until the too easy slaughter of trout made him give up angling for ever. The Fettes of my time gave no encouragement to literary excursions of this nature.

Looking back on my school-life, I am sometimes inclined to ascribe this rigidity of attitude to lack of imagination and to the cramping limitations of a classical education. Then common-sense comes to my rescue, and I think of the unfortunate master who would have been called upon to superintend these literary pilgrimages. He would have been well-meaning, and well-meaning masters are rarely good disciplinarians. The pilgrimage would have lent itself inevitably to ribaldry and "ragging". The comedian, who exists in every form, would have had a field day, and, so far from being stimulated, any latent literary enthusiasm among the other boys would have been killed for ever.

It is, I think, better that boys should remain boys until they leave school, even if this means a prolongation of the Philistine stage. And in my time Fettes boys, with very few exceptions, had "boy" written all over them even when they were tackling grown men. It is true that they possessed certain advantages over the modern boy. Better developed physically but more circumscribed in their mental outlook, they had no radio nor even a gramophone to disturb the water-tight compartments of their minds. They were not exposed to the frenzied canvassing of Navy Leagues and

Peace Pledge Unions. If their enthusiasms were confined, they were free from cynicism. The storm of politics never ruffled the tranquil back-waters of their lives, and certainly no boy would have dreamt of criticising Joseph Chamberlain or Arthur Balfour in the same manner in which the modern boy contemptuously dismisses Mr. Churchill as a firebrand and loftily condemns the diplomacy of Mr. Eden. Perhaps we were not rebellious or challenging enough, but in every generation youth has the defects of its age, and in course of time the boy of to-day will be amazed by the cocksure confidence of the next generation in the same way in which I sometimes marvel at the mental precocity of this one.

In the Easter Term of 1904 I saw the school football team win the championship for the second year in succession and the Scottish Fifteen, helped by three formidable Old Fettesians, score a narrow triumph over England at Inverleith. Of those glories I was only a humble spectator. But with the advent of summer I tasted the first fruits of personal success. Although there were several old "caps" back, I gained an early place in the school cricket Eleven and succeeded in keeping it.

This exaltation brought many privileges: white cricket boots which were cleaned by Geordie Howell, the school professional; long talks with Geordie himself, a shrewd judge of men and a cynical philosopher; pleasant trips to Perth to play Glenalmond, and to peaceful Lasswade, where the nearest Scottish approach to English country-house cricket existed, and, last but not least, the thrilling but nervous ordeal of walking out alone from the pavilion to the plaudits of one's schoolfellows. It meant, too, new friends, for cricket is an exacting pastime, and the Eleven were naturally thrown much together.

In this way I renewed my acquaintance with Kenneth McLeod, with whom I had spent my first year in the Lower Fourth. He had then gone on to the Modern Side and, rising early to dizzy heights of athletic distinction, had soared out of my life. Although not yet captain, he had already been three years in the Eleven and was still the youngest member of it, a distinction of precocity never attained even by M. R. Jardine, the father of England's Test Match captain and the greatest cricketer that Fettes has ever produced. McLeod was a pleasant and amusing companion, conscious of his own prowess, yet free from frills, independent in his attitude towards masters and boys, happy-go-lucky and care-free except on the field of play, where he never admitted defeat until the last ball was bowled or the whistle blown for time. I liked him and, of course, regarded him as the greatest of my contemporaries.

As there were so few vacancies in the Eleven, I trained very seriously. Hitherto the swimming baths had been my chief delight in the summer term, but now I shunned them lest the water might affect my eye. I was fortunate enough to make a good score in an early match, but I had many anxious moments, when, coming out from breakfast on the morning of a match, I scanned the notice-board to see if my name had been omitted or if I had dropped a place in the order of merit.

Perhaps the most anxious of these moments came on the eve of the match against Merchiston. I was doing my preparation in my study when the school porter knocked at the door. The Headmaster wished to see me at once. Vaguely disturbed and examining my conscience, I walked over to the Lodge. The Head held a telegram in his hand. There was a grave but kindly look in his eyes.

"I'm sorry to tell you", he said at once, "that your grandfather is dead." I looked down at the floor, and he continued:

"Your father is coming to Edinburgh at once. You may of course go to him on Sunday and you may tell your housemaster to make the necessary arrangements for you to attend the funeral."

He made some kind references to my grandfather's public

career, and with eyes still downcast I thanked him. Then I looked up.

"What about the match against Merchiston to-morrow?" I blurted out nervously.

The Head had not thought of this contingency. He hesitated for a moment. Then he asked me:

"Do you think your father would like you to play?"

I did not know, but decency seemed to demand a negative, and I gave it.

"I am sure you are right," said the Head with a more gentle voice than I had ever heard him use before. "You had better tell the captain of the Eleven at once."

That night I slept fitfully and lay awake for hours, a prey to a new and strange nervousness for which my grandfather's death was only indirectly responsible. Although I struggled against it, the dominant thought which disturbed my sleep was fear lest my substitute should do so well in the match the next day that I should lose my place in the team.

Cricket was banished from my thoughts when on the Sunday I went with my father to the house near Merchiston, and was taken into my grandfather's bedroom. His was not only the first death among my near relations during my lifetime; in his person I saw death face to face for the first time. He looked very strange, for during his illness he had grown a beard. The lines had vanished from his face, leaving the skin as smooth and as polished as wax. The last years of his life had been troubled years. A diary which he had left showed that his second marriage had been a failure. Now that he looked happy and peaceful I felt relieved.

Two days later I followed the coffin to its last resting-place in the Grange Cemetery, where lie buried Dr. Chalmers, Dr. Guthrie and many another Scottish divine. My grandfather had played a considerable part in the public life of Edinburgh, and *The Scotsman* had devoted a column to his obituary notice. He had been chairman of the Edinburgh Chamber of Commerce and a governor of the Infirmary, and at the time of his death he was a member of the Edinburgh Town Council. The City Fathers, dressed in their civic robes, attended the funeral in full force and rode before the hearse in carriages with officers carrying the City Sword, mace and halberds covered with crape. As the only grandson present, I was one of the pall-bearers and helped to lower the coffin into the grave. I was cold and ill at ease in the presence of the large crowd of mourners. I felt as if I were taking part in a dramatic performance and was overcome by stage fright.

Still nervous and strangely silent, I drove back with my father to the house and was given a glass of milk and a piece of cake while the lawyer read the will to the assembled relations. It was a typical Scottish will, rigidly just in its even division of the estate between the five surviving children. My father was the only son. His education, paid for by the scholarships which he won, had cost my grandfather almost nothing. Yet from my father's share of the inheritance was deducted the advance which he had received to enable him to complete the purchase of Seafield.

Only half understanding the legal rigmarole, I listened inattentively while the lawyer droned his way through the maze of figures. Then I heard the word grandchildren. My grandfather had left us all a hundred pounds each, to be spent on travel. I felt a sudden twinge of remorse. My grief had been inadequate. It is true that my grandfather had never won my affection. He had few of the attributes which gain the confidence of boys. He took no interest in games, nor did he enter easily into the spirit of boys' amusements. His house was a place where one's shoes had always to be free from mud and where one had to wait until one was spoken to before speaking. But he had inspired me with a certain respect for the serious things of life and at least he had always taken an interest in my intellectual welfare. And of that interest he had now given a tangible proof. I felt sorry that I had not shown him more devotion. I felt still sorrier for my father who looked suddenly ten years older, and for once I was angry with my mother who had never liked her father-in-law and who, even in the presence of death, saw no reason why she should make a pretence of having done so.

Full of rather morbid thoughts I made my way back to Fettes and changed into ordinary clothes. The emotions of normal boys are skin-deep, evanescent, and easily influenced by what to-day seem trifles. With the casting off of the outward signs of mourning, my morbidness vanished. Nor were my alarms about my First Eleven colours in any way justified. Fettes won a comfortable but unexciting victory over Merchiston; my substitute did nothing to disturb my equanimity. I resumed my place in the team automatically and a Sunday or two later, as I was coming down the steps from Chapel, the captain of the Eleven walked up to me, shook hands with me, and said: "Congrats on your First."

My new cap and blazer arrived on the eve of the Loretto match, a two-day affair which in that year was played at Fettes. Superstition and fear of being accused of indecent haste compelled me to leave the glaringly new blazer in my locker. My modesty was rewarded. Fettes won the toss, and, although we had two remarkable schoolboy cricketers in McLeod and Gerald Turner, a brother of the former Essex player, we made a wretched start. Both our stars were dismissed cheaply, and at luncheon time we had lost seven wickets for only 91 of which my share was 28 not out.

On going out to bat after luncheon, I was told to make runs quickly, because our tail was weak. I hit at everything and with the aid of good luck and bad fielding, the last three wickets added nearly a hundred runs. I walked in as modestly as I could, but of course I enjoyed my success. Boys who had hardly noticed my existence before came up and spoke to me. Masters added their congratulations and said that in the circumstances my score of sixty-six was worth many a century. A score of seventy-five in a school match would have entitled me to a presentation bat, and great was my joy when my house master informed me that I could order one at his expense. Perhaps my happiest moment was when Gerald Turner, our captain, asked me why I was not wearing my First Eleven blazer. I put it on next day, and nobody jeered or pinched my arm.

It was not a thing that one could wear often, for by some strange lack of imagination the early authorities at Fettes had selected for the First Eleven cricket colours a blazer which even at a close distance was indistinguishable from a Cambridge Blue. Wags used to say that, when the colours were first chosen, Fettes had not heard of Cambridge. Personally I suspect that our English masters, driven mad by their efforts to teach Scottish boys the rudiments of the game, chose Cambridge blue as a cruel joke at the expense of Scottish cricket.

My triumph was short-lived, for on the Saturday Kenneth McLeod made a century and we won easily. But it was dangerously intoxicating. I enjoyed the rest of the term hugely. Founder's Day was a different affair when we spent the best part of the day playing cricket on the "Turf" against the Old Fettesians. It was a sweet revenge to find that old boys, who in one's first two years had seemed unconquerable giants, were not only vulnerable on the cricket field but ready, and, indeed, almost glad, to claim one's acquaintance. There was, too, a sensuous satisfaction in strolling along the Green Walk on Sunday evenings after chapel and stopping to gossip with "bloods" in other houses. It was a change from the days when I walked shyly with "Poodle" Black or some other small boy in "College", not daring to speak to anyone who was not of my age or term.

I appreciated these amenities of success. But my work suffered as, indeed, it was almost bound to suffer. In the summer term we had three half-holidays in each week, and, as Fettes was so close to Edinburgh, the First Eleven played numerous matches. In school matches the Eleven frequently were let off an hour or more of morning school in order to start the game at noon. In matches against clubs, stumps were drawn at six-thirty. Preparation began at quarter to seven. It was too much to demand from members of the Eleven that they should be able to change, have tea—for one always wanted more tea—and settle down to work within quarter of an hour. On the contrary, most of the team used to linger over changing in order to gossip about the match. I was a definite lingerer, and, although I was in the Upper Fifth and therefore exposed like a tee'd golf ball to the full force of "K. P's" drive, I fear that on match nights I did little preparation. This backsliding produced its inevitable result in the examinations. When the final order was read out at the end of the term, I was far down the list. Worse still, I missed my remove into the Sixth Form.

This was a serious blow to my prospects, for my failure not only meant that in all probability I should have to remain for another year in the Upper Fifth, but it was also the death-knell to my chances of a scholarship at Cambridge. I was a little ashamed of myself and went home for the holidays with a new determination to amend my ways.

These holidays provided an incident which throws a revealing light on the difference between my brother Rufus's character and my own. During the summer term the South African cricket team visited Scotland, and during their visit Reggie Schwarz, the famous googly bowler, and an old friend of Cumberlege, our games master, came down to Fettes and bowled one evening at the nets. He showed us how the googly was bowled.

When I went home for the holidays, I demonstrated the finger action very clumsily to my brother and then banished the "googly" from my mind. Not so my brother. Taking a ball, he practised the new art for hours and, indeed, weeks by himself until he had mastered it. When he went up to Cambridge, he had his reward, for, after taking what I think is still a record number of wickets in the Freshmen's match, he went straight into the Cambridge eleven.

He has, and always has had, an immense capacity for taking pains, and thoroughness is the keynote both of his character and of his success. At school perseverance was not my strong quality, and many years were to pass before I learnt to acquire it.

CHAPTER SEVEN

IT IS A characteristic of the British public-school man that when he leaves school he likes to picture himself as a lazy dog whose school days were spent in dodging work. This trait is not confined to the successful business man who, enviously contemptuous of intellectuals, glories in the fact that as a schoolboy he never rose above the Lower Fifth. I have noticed it frequently among dons and meek professors of theology, and even among schoolmasters, who in their moments of expansive reminiscence like to be remembered by their school contemporaries, not as the successful scholar, but as the boy who crowned the founder's statue with a chamberpot. It is a foolish vanity which has nothing but tradition to recommend it. For the plain truth is that no boy, especially if he is the son of poor parents, likes to come home with a bad report.

All my life I have had a facile capacity for making good resolutions. It is not a quality which I admire. All too frequently the making of good resolutions is merely an escape from our own weakness, and after repeated failures becomes little more than a habit. We see older men who rise every day with a vow never to touch alcohol or tobacco again and who by 11 a.m. are drinking their first cocktail or smoking their fifth cigarette. We realise that they have lost their will-power and wonder sadly when the period of our own inevitable decline will set in.

Having missed my remove into the Sixth Form at the end of the summer of 1904, I duly received a bad report. I was full of remorse. During the holidays I took myself severely in hand and for once I succeeded in keeping my good resolutions. When I returned to Fettes for the Christmas term, not only had I made up my mind to work, but, vaguely perhaps, I had acquired the first consciousness of a sense of responsibility.

And work I did, if not as hard as I might have worked, at least harder than I had ever worked before. As a schoolmaster my father had a profound contempt for boys who "cribbed", and even in my laziest period at Fettes I had never used illegitimate aids to work. Now in my regenerate days I made a vow not to read during preparation until I had finished my work for the next day. No longer did I leave the learning of my Latin and Greek repetition to the last five minutes before school. I took my Virgil or Odyssey with me to bed, learnt my lines before "lights out" and rehearsed them the next morning over my cocoa.

The results of my new industry were not long in showing themselves. In the first week's order list I came out top of the form and, encouraged as well as driven by "K.P.", I maintained my place for the rest of the term. Of my fourteen terms at Fettes this was the most satisfactory to myself and the most beneficial to my character.

Of course, as in the case of many schoolboys, my sense of values was topsy-turvy. My courage was of the wrong kind. With my thwarted passion for popularity I was always ready to commit some reckless act of bravado against the school regulations. For the same reason I found it hard to say "no" to almost any kind of temptation. For a boy with this kind of character hell waits with yawning mouth.

The heroes of my microcosm were not the boys who were to make their mark in later life. Indeed, I doubt if even the masters could have picked these out. They were not necessarily to be found among the boys who excelled at work. Of the five heads of the school during my period at Fettes all have done reasonably well in life, but only one, John Stevenson, who is the *Times* Canadian correspondent and a well-known Dominion journalist, can be called in any way a public figure.

Looking back to-day, I find it hard to generalise, for of my contemporaries at Fettes no less than seventy-seven fell in the

Great War. On the whole I think it fair to say that it is not the athletic leaders but rather the unnoticed boys who have made the greater success in life. I do not forget distinguished scholar-athletes like Sir George Cunningham, but of my contemporaries the most prominent to-day is Lord Normand, who as Solicitor-General for Scotland has been a Minister of the Crown and who is now Lord Justice Clerk. At school he was an open scholar and a school prefect, but his nickname was "Cuddy" because of a certain plodding perseverance both in his character and in his gait. Some of the masters may have realised his striking qualities—he took a First in Greats at Oxford—but I doubt if many boys did. He was in Glencorse, and beside the great games "bloods" of that house he seemed small beer.

Another distinguished Fettesian contemporary is Monsignor Heard who to-day holds high office in the Church of Rome. Like Lord Normand he was an open scholar and a school prefect. Like Normand, he was an undistinguished member of the Second Fifteen, and as the son of the headmaster, living in his father's house, he, too, was a remote and solitary figure with little influence on the lives of his fellows.

Rugby football and athletic prowess were not alone in providing the supreme test of courage. Of the four Anderson brothers, all of whom were killed in the Great War and whose record, including a Victoria Cross, was pre-eminent, not one achieved any athletic distinction, and two of them were called "Crocky" because of their frail physique. Even more remarkable is the case of another contemporary whom I remember as P. A. Cooper. At Fettes his nickname was "Cowpat", and he went through his school career without revealing either to master or boy any promise of the great things that were to come to him. Yet he did brilliantly in the War, rising to be Deputy Controller of Trench Warfare.

With him I underwent a humiliating experience a few

years ago. Soon after I had written *British Agent* I was a guest at a large dinner party in London. At the end of the meal a tall figure came up to me and smiled. I failed to recognise him.

"I was at Fettes with you," he said slowly.

"I'm sorry," I said, "I'm afraid I can't place you."

"I'm Cooper," he explained. "I was in Moredun."

I remembered and was condescendingly gracious. "I'm very busy," I replied, "but you must come and lunch with me one day. Where can I get hold of you?"

"I'm rather busy too," he answered, "but a message to the Bank of England will always find me."

"Pat" Cooper had become P. Ashley Cooper, director of the Bank of England, close counsellor of Mr. Montagu Norman, arbiter of the fate of goodness knows how many great companies, the leading "doctor" of industry in Britain, and the Governor of the Hudson's Bay Company.

It takes all kinds of boys to make a school. Some develop early and others late, and on the whole the late developers have the last and longer say. But there is nothing untoward in the hero-worship of games "bloods". They are the natural leaders of their time and in their school and university days reap the full reward of their short-lived reign.

For my own hero-worship there was an additional excuse. Successful as the school football team had been in the two previous years, it was to win still greater triumphs in the season that was just starting. In this Fifteen I gained a place, playing half-back with Arthur Gallie, a member of a family which has given to Fettes and to Scotland several stout-hearted footballers. He had the courage of a terrier, and we became great friends, spending hours together practising "blind-side" and other tactics on the field. The position of us half-backs was no sinecure, for we had to serve a brilliant three-quarter line which contained three future Blues, two of whom also gained International caps. Even then it was up to the best club standard. Its brightest star was, of course, "Grunt" McLeod, and when "Grunt" was not being given his fair share of the ball he let you know it.

I have met Englishmen who played under "Grunt" at Cambridge and who confessed that they were rattled by his free flow of invective. But I never minded it, and when he grunted out a fierce "can't you get that ruddy ball out" I would clench my teeth in grim determination. There was a tremendous driving force in "Grunt" which communicated itself to the whole team, and for a good pass or a clever opening his praise was as freely given as was his blame. After the first match, when we drew with the full strength of Heriot's F.P.'s, to-day one of the leading clubs in Scotland, the Fifteen went from triumph to triumph, winning all its club matches with one historic exception, and defeating all the other schools without having its lines crossed.

Inter-school matches were like miniature internationals and attracted what in those days was a considerable crowd of spectators. In my time Merchiston was our most formidable opponent. But the most amusing matches were against Loretto. When they were played on Loretto's ground, scores of Musselburgh fishermen and local miners turned up to support the home team. The support was sometimes physical as well as vocal, especially if Fettes were winning. On such occasions the Fettes wing-threequarter nearest the fishermen was lucky if the abuse hurled at his head was not accompanied by a shower of turf-sods.

Membership of the Fifteen brought certain privileges. One of these was beer, or "swipes" as we called it, after matches. I tasted it only once. Apart from the fact that I did not like it, I was afraid lest it might be bad for training. I observed the same restraint when we went to play Glenalmond, a long journey which lent itself to undetected indulgence in tobacco and alcohol. But nobody drank or even smoked. Certainly Arthur Gallie and I did not. We took our football in deadly earnest, wanted to get our "caps", and regarded physical fitness as the essential approach to that coveted goal.

It was from Arthur Gallie that I learnt the trick of sleeping with a knotted handkerchief in the middle of my back. Boys are sophisticated innocents. Someone had put forth the fiat that nocturnal sexual disturbances came from sleeping on one's back. The knotted handkerchief was intended to prevent any possible diminution of our physical strength.

In that Christmas term of 1904 the average age of the team was just a month under eighteen. Five of the Fifteen subsequently gained their International "caps" and within a year three of them were playing for Scotland against New Zealand at Inverleith. Yet in spite of their physical strength and prowess, they were a team of boys, boyish in mind and outlook, never claiming the privileges of manhood, and blissfully unconscious of many things which to-day disturb the mind of the modern boy of fifteen.

If I seem to dwell unduly on the athletic side of my school life, it is not merely because my last three years at Fettes were marked by a series of football and cricket triumphs unparalleled in the history of the school, but because I myself allowed too much of my time and attention to be absorbed by games. In this attitude I was, I think, slightly abnormal. If the scholar-athlete was the ideal which every decent Fettesian admired most, the clever boy who was not good at games had no reason to feel himself an outcast. For, if prigs were not tolerated, brains at all times commanded a full measure of respect even from the "rugger" Goths. But it is true that the sensitive boy who excelled neither at games nor at work must have suffered, especially if he had musical or artistic tastes. Fettes was not a picture palace for aesthetes nor a happy home for poets, and parents who expect a public school to cater for the abnormal boy had better send their sons elsewhere.

Since the War public schools have been attacked from many quarters and from many angles. Socialists condemn them as a breeding ground of class privilege and as a patriotic forcing bed for cannon-fodder. Self-made business men have no use for them because the curriculum does not include book-keeping and shorthand, and I have heard a professor of Economics in a North of England University declare that of all his students the public-school product is the most intractable to teach and the worst equipped mentally. Many critics, too, deplore the neglect of Science, and even more serious is the widespread accusation that public schools accustom boys to a standard of luxury which they are afterwards unable to maintain by their own earning capacity.

As a boy I took my public school for granted, an institution to be accepted unchallenged as the best in the world. To-day, having so many schoolmaster relatives, I have formed rather different ideas about both Fettes in particular and about public schools in general. I have been among the critics, and on the whole I believe in the challenge of youthful rebels provided that their criticism is constructive and not merely the destructive nihilism of disgruntled idlers who plead lack of opportunity for their own lack of effort. I do not believe that any system which stands still is perfect, and I have no sympathy with the type of old public school boy whose educational philosophy begins and ends with the last sentence of the Gloria.

But I am confident that the British public-schools are not standing still. During the last thirty years I have seen much of school life in many foreign countries, not only in Europe but also in Asia and the New World, and I am convinced that the best product of the British public school has little to fear from a comparison with the best type of Continental and North American schoolboy. It is significant that in the United States the number of schools run on British lines is steadily increasing. I have noticed, too, with quiet amusement that those of my friends who are loudest in their condemnation of public schools have sent their own sons to such institutions.

I dislike privilege in any form. I believe in the disappearance of classes; that is, in the form in which they now exist. But in every human society there will always be a hierarchy which in itself constitutes a class. There is such a hierarchy not only in Russia, but in the dictator countries, and the same is true of all countries and of all political Parties. If the British public-school system has justified itself, I should like to see the opportunities which it provides extended as widely as possible, and I welcome the increasing provision which most public schools are now making for the admission of poor boys. But I am no believer in the virtues of a mass-education which, while it may raise the general, must affect adversely the highest standard. Culture is and always has been the creation of the few. It is the function of the public schools to spread and maintain this culture, and, when they no longer fulfil this first duty, they will cease to justify their existence.

As for the charge that public schools produce cannon-fodder, I cannot understand the Socialists and so-called internationalists who make it. Pacifists on paper and opposed to every form of military training, they are always pugnacious in their demands for strong British action against any foreign state whose constitution does not conform to their own ideal of government. The country which many of them profess to admire has produced in the Red Army the greatest supply of cannon-fodder in existence to-day, and in a world of wolves our Socialists try to bark and to be sheep at the same time. I loathe the very idea of war, but I do not believe that our public schools are cannon-fodder factories. Indeed, my own experience of talking to public-school boys has convinced me that they are almost too strongly impregnated with the internationalist ideal and that in political outlook they are far more tolerant and advanced than the schoolboys of any other country.

I am not blind to the defects of the public-school system. There is a whole world between a good school and a bad one, and the highly individualistic nature of their constitution makes it difficult for the parent to distinguish between the two. Every school, too, suffers from the large number of schoolmasters who enter the profession with no zeal and no capacity for teaching, and from the strange British characteristic, prevalent in almost every walk of British life, which prevents headmasters from getting rid of the inefficients. A bad form-master can cause untold harm, and, when one remembers the natural receptivity of boys, it is sad to think of the good material that is allowed to go to waste.

In a changing and rather hysterical Britain, public schools are right in trying to conserve what is best in the old traditions. But they must move with the times or go under, and I am not sure that a special university degree for schoolmasters with a year's course in practical teaching is not an overdue reform. Even more urgent is the need for some system which will enable young masters to be moved regularly from one school to another. At present the profession in the public schools is like a restrictive Colonial or Consular service, and through being rooted to one school a master loses his keenness and his breadth of outlook long before he has served his time.

But, when all has been said both for and against, I believe firmly that the greatest enemies of the public schools are the old boys and the parents. It is one of the weaknesses of the team spirit instilled by public schools that nearly every old boy sees his own school days through a mist of sentimentality. He is the most obstinate opponent of change and is largely responsible for the cheap sneers about the old school tie. As for the modern parent, responsibility for the charge of luxury-breeding which is frequently levelled against the public schools rests largely on his shoulders. Wealth still feeds the public schools, and the wealth of Britain is to-day concentrated in the South of England. And to the Englishman in the south, prosperity has brought an indolent ease of living which transfers itself all too readily to his son.

I know scores of fathers who allow their sons to drink cocktails and smoke cigarettes in the holidays, who tolerate their staying in bed till luncheon time and up till all hours of the night, who lavish small fortunes on their sons' amusements, who smile indulgently when the little Willie or little Richard holds the conversation at the dinner table, and who, anxious to remain young themselves, encourage the son to call the father by his christian name. Home is still the dominant influence in a boy's life, and against home influences such as these even the best schoolmaster has a hard struggle.

In one respect the parent is entitled to some sympathy, and this is in his difficulty in choosing a school. Like most other institutions public schools and especially school houses have their ups and downs. Yet under the hotel-keeping system a parent has to put his boy down for a school almost as soon as the child is born. Here even the most painstaking parent has to take a risk. Having selected his school, he does his best to find out which is the best house. The opinion which he consults seems to favour Mr. Johnstone, and down goes the boy for Johnstone's. By the time the boy is thirteen, the exemplary Mr. Johnstone has probably become a headmaster, and the parent is lucky if Johnstone's, from being the best house, has not become the worst.

This parental difficulty is no excuse for the reprehensible tendency of the modern father to leave the choice of school, and especially of house, to the mother. It is true that the modern father has to work far harder than the fathers of thirty years ago. But there are many historical examples to show that the first sign of decadence in a nation is when the woman becomes the superior animal. Apart from the fact that a mother generally judges a school as she judges an hotel, there is, I fear, a definite lack of will-power and virility in a father who voluntarily abandons the superintendence of his son's education. A nation has the youth which it deserves, and if they accept this principle many fathers, especially those who decry modern youth, should have rather sorrowful reflections.

These strictures apply to Scottish parents in a vastly lesser degree. But I notice a tendency among them which I cannot help deploring, and this is the growing tendency to send their sons to English schools. Eton stands apart, a half-way house between a public school and university, unique in its advantages and drawbacks. But, with the exception of the aristocracy, Scottish parents, as a rule, do not patronise Eton. It is to other schools that with doubtful advantage they send their sons in ever increasing numbers.

The motives for this change are, I think, partly snobbish, partly selfish and partly self-defensive. During the nineteenth century the educational strength of Scotland was largely in its day-schools, and even to-day schools like Edinburgh Academy and Watson's College, which rank as public schools, have a vast preponderance of day-boys. The success of these and other Scottish day-schools was in a large measure the result of the interest which the average Scottish parent showed in his son's work at home. In those days the Scottish parent stayed at home and found his pleasure in books. Since the beginning of the new century the advent of the motor-car and the cinema has transformed home life even in Scotland, and little Jock—in the new circumstances probably much to his benefit—has to be sent to a boarding-school.

At first Fettes, Loretto, Glenalmond and Merchiston were good enough. But parents do not send their sons to the boarding-school near which they happen to live. They know too much about it; they hear all the gossip. They therefore go farther afield to exchange the dangers which they know for the perhaps greater dangers which they do not know. In their choice of a school social considerations as much as a laudable desire to do their best for their sons influence the final decision, and to-day the cry is England.

I am far from denying the merits of English public schools.

I am informed, too, by Mr. H. G. Wells, that I must forget Bannockburn, and I gladly add my testimony, based on a long first-hand experience of post-war Europe, to the dangers of excessive nationalism, but for the life of me I cannot see what benefit is to accrue to Scotland from a slavish aping of the luxurious habits and high living of the Englishman, and as a cultural nationalist I believe in Scots supporting Scottish schools.

Headmasters who have had personal experience of both English and Scottish public schools have told me bluntly that, if Scottish schools are to win back Scottish parents, they must raise their standard of work and must provide the same wide range of educational facilities which to-day exist at the best English public schools.

This assertion presupposes a definite superiority in favour of the English schools, and the fact that so many Scottish parents now send their sons south may be accepted as Scotland's recognition of this superiority. I can speak only of Fettes and of that without authority, but I think it would be hard to find any school of the same size in England which can show as fine a record of scholarship or as long a list of distinguished scholars. Year after year Fettes boys have gone to Oxford and Cambridge with open scholarships or exhibitions. During more than half a century the number of scholarships gained has varied very little, and very rare indeed have been the cases where the final results achieved at the end of the university course have not justified the original award.

I believe, too, that Fettes has kept pace with the march of time more than most schools. Yielding to the insistence of the scientists, she has greatly improved her Modern Side, and to-day the annual list of classical honours is supplemented by scholarships gained for science and mathematics. She continues to produce her special type of scholar-athlete, and two of the most distinguished, G. P. S. Macpherson and N. K. Hutton, belong to the post-war period. "Phil" Macpherson, who captained Oxford and Scotland at "rugger", took a First in Moderations and Greats at Oxford. N. K. Hutton, an Oxford rowing Blue, won the Craven scholarship and the Chancellor's Prize for Greek verse.

It may be said with truth that scholarship and games prowess do not make a school, and I should be reluctant to admit that the merits of Fettes were confined to these two qualities. In spite of its English top-hats, tail coats and Eton jackets, which I think might now be abolished with advantage, it is and always has been a typically Scottish school, providing a typically Scottish education, in which the moulding of character and the encouragement of initiative have always counted for as much as work. Its boys have always come from middle-class families and have had the virtues and, if you like, the defects of their class. Wealth was represented, but it was the wealth of the self-made, not the accumulated wealth of the accident of birth. In my time the richest boy at Fettes was the grandson of a cooper. He was popular, but not on account of his wealth which was certainly not worshipped. Grit and energy have always been the two great Fettes virtues; slackness and self-advertising the two great sins.

In my time every boy who came to Fettes had to learn not merely to take hard knocks without flinching, but also to subjugate his own individual interests to the benefit of the common weal. On every boy there was a common obligation to do his best in whatever he undertook, and those who failed to accept this obligation suffered.

Fettes may have produced few geniuses, but year after year she has sent forth sons distinguished by their sanity of outlook, their mental and physical vigour, and their practical competence to deal with any emergency. They are to be found in such professions as the law and medicine, in commerce, and in all branches of government service. I have met them in all parts of the world and have been amazed by the general standard of reliability and the infrequency of failure.

This is the supreme service which Fettes and other Scottish schools have rendered to the British Empire, and surely they deserve the approbation of the Scottish parent. I am aware that the poverty of my country forces many Scots to go abroad and that, in particular, the fertile plains of England act like a magnet on the predatory instincts of a race of mountaineers. We are proud when a relative of Theodore Roosevelt refers to the Scots as "the spinal cord of America", although we conveniently forget that continuous exportations of spinal cord expose the Scots at home to the risk of becoming invertebrate. We are content to become hewers of wood and drawers of water for the English, admittedly in return for a remunerative consideration. But even this ambition has been achieved largely by the special educational advantages which the Scot has hitherto enjoyed. These advantages will be difficult to maintain if Scottish parents, instead of sending their sons to Scottish schools, develop the habit of converting them into Englishmen at the age of thirteen.

To my mind the problem is a simple one. No Scot who thinks about his country can fail to be disturbed by the present state of Scotland. Her survival as a nation hangs in the balance. I believe that the Scottish schoolboy of to-day has many advantages over the boys of my time. We were a happy-go-lucky generation. Social problems did not enter into our ken. Scotland herself was something that we took for granted, and, if my memory is accurate, no Scottish history was taught at Fettes. The modern boy has a deeper understanding of the difficulties which beset others besides himself. He thinks more of his country; he is, I hope, more Scotland-conscious. It is to the Scottish schools that we must look to provide the leaders of a national revival.

For myself I shall make a frank confession. I was a failure at Fettes in that I never fulfilled the scholastic promise of my early years at Seafield. Although I eventually reached the

Sixth Form, I never brought my classics to the point where I could read them for pleasure. Ten years of intensive study of Latin and Greek never made those subjects familiar to me as languages. A little later in life the rebel that has always been in me made me react violently against a classical education. I became a modernist of modernists. I learnt a large number of foreign languages and attributed my proficiency to a natural genius which had been starved at school. I regretted my abysmal ignorance of science and in my bitterness I ranted against public-school education as a kind of mental gymnastics taught in the same soulless manner as a Prussian sergeant teaches drill. Assuredly there is nothing easier for the public-school failure than to attack the public schools.

Many years ago, having survived this period of vanity, I reversed my mental engines. Soon I came to realise that the learning of modern languages is a matter of opportunity, available mainly to diplomatists and waiters, and that, apart from the pleasure which it confers on anyone living abroad, it has little or no educational value whatsoever. I saw a world in which scientists, neglected for many years, not only had assumed their rightful place but were also claiming dominion over matters which lie outside their province. I did not and do not like the idea of a world run entirely by scientists. I resented and resent their rather pompous assertion that the advance of science is synonymous with the progress of civilisation. I hope fervently that some day the assertion will come true, but one has only to look at the uses to which science is being put in every country in the world, or to take part in a gas drill in Prague or Berlin, to realise that so sweeping a claim will not stand even a superficial examination. If there is one lesson which a classical education teaches, it is that the progress of civilisation is largely a figment of the imagination and that by the immutable laws of life our present civilisation will vanish as the great civilisations of the past have crumbled into dust.

To-day my taste for the classics has returned to the exclusion of most other things. Stimulated by the books of the excellent Dr. Glover, I have taken up again my study of Greek and Latin, but especially of Greek. I began by making a duty of it, working for a fixed hour every morning and "sweating up" thirty or forty lines with the aid of a dictionary in much the same way as I did at school. There were moments when I nearly lost heart. But I persevered. I am no scholar. I skip all difficulties of construction. But to-day I can read with tolerable ease as much of the classics as I am ever likely to master. Herodotus has become my favourite author. He has added enormously to the zest of my travels and to my comparative study of the present. I hope that he and other writers of the classical past have given to me a little of that detachment of view which is essential to any professional observer of the European scene. It is certainly a salutary corrective to any complacent thoughts about our own allegedly superior civilisation to remember that barley water was prescribed by Hippocrates for his over-indulgent patients, that the straws, through which we moderns drink it, were in use for the same purpose over two thousand years ago, that the rules for the dietetics and the physical jerks which we now practise were laid down by Diocles and other Greek physicians, and that practically every political panacea advocated by modern politicians is to be found in Aristotle and Plato.

Do I owe to Fettes the new pleasure and interest in life which I have derived from this return to the classics? I think I do. At any rate, never at any moment have I regretted that my father did not send me to some other school. I study the various honours lists for news of her sons. When November comes round, I turn instinctively to the sporting pages of the newspapers to see if the new generation has triumphed over Merchiston and Loretto. And Twickenham and Murrayfield are not the same if there is no Fettesian in the Cambridge or the Scottish pack. Although I have drifted far away from the centre of Fettes life, I am profoundly conscious and proud of the fact that, however insignificant, I am a member of a corporate body which in a world of scepticism and petulant criticism still stands for certain definite ideals of action and for certain definite Scottish standards of conduct. And I hope and believe that every Fettesian thinks and feels as I do.

CHAPTER EIGHT

AT THE END of the Christmas term of 1904 I obtained my promotion into the Lower Sixth, returning home for the holidays with the form prize and good report. Undoubtedly, I had had a good term. Everyone was pleased with me, and I was therefore rather pleased with myself.

At the same time my own self-satisfaction was tempered by certain troubling doubts. Although I was now over seventeen, I was still very much a boy. My home life was still very simple. Pocket-money was still meagre. My visits to the theatre were so rare that they stand out as landmarks in my life. During the ten years that I spent in Broughty Ferry I was taken only twice, and, although I have seen the play a score of times, I can remember my first performance of *Romeo and Juliet* by the Benson Company as clearly as if it were taking place before my eyes at this moment.

I had never been to a concert or to a picture gallery. I still disliked parties and dances. My second brother Rufus was still my greatest friend, and the summer holidays were more than ever the chief event in our lives. I had no wish to ape grown-ups. I had no desire to smoke or drink. My personal vanity had not survived one disastrous experience when, modelling myself on a photograph of a Cambridge rowing Blue in an illustrated newspaper, I had appeared at dinner with my hair parted down the middle and had been received with hoots of laughter. In a drawing-room I was as awkward as an elephant. Above all, I had no thought about the future, assuming vaguely that I should have another year at Fettes, that with additional experience I should excel at football and cricket, and that I should then go to Cambridge with the same hopes of a "rugger" Blue as coloured the dreams of most members of a successful Fettes Fifteen.

But even I realised that this unambitious dream could not come true without money. Cambridge, as my father had often pointed out to me, would be possible only if I won a scholarship. When I summed up my position in school at Fettes, I found little cause for satisfaction. Several boys whom I had beaten in the foundation examination had sailed right away from me in the race for promotion. Worse still, boys who had entered the school a year and even two years after me had left me behind. Winning the Upper Fifth form prize was no compensation for previous failures. It meant merely that I had regained a little of the lost ground. Carelessly optimistic as I was by nature, even I knew that the Lower Sixth was not a form from which boys won scholarships.

In my family there has always been a tendency on the part of nearly all its members to trust in their luck, to hope that something will turn up and to feel confident that in the hour of need someone will pay. Strangely enough, the trust, the hope and the confidence have rarely been misplaced. But at that moment the odds were heavily against me. There was a financial crisis in the affairs of all my relations. My grandmother's fortune, sunk in the new and unproved plantation rubber industry, was then completely immobilised. My father's school at Seafield had never realised expectations, and already he was thinking of another change. At Broughty Ferry the family had received another addition in my brother Rupert, and with five sons to educate my father was too poor to send me to Cambridge without a scholarship. Assuredly the chances of adventitious aid were unfavourable.

During the Christmas holidays I had several conversations with my father about my future. Looking back to-day, I feel sorry for him. There can be nothing more distressing to a father than to have to plan the future of a boy who has no ambition. And in those days I was wholly ambitionless. Had he arranged for me to be a bookmaker or a bank-clerk, I believe that I should have accepted the arrangement without demur. But his methods were insidious rather than insistent. He had three cousins in the Army. They had made their own way and they had done brilliantly. Their careers were recounted to me in the hope of stimulating my interest in a soldier's life. He had two great friends who were successful advocates. One was the leading Scottish junior. The other had recently been made a law lord. And their example was also dangled before my eyes. There was another friend who had large shipping interests in Glasgow. My father wrote to him, but I do not think that the answer was very encouraging. In any case it would have made little difference. I had no idea what I wanted to do with my life, and my father's well-meant suggestions made no appeal to me.

If I had any wish of my own, it was to be an estate agent to some big landowner in the Highlands. Estate management ran in the family. On my father's side my great-grandfather and my grand-uncle had been factors to the Duke of Portland. Two of my mother's relations had held the same office under the Earls of Seafield. In my own case the impulse came from my love of fishing and shooting. It was not a very satisfactory situation, and I went back to school with the problem of my future still unsolved.

The term began with a great disappointment which, later, was to be set off by a minor personal success. During the Christmas holidays my father had taken me to Edinburgh to see a football match. On my way home I developed a serious attack of influenza. My temperature rose so high that my mother arranged a bed for me in her own room so that she could nurse me. During the night I became delirious, wandered in my sleep, and crashed into a large plate-glass window, cutting my head badly.

I came back to school late and found everyone talking about the great match which was to take place the next day. I was of course not yet fit to play football and thus, as a touch-judge and not as a player, I took part in the game, memorable in the annals of Fettes, when the school Fifteen played Scotland as a preliminary practice for the international match against Wales.

The match was played at Fettes, and a large number of spectators, including the members of the Scottish Rugby Union, came to see it. It was a more thrilling battle than any international, and by one side, at least, it was fought with international fierceness. The school three-quarter line was nearly as good as Scotland's. Scottish boys from Merchiston and the Academy have more than once worn Scotland's jersey while still at school, and in that spring of 1905 Kenneth McLeod would certainly have enjoyed this honour but for a wise rule which prevented Fettes boys from taking part in an international. We were, of course, heavily out-weighted forward, but the boys, with everything to gain and nothing to lose, played like tigers, and for a long time the struggle swayed with changing fortune. Stoppages for injuries were frequent, but the injuries were all on Scotland's side. Indeed, Jimmie McDonald, Scotland's wing three-quarter, had two teeth kicked down his throat and was only just able to take his place in the match against Wales.

At first Scotland scored two rather easy tries, but the school fought back heroically, and when Moir Mackenzie, his auburn hair shining like an oriflamme, twice forced his way across the line with two Scottish forwards clinging to him there was a roar of cheering which could have been heard at Holyrood. Even if Scotland's chosen did not at first exert their full physical strength, they were forced to do so long before the end. Although they won, the final score was only fifteen points to six, and this narrow margin represented a wonderful performance on the part of schoolboys of which Press and public alike were generous in their praise. I would sooner have played in that match than have won a Scottish cap, and to have been deprived of my chance by influenza rankles to-day more bitterly than many a major disappointment in my later life.

I soon recovered from my illness and took my place again in the school side. Football, however, had lost some of its savour. We were in no danger of defeat by any other school.

Arthur Gallie, my brilliant partner at half-back, had left at Christmas, and without his skill in getting the ball away from the scrum my own part in the team's success was less satisfactory.

On the other hand, elevation to the Lower Sixth gave me a new interest in work. Here, except for rather rare occasions when the Head took both Sixth Forms together, my mentor was G. H. Keeton. His methods were different from those of "K.P." In the Sixth there were no impositions, no "extras", and, indeed, no fear of punishment. Teaching was by suggestion rather than by precept. Keeton would have you up to his desk and for five or ten minutes would go through your Latin or Greek prose more with a view to recommending improvements of style than to stressing inaccuracies. He praised when he could, and, although there was not perhaps the same "drive" as in the Upper Fifth, I appreciated these attempts to enlarge my mental outlook.

Keeton, too, enlivened the hours of work with references to present-day events, and under this stimulus I began to read the newspapers in which previously I had studied only the sporting pages. The Russo-Japanese War was then at its height, but, although I was now four years older, I do not think that it ruffled the surface of my life any more than did the Boer War. Like everyone else, I was patriotically pro-Japanese, and in the popular pantomime songs of the year Japanese themes took the place of "Goodbye, my Blue-bell" and the other sentimental ditties which cheered Tommy Atkins on his way to South Africa. At the singing after school matches fags favoured a song called "Farewell, Little Yo-san" of which the chorus ran:

> "Farewell, my little Yo-san,
> Goodbye, my sweetheart true,
> Over the mighty ocean
> There's a duty there to do.
> Sometimes will you remember

> To-ki, your sailor-man,
> Who is going out to fight
> For the cause of the right
> And the freedom of dear Japan."

The great British public does not change very much. The fever of ignorant excitement and the passion to intervene were then as tensely and as hysterically pro-Japanese as they are to-day anti-Japanese in the present Sino-Japanese conflict. Yet it was and is the same Japan.

I also took a new and more intellectual interest in the various entertainments with which we were regaled during the winter terms, and I remember with gratitude Percy French, an Irish genius, who could play, sing, draw and write verse. One of his fishing poems has long been a favourite of mine and, doubtless, of many anglers. I refer to the six lines which I believe he scribbled in five minutes at the request of an Irish hotel-keeper who wanted some message for his visitors' book:

> "Pack up my rod. The air is chill.
> The hills are turning grey.
> To-morrow I must pay my bill
> And haste me far away
> Back to the world again. But still
> Thank God for such a day."

Half-way through the term came the house "rugger" matches and the personal success to which I have already referred. "College" succeeded in winning their way into the final, but I do not think that there was a single boy or master in the school who would have given a firelighter for their chances. Their opponents were Glencorse, and Glencorse had not only the great McLeod but an all-powerful, well-balanced side which included a large percentage of the Second Fifteen. "College" had some good forwards and a superb leader in Moir Mackenzie. Our backs, however, were small and inexperienced. I was the only boy behind the scrum who had ever played on Big Side.

Before the match we had a discussion in which Moir laid down the tactics for the game. The forwards were to keep the ball tight; I was to do my "damnedest" to prevent the Glencorse halves from feeding Kenneth McLeod. Our chief hope would be a wet day.

Unfortunately for us, the weather did its best for Glencorse, and the final was played on a day such as rarely graces an Edinburgh winter. The turf was as firm and true as a billiard-table. There was not a breath of wind. House matches, however, have a psychological effect of their own, and frequently boys who never shine in a school game perform prodigies of unexpected valour. And so it was on this occasion.

"College" played as it had never played before and could never play again. From the beginning our forwards dominated the game, keeping the ball tight and penning Glencorse in their own "twenty-five". Moir himself was everywhere. He was like a giant possessed and did the work of three men. My own special duty was to pounce on the ball if ever it came out, and, playing close to the scrum, I had a comparatively easy task. By a preconcerted signal with Moir, our forwards would let the ball out every now and then, and I would make ground by touch kicking. On the rare occasions when Glencorse managed to heel, I was on their scrum half like a flash.

In the past, House matches at Fettes had been marked by play so rough that more than once the Head had intervened. Indeed, only a year or two before there had been a special "pi-jaw" about coarse play and bad language. But this game was played in the best spirit. There was one moment when Moncreiff, a big Glencorse forward, was so enraged by my spoiling tactics that he exploded savagely: "Keep onside, you little brute, or I'll wring your neck." But Moir was there. "Keiff," he said quietly, "if there's going to be any neck-

wringing I'm starting on you," and Moncreiff, a good fellow, growled an apology.

At half-time there was no scoring, and Moir was well
pleased. "Grunt" McLeod had not touched the ball more
than thrice, and each time he had been downed before he
could turn. Moreover, he was getting a little rattled at the
failure of his forwards to obtain the ball. We had nearly
worn them down. The probability was that in the second
half we should complete the process. Before the match we
had hoped for no more than to make a brave showing. Now
victory seemed a distinct possibility.

As the game was about to restart, Moir whispered to me:
"When we get near their line, we'll let the ball out. Then try
and go through on your own." My chance came, but not in
the manner that Moir had indicated. Between half-way and
his own "twenty-five" a Glencorse forward made a wild
attempt to sling the ball out to McLeod. I intercepted the
pass and was through the Glencorse three-quarter line before
anyone realised the danger. As I ran up to the full-back, I
punted over his head and, the ball bouncing well for me, I
was over the line. It was a spectacular score but, characteris-
tically enough, Moir cursed me for not getting round behind
the posts. He was right. My over-anxiety cost us two points,
for our goal-kicker failed to convert my try. Still, we were
three points up, and there were only fifteen minutes to go.

Spurred on by the frantic cheers of our supporters, we
continued to keep Glencorse in their own "twenty-five",
and, as scrum succeeded scrum, the referee began to look at
his watch. Then Fate, having upset all preconceived ideas of
form, made a mockery of her own jest. Four minutes before
time our forwards, wheeling a scrum, rushed the ball over the
Glencorse line. A score seemed certain. Then someone kicked
the ball too hard. A Glencorse boy was about to touch it down,
when there was a sharp roar from McLeod of "sling it here".
The boy threw a bad pass, but "Grunt's" hands could gather
anything. Receiving the ball behind his own goal posts, he

was in his full speed in two strides. A quick turn to the left and then a sudden swerve inwards, and he was through. Once he was clear, there was no full back living who could have touched him, and, easing up after he had outrun all pursuit, he trotted the last ten yards before touching down behind our goal posts. Of course he kicked the goal, and "College" were beaten.

For a moment I was dazed with disappointment. I felt my heart beating fiercely against my jersey. My temples throbbed and I realised that I had a splitting headache. In a dream I heard the final whistle go. It was followed by a renewed outburst of cheering, and to my surprise the cries of "Well played, College" from the whole school drowned the cheers for Glencorse. Moir, generous in all things, patted me on the back. And when "Grunt" McLeod, after congratulating us and admitting that he had almost abandoned hope, said to me, "why the deuce don't you always play like that?" I felt that our defeat was indeed greater than victory, for never again, if we had replayed the match a hundred times, could we have run Glencorse so close. As I sank into my hot bath, a delicious feeling of well-being pervaded all my limbs. That night the world, and to me Fettes was then its capital, seemed the best of places.

My joy did not survive the next morning. For the second time in my school career I received a summons from the Headmaster. It came while I was in school, and this time I did not go to the Lodge. The Head was in his little study next to the Sixth Form library. As I knocked at the door, I felt the momentary trepidation which he inspired in most boys. But I was not worried, and what followed took me completely by surprise.

It was my character and my future which were under review. With more sympathy than I had thought him capable of, he pointed out rather sadly how I had failed to fulfil the hopes which he had placed in me. I had wasted my energies on things that did not matter. He knew, and I must know,

that my father had set his heart on my winning a scholarship at Cambridge. Because I had wasted my opportunities,
this scholarship was now beyond my mental reach.

He turned away for a minute or two and looked out of the
window. Vaguely I let my eyes wander round the narrow
walls, the round table bare of papers, and the two armchairs
ranged symmetrically on each side of the fireplace. All that
was wanted to turn the place into a dentist's waiting-room
was a pile of *Punches* and *Illustrated London News*. Then I
concentrated my gaze on the burning grate.

The Head was speaking again. He had a list in his hand.
Doubtless it contained the names of the candidates for next
term's foundation examination. There was, he said, another
matter which he had to consider. Fettes was giving me a more
or less free education. I was keeping someone else, perhaps
someone more deserving, from those benefits. There could
be no question of my remaining at Fettes for another year.
He was writing my father to that effect.

He said no more. The interview was ended, and I left the
room. But before going back to the Lower Sixth I went
down to the lavatory to regain my composure. I was too
numbed to concentrate my thoughts, but dominating everything else in my mind was the premonition that Fate had
taken the decision regarding my future out of the hands of
both my father and myself. Vaguely I felt that it would not
be the only time that Destiny would intervene with the same
suddenness.

When I went back to my place in form, my neighbour
whispered to me: "What did the old Bulge want?" I whispered back with a smile: "Oh! a lecture about my work."
For the rest of the term I maintained this outward indifference, but in my heart I was subdued and uneasy.

CHAPTER NINE

WHENEVER ONE OF my Macgregor relatives runs into debt, makes an ill-assorted marriage, or gets into trouble of any kind, he may expect to have his affairs discussed in detail by the rest of his family. He will be helped, but he will be criticised with candour. It is the clan custom, with all its defects and all its compensations.

When I came home for the Easter holidays, I was in some anxiety lest my own failure should be subjected to an unpleasant family publicity. But I did not know my father. Fully informed of all my shortcomings by the Headmaster, he had told my mother that my work had been unsatisfactory and that my foundation scholarship could not be continued. But my welcome was as warm as if I had come home with a bagful of prizes.

I knew, of course, that my father was worried. He has always had a natural dislike, amounting almost to an inhibition and very rare in schoolmasters, of saying unpleasant things to people. He has, at all times, preferred the written word to the spoken in his relations with his own children even when they are staying under the same roof.

I now began to receive a succession of these written messages. Some were helpful, dwelling on the advantages of self-discipline and giving hints on the best means of acquiring it. Others again were encouraging and stressed the importance of a first failure as the best stepping-stone to success. But in these notes there was little or no mention of my future career. The truth was that my father was engaged in another correspondence.

This exchange of letters was between the Headmaster of Fettes and himself. Several times I had come down early to breakfast and had recognised the Head's clear handwriting among the pile of letters on my father's plate. But I was told nothing. In due course my term report arrived. As far as my other masters' criticisms were concerned, it was not bad. But it was signed by the Head without comment, and the correspondence between him and my father continued.

Then one day towards the middle of the holidays my father sent for me. He was, as usual, a little nervous in coming to the point, but, when he did, he was quite firm. His mind was now made up. I was to leave Fettes. He had decided, on the Head's advice, to send me to Germany. He handed me a prospectus written in English.

I took the folded sheet of paper and read it through. It was headed: Institut Tilley, Ringstrasse 40, Gross-Lichterfelde-West bei Berlin. There was a formidable programme of work providing for a full course of instruction in the German language in the mornings and lectures on art and music and visits to museums in the afternoons. Another paragraph dwelt on the virtues of a vegetarian and fruit diet. No drinks of any kind were provided at meals, and cocoa, drunk two hours afterwards, was recommended in preference to tea or coffee. The introduction of alcohol into the house was forbidden. The woollen underwear of Dr. Lahmann, the well-known German food and clothing reformer, was warmly extolled but not enforced. Heavily underlined and in the most prominent place was the basic rule of the "establishment". "Every student of the 'Institut' pledges himself from the moment of his arrival to refrain from speaking and reading a word of his own language not only inside the house but outside it. It is understood that any breach of this rule will involve instant dismissal." An exception was made in the case of private correspondence.

I handed the paper back to my father with a half-hearted smile. Even if I did not like it, I could appreciate the humour of the situation. There was no mention of exercise in the prospectus. I was to be sent to a place where there was no football. It would be the complete antithesis to Fettes.

A day or two later I made the journey from Broughty Ferry to Fettes in order to collect my belongings. The place was deserted, and it was some time before the school porter could find the key to unlock the door of my study. Carrying my tin trunk, we climbed the stairs to the fourth floor, and, as we climbed, the echo of our footsteps on the stones resounded through the empty building. I looked round the shabby, little room. There was not much that seemed worth taking away. A few books perhaps; a hockey stick. The rest —the kettle and the pan for "brewing" cocoa—could be left unsold to the next occupant. Then I turned to the pictures. There was my photograph of the cricket Eleven. I should want that. As I took it down, I suddenly remembered that the photograph of the school Fifteen, which should have been taken at the end of the Easter term, had been postponed until the summer because of someone's illness. It was a Fifteen which had won all its matches except the historic encounter with Scotland. I had been a member of it. Now I should be missing from the photograph.

Quickly I slung my effects into the trunk. Then, leaving my cab at the door, I walked down to the field. The air was soft and balmy, and the trees wore the first green of spring. The goal posts on Big Side were down. Even the muddy patches made by prolonged scrums had disappeared under the new growth of green grass. I saw again the closing scenes of that final House match with Moir Mackenzie battling to the last and Kenneth McLeod running and twisting in a great burst of speed. They were to win far greater triumphs. I had played my last game of football on Scottish soil.

As I walked back to the pavilion, I crossed the turf, already cut and rolled for the coming cricket season. Again I remembered that next term I should have been cricket captain of "College". Rather nervously I hoped to find in the pavilion Geordie Howell or someone to say good-bye to. But the pavilion was locked. Even Geordie was on holiday.

It was a sad and sentimental visit, and, like Loti, I let my thoughts run melancholically on the irrevocable past. What the Head had said was only too true. My father, who takes

all family shocks with wonderful courage, had never reproved me either by word or by look. But I knew that my
mother, whose nature was like my own, was unhappy. Her
Highland pride in the success of her sons had been hurt, and,
although we rarely pity those whom we love, I was grieved
because of her.

My sadness did not last long. Except on the score of neglected opportunities I was not conscious of any great wrong-
doing, and, thanks to "K.P.", even my slackness in work had
been made good during my last two terms. Now that the decision about my immediate future had been taken, I was determined to make the best of it. There are moments when all
men are afraid of life. Some cling in their fear to the known
and familiar. Others seek their escape in new and strange
surroundings. And so we divide mankind into the traveller
and the stay-at-home. I myself have always been among the
travellers, and already there was a pleasant sense of freedom
and of suddenly acquired manhood in the thought that I had
done with school for ever. Tilley's, after all, was not a prison
for youth but a seminary for students of all ages. They included
dons, professors, schoolmasters, General Staff colonels, doctors, and even world-famous philologists like Otto Jespersen.
I felt a new dignity and a new self-respect. Only one thought
troubled me—the rule about abstaining from the use of my
own language. As I did not know a single word of German, it
seemed as if I should be dumb for months. As a matter of
fact the rule was rigidly enforced and was the reason, apart
from Tilley's genius as a teacher, why the "Institut" was the
most successful establishment of its kind that has ever
existed.

There was, too, all the excitement, far more thrilling than
going to school, of setting out to a new country and the
pleasure, which constant repetition has never staled, of
ordering one's ticket and choosing one's cabin.

These preparations did not damp my ardour for the ordinary amusements of the holidays. There was golf and, with

the approach of May, tennis. But even my zest for games had undergone a change. I found myself shyly suggesting to my mother whom she should ask to our tennis parties.

The reason was a young girl of my own age who lived at Broughty Ferry. She used to come to Seafield to dances and to tennis parties, but, except that I was bored by having to take part in mixed doubles, I had never given her a thought. Now I discovered that mixed doubles were preferable to singles with my brother Rufus.

I never spoke of my attachment. But it was not Rufus whom I took to play golf at Carnoustie. She had a slightly upturned nose and a most attractive smile. She even taught me to dance.

On the day before I was to sail for Germany, we went for a walk along the narrow rocky path which skirts the sea-front of Broughty Castle. There, hidden from all eyes, and with the sea almost lapping our feet, I had my first kiss.

She gave me a tiny snapshot which seemed all smile and snubness, and I put it beside my tickets in my new pocket-book.

Early the next morning I left for Edinburgh with my father. I was to go to Berlin by sea via Hamburg. My port of departure was Leith, and my father accompanied me to the docks. After putting my luggage on board, I came down to the quay to talk to him. In spite of his efforts to control himself, his emotion kept rising to the surface. In his long life he has come to say goodbye to his sons on countless occasions. And in failure and in success his attitude has always been the same. He always waits till the last minute. First, there is the long interval during which he talks commonplaces and tries to appear unconcerned. Then he looks at his watch. Two minutes more. Suddenly he takes you by the arm. He holds you very tightly. As you go on board, he shouts some last-minute instruction—an address to be remembered or a friend to be looked up in Moscow or Peshawar. As the steamer recedes from the dock, the last you see of him is a bare-headed man with bent shoulders scanning the deck with peering, short-sighted eyes.

But mine was a special farewell. It was the departure of his eldest son on his first adventure in a foreign land. Although my father was then only forty-seven, his procedure was then much the same as it is to-day. As we walked up and down the quay, he kept repeating to me minute instructions about my journey. Then, as the siren shrieked, he gripped my arm very fiercely. Something of his emotion he communicated to me. I ran up the gangway, not daring to look back. When I came up on deck again, he was gone.

I felt a little friendless and alone. The weather was superb, and under the clear blue sky the Firth of Forth, set in a brown and olive green frame formed by Edinburgh and the Pentlands, shone like a silver mirror. Twelve years later I was to sail down this same Firth of Forth in a British cruiser accompanied by two destroyers on my way to Russia. Now I was the most insignificant creature on board.

Even at this early stage Fate had seemed to decree that my life should be a series of comings and goings. Already I had had four homes: Anstruther, Beith, Broughty Ferry and the Highlands. I had lived in close proximity to Scotland's three leading cities. Now, without having ever crossed the English Border, I was going to a capital which was larger than Edinburgh, Glasgow and Dundee put together. Germany was to make me, in so far as I can call myself made, for it was to complete the process begun by K. P. Wilson and to teach me the only virtue I possess: the capacity for hard work.

But I doubt if Germany made any concrete picture in my mind. My thoughts, tinged by a not unpleasant melancholy, were full of the unknown adventure that lay before me, and, of this unknown, Germany was only a part. I thought of the countless numbers of my compatriots who had sailed from Leith with similar hopes and fears in their hearts. I saw myself as a modern David Balfour and remembered with some grimness that at Tilley's I should not be able to read my *Catriona*. In my mind curiosity struggled with regret. Vaguely I realised that I had been given a great opportunity, and the thought kindled the first spark of ambition in my heart. I was grateful to my father for the sacrifices he had made for me. At the same time I understood that this journey meant a complete break with my past and that I had gone out into the world for ever.

I was leaving Scotland, too, for ever, although at the time I had no knowledge of my father's future plans. Now I live in the hope that one day it will be my home again.

I owe an immense debt to my father, who is the most understanding man in the world. But my heart is my mother's. Of all my sins one lies heavy on my conscience. It was my mother's wish, frequently expressed in life, that she should be buried at Cromdale, beside the Spey. When she died, in 1928, she was buried, for various reasons, at Sandhurst, where my father moved in 1906. To-day, I never pass her grave in that peaceful little churchyard and read that name— Florence Stewart Macgregor—without being profoundly conscious of the incongruous discordance of the Stewart and the Macgregor beside the Hodges, the Butlers, the Woods, and the scores of other English names—without feeling the friendless loneliness of that granite Celtic cross among the English graves of imported marble.

I hear again her cry: "I wish to lie among the mountains with the Spey running by my head." It is also my wish. My ancestors came down from the mountains to the plains, but I, who have seen too much of the great cities, want to go back to the mountains. And, when the hour comes, I too desire that I may find eternal peace beside the running waters and the everlasting hills.

INDEX

INDEX